About the Authors

Derek Taylor, OBE has a history degree from Cambridge University and has written a number of books on Jewish topics; British Chief Rabbis, 1664-2006, Don Pacifico, Solomon Schonfeld and Jewish Parliamentarians (with Lord Janner). He is married with four children and 14 grandchildren and lives in Hampstead.

Harold Davis, a medical graduate from Durham University, is an amateur historian and geneologist specialising in the Jewish Communities of the North East of England, especially of his home town of Sunderland. He has edited a book of Sunderland Jewry at War. He is married with four children and 13 grandchildren and lives in Hampstead.

The Sunderland Beth Hamedresh 1889 - 1999.

The Road to Gateshead.

Derek Taylor & Harold Davis

Published 2010 by arima publishing

ISBN 978 1 84549 435 3

Printed and bound in the United Kingdom

Typeset in Garamond

arima publishing
ASK House, Northgate Avenue
Bury St Edmunds, Suffolk IP32 6BB
t: (+44) 01284 700321

www.arimapublishing.com

Contents

Introduction

בס"ד

Dayan Ch. Ehrentreu
Rosh Beth Din

חנוך עהרנטרייא
ראש בית דין

14. 7. 10
ג' מנחם אב תש"ע לפ"ק

I read with interest the book The Sunderland Beth Hamedresh which revived in my mind grand recollections of the past history of the Sunderland Community. It brought back to my mind memories of the years my family spent in Sunderland in general and in the Beth Hamedresh in particular.
The authors certainly have a very fine grasp of historical events and their implications. The Sunderland Beth Hamedresh, Yeshiva and Kolel were admired internationally as they exerted a major influence on Jewish Communities the world over. The Alumni of the Kolel and the Yeshiva occupy prominent positions in the Rabbinate and have also produced many Torah trained laymen.
Any reader reading this book will draw inspiration from the staunch Torah adherence of the early builders of the Sunderland Beth Hamedresh and we are indebted to the authors of this book for the clear insight they have given us on the story of this very special community of Sunderland and of the Beth Hamedresh in particular.

H Ehrentreu

Daayan Ch. Ehrentreu

Foreward from Vivian Wineman
President of the Board of Deputies of British Jews

The 20th century was remarkable for a complete revolution in the distribution of Jewry throughout the world and the passing of many and long established Jewish communities. In many parts of the world this was the result of tragic persecution, destruction or expulsion.

In the United Kingdom also many communities have vanished but here the cause has been demographic evolution. Most, if not all, provincial communities in the United Kingdom are now facing challenging times - some of them are in terminal decline or have ceased to exist entirely. Their legacy lives on however in their members who have often gone to enrich other communities whether in this country or overseas - particularly in Israel. One such community is Sunderland - one of the oldest and most distinguished provincial communities in this country.

The Sunderland community particularly in its later years was remarkable for its homogeneity, its orthodoxy and its worldliness. Almost all its members came from families deriving from Lithuania and many even came from the same village, Kratinga (or in its German form, Krottingen). They even brought with them the traditions of Lithuanian Jewry, its piety and learning and combined these with a self-reliance and a benign attitude towards their non-Jewish neighbours which made them distinctive.

There were two Synagogues in Sunderland. Although they were both Orthodox - relations between the Beth Hamedrash, the strictly Orthodox establishment, and the Sunderland Hebrew Congregation, the equivalent of the United Synagogue, somewhat derisively termed the 'Englisher Shul' were not always easy. The members of the Beth Hamedrash, the subject of this excellent account, absorbed many English virtues but the art of compromise was not of them. It had been agreed in principle at the beginning of the last century that there should be a joint Board of Shechitah between the two synagogues. Moving from that agreement to setting up the Board itself took a mere thirty years. One can only be awestruck by the stamina of those involved.

The members of the Beth Hamedrash were proud of their Litvak traditions, of the standard of learning of their rabbis as well as their own dedication and institutions. They were proud also of their relations with their neighbours and were respectful of their principles. Established in Quaker Durham they felt an affinity with the local Christian population and respected their sensibilities. They would not willingly offend their neighbours by, for instance, displaying washing on Sundays.

These traditions of faithful adherence to Jewish law combined with a respectful attitude to outsiders carry a very important message for our community today. Sunderland community is no more but hopefully its influence as presented by its members and their numerous descendants will be felt throughout the Anglo-Jewish community and for that matter throughout the Jewish world.

Vic Wineman

Preface

If you want to find the relics of the Sunderland Beth Hamedresh today, you'd have to search far and wide. The bimah graces the synagogue in London's Woodside Park. There's a sefer torah in Gateshead. The Shtender is in Newcastle and the old members can be found scattered all over the world; in London, Antwerp, Israel and points North, South, East and West. There's a time capsule under the school science block which covers the site of the old synagogue and plenty of tomb stones in the Bishopwearmouth cemetery.

Yet, in its day – and it lasted from 1889 – 1987 – the most knowledgable rabbis in Israel would say that Sunderland Beth Hamedresh was very special indeed. This book sets out to tell its story.

It's a story of commitment to an ideal; the practice of Judaism in all its complexities in a part of the world where there was no tradition to build upon of a similar determination. It shows what can be done to obey the mitzvot, even if the odds are all against you. It tells of a village in Lithuania, from which most of the congregation first came; poverty stricken, not speaking English, with only their own resources to rely on in a totally strange environment. Their only advantages were their commitment and the kindness and tolerance of the local English people in Sunderland.

From such unfavourable beginnings the Beth Hamedresh made the Gateshead Yeshiva possible, they provided Mayors and Leaders of the Council for Sunderland, brought up their children to be pillars of the local community, doctors, specialists, lawyers and accountants. In a steadily more secular environment they maintained their strict observance of the laws laid down in the Talmud. Their success in achieving this deserves a permanent record.

We should like to acknowledge the help we have received from Mordaunt Cohen, Shirley Davis, Michael Davis, Dayan Chanoch Ehrentreu, Peter Gillis, Max & Eva Guttentag, Lionel Kopolowitz, Rabbi Abraham Levy, Diane Lopian, Jack Lopian, Chaim Pearlman and Meyer Pearlman. The Jewish Chronicle archive has been invaluable and we have drawn heavily on the records of the community and the work of other authors many years ago. Thanks are also due to the photographers: Dr Nicholas Posner and Phil Dougan.

The community was full of characters. Effective rabbis who led their communities rather than being led; rabbis like Hirsch Hurwitz, Moshe Rabbinowitz, Abraham Babad and Shammai Zahn. The laymen too; Chatze Cohen who raised 22 children when not leading the daily study of the entire Gemorah. Joseph Pearlman who could cheerfully survive a Slump. Joseph Landau, Militia Man No: 1, because he wouldn't report to his camp on Shabbat, travelling instead on the previous Friday. The members followed the din to the letter and many of the most obscure rulings come to life as their origins are explained.

The Sunderland Beth Hamedresh was not just another Jewish community which arrived, grew, declined and eventually disappeared. What it stood for influences the behaviour of the descendents of the congregation all over the world to this day. Large numbers of them remain true to the faith of their ancestors. In this, they followed in the footsteps of many other Jewish Orthodox congregations over the centuries and that is the bequest of the Sunderland Beth Hamedresh to coming generations.

Chapter 1
The story so far

Except for the largest towns and cities, sizeable Jewish communities don't stay around for long. Admittedly, the Jewish idea of "long" is somewhat more extensive than that of most people. A couple of hundred years, when you can easily prove you've been in existence for thousands, is but a blink of the historical eye.

So in Britain we can find the sites of old Jewish cemeteries in Bath, Chatham, Dover, Exeter, Falmouth, Gloucester, Northampton and Norwich, Penzance and Plymouth, to name just a few. They may have been disused for decades and centuries, but they bear witness that there was once a Jewish community which worshipped and worked, lived and died, where now the contribution of many of them has faded from memory as the years have drifted by.

In the disappearance of these Jewish communities, there can be satisfaction as well as sadness. Some of the descendants moved on and helped create or strengthen other Jewish communities. Judaism itself didn't die. The efforts the members of the old communities made to ensure the religion survived were not wasted. And for Orthodox Jews that is absolutely everything. Nothing else matters. Just that they have children to inherit the faith and that it will continue in its Orthodox form after they have gone. Which has been unlike the worship of Egyptian, Greek and Roman gods and unlike the Albigensians, Hussites, Sabbateans and any number of other sects who are now just names in history books. Those who wanted to destroy the Jews were every bit as determined as those who destroyed the other sects, but when it came to Judaism even the most powerful empires failed in their attempts.

Jewish communities disappear for many reasons. The most common is that the Jews assimilate and are lost to whichever faith is most common among the wider population. They also disappear through massacre and expulsion. They might abandon a town because it has been destroyed or lost its economic base. They might emigrate or be taken into slavery. If there were something like five million Jews at the time of the Roman Empire, the best guess is that this figure had dropped to about a million in the Middle Ages. It recovered to some nine million in the mid 19th century. Two hundred years later, there are now not more than 15 million and that depends on what you regard as a legitimate Jew. In Britain, unless their synagogues and cemeteries have been protected as part of the heritage, they leave few traces. The Board of Deputies of British Jews takes responsibility for some disused cemeteries, but not all of them.

There are also a few old Jewish houses, like Abraham's in Lincoln - the oldest stone house in the country - and a number of streets still bear witness to their former inhabitants, with names like Old Jewry. There may have been a mediaeval synagogue in Guildford and the present community's website proudly claims "Haimishe since 1140!" The new small Lincoln community does, in fact, meet in what could have been the 1150 synagogue. This would make it the only pre-expulsion synagogue in England.

Another of the disused cemeteries is that of Ayere's Quay in Sunderland. It was in use between 1770 and 1856. The ground rent was £1 a year, which was raised to £1.50 when some extra land was taken in 1848. Alas, today it is a tangle of high grass and weeds. Almost all the stones have vanished and all that really remains is a lofty stone pillar, a memorial to one, David Jonassohn, which stands high and crooked in the wilderness. The next Jewish cemetery section at Bishopwearmouth is, at the moment, in much better shape.

In our more enlightened days it isn't difficult for a religious denomination to get the help of the local authorities to find some land for a cemetery, but in the 18th century, there was considerable dislike of Dissenters, a feeling which could affect the treatment of Jews as well. Although this did not create a problem for them in Sunderland, The Antiquarian Society of Sunderland in 1915 recorded:

> One of the most difficult positions the early members of the Society of Friends and other dissenters were placed in, was the burial of their dead... It is said that some of the clergy refused to bury any of them, and a story is related of one clergyman who, when accused of such conduct, denied the accusation and said that he would cheerfully bury them all!

There were Jews in the North East of England in Norman times. What is now Silver Street in Newcastle, was called Jews Gate. Jews in Newcastle were taxed by Henry II and the whole community was expelled from the town in 1234. This gave Newcastle's Jewish history several centuries start on Sunderland, but when the Jews were allowed back in the country by Oliver Cromwell, it took them some time to move back to the North East. Sunderland had been transformed by two events. The first took place during the

Civil War in 1642. Newcastle was for the King, but the good and the great in Sunderland had been persuaded to support Parliament. As a result, when the Roundheads won, the coal shipping industry which had been Newcastle's prerogative was given by the Parliament to Sunderland.

Cromwell is usually given the credit for allowing the Jews to return to Britain but he didn't pass a law to that effect. This was fortunate for the Jews as Cromwell's laws were abrogated by Charles II when he regained the throne. It was when Charles refused a petition from the City of London to expel the Jews again in 1661 that, de facto, they were permitted to settle in the country.

As a coal port Sunderland grew considerably, and then expanded again when coal began to be mined in the area around Durham. A few people did very well financially. The condition of the others was wretched. The struggle for existence among the poor, and particularly among the children, is hard to conceive in these days of a welfare state. Even in the earlier part of the 19th century, poor children would collect acorns in the woods in order to roast and eat them. It was one way to avoid starvation.

By 1744, though, there is a record of Jewish pedlars in Morpeth in Northumberland and evidence that many inns had a locked cupboard in which were housed the utensils which could be used for cooking and eating kosher food, by those who plied their trade in the local villages. The first Jew we can name as settling in Sunderland was Abraham Samuel who was there from at least 1750. He was described as a Silversmith and this was one of many professions in which the Jews specialised. It was easy to transport the stock, the skills in manufacturing resulted in prices which were far above the cost of the raw material, and jewellers could be pawn brokers as well. Running a business, however, had all the risks of today and many failed to survive, including Abraham Samuel who went bankrupt in 1783 before dying in 1794.

The fact is, however, that there must have been many other Jews there at the same time as Samuel. In 1781 there was a split between the original settlers who came from Holland, and the Poles who had fled from the Empress Catherine's Russia, when she made their lives impossible. Many fled to the North East of England and settled, of course, in the same parts of the town. Orthodox Jews may not ride on the sabbath and, therefore, it is customary for them to live in close proximity to wherever they pray. Until 1828 Crescent Row, Sunderland was known as Jews Street. The Dutch Jews made a living near the port when they found that if they had the ability to speak more than one language, they could work as middlemen and interpreters, which was lucrative enough to keep them going.

The synagogue in Vine Street in Sunderland was established in 1781 when there were no congregations of Jews in towns like Manchester and Leeds. By 1790 it was officially known as the Adath Yeshurun or the Israelite Congregation. By 1820, the Poles though were meeting in Lilburne House in Vine Street. Lilburne had been one of Oliver Cromwell's supporters and indeed it was said that Cromwell had stayed overnight in the house when he came North to fight the Royalists. The Jews also had a cemetery in Hetton Staiths, though it was not unusual at the time to be buried in your own garden.

The cause of the split in the community is not known, though it could have been because the Poles belonged to a Jewish sect called the Chassidim and were more religious than the earlier Dutch settlers. Those who came from Germany were probably Misnagdim - a word which means opposition. What they were opposed to was, indeed, the Chassidim. Levels of religious observance are a common cause for dissent within Jewish communities. There can be a problem that trying to live a full religious life can be distorted into an effort to be holier than thou, and thereby gain status Brownie points.

Like those of many other cultures, Jews are not always conscious of why they behave in particular ways. For example, they have an international outlook. An Englishman could be born and live all his life in a village in Britain in the 19th century. Only the invention of the railway opened up new vistas. If, however, you were a Jew at any time after the expulsion from the Holy Land in the 2nd century, you could be expelled, persecuted and attacked, until the only way to save your life was to flee to another country. To travel vast distances was, therefore, perceived as perfectly possible, instead of out of the question. Jewish merchants were trading with China from North Africa in the 10th century. The Indian Jewish community didn't celebrate the winter festival of Chanukah because they had left the land of Israel before the Greeks invaded the country in biblical times. It was the eventual defeat of the Greeks by the Maccabeans which triggered the celebrations and the Festival.

The Jews were traders even in those far off days. The Holy Land was on what was just about the only trade route from North Africa to Asia Minor unless you went by sea. The Jews would always try to go where the trade routes developed and they took advantage of new industries to build their fortunes. They were in the Brazilian wood trade in the 17th century and the Indian diamond trade in the 18th. To avoid customs duty, Jewish traders in Falmouth, in the time of James II, were shifting Dutch cargoes into British ships in the port, before sailing on to the West Indies, where Dutch products in Dutch ships would otherwise be subject to a hefty levy. The Customs tried to prosecute but the jury acquitted them because:

> The Jews are a very rich sort of people, their trade is very great, they employ many ships etc., and should that be cut off, abundance of people, both here and in the plantations would feel the want of them.

The Jews were useful in oiling the wheels of commerce. They always preferred to be self-employed. They were too likely to face discrimination if they went to work for non-Jews. This went on for a long time. In 1954 a Cambridge graduate had an interview for a job with Unilever after leaving University. The interviewer told him out of the blue "I would like you to realise that there is no anti-Semitism in Unilever!"

Another profession which Jews favoured was medicine, where they were appointed to look after popes and emperors, kings and, for two periods in her reign, Queen Elizabeth. They were also money lenders, - now called bankers - when charging interest was forbidden to Christians. They were also very well organized traders because they possessed an international network of co-religionist contacts and a universal set of rules for conducting business. These were set down in the Talmud, the source of Jewish law.

All these factors came into play in the 18th century when Sunderland suddenly grew in importance because of the industrial revolution. It had been a fishing village in 1100 and had a few hundred inhabitants in the Middle Ages. Salt and shipbuilding were its industries in 1400, though it was exporting some coal by the end of the 16th century. By 1700 the town had 1,500 citizens and its shipbuilding capacity boomed in the 18th century.

In Newcastle, the local paper, the Newcastle Courant, occasionally mentioned Jewish weddings. They found dealing with the fact that there was still a religion called Judaism difficult to describe. In 1791 they announced "A wedding was celebrated at Sunderland, agreeable to the rites and ceremonies of the Jews, between..." a Jewish dentist from Edinburgh and a Jewish widow from London. On the assumption that they weren't just meeting halfway, the likely reason for their choice was that there was a community in Sunderland of some size. When Abraham Samuel died, the paper recorded that he was "one of the Jewish persuasion".

In the Navy List of 1814 Levi Samuel of Sunderland is included as a licensed Navy Agent. Much of the attraction of serving in the Navy at the time was the possibility of looting captured enemy ships. If, however, you could avoid the Admiralty confiscating the booty, you still had to sell it to make the profit. Finding punters - and the provisioning of ships - was the kind of work which made the occupation of Navy Agent well worth while.

Navy agents were also involved in collecting prize money for a large number of sailors. When the Board of Admiralty was asked to distribute prize money from the sale of captured enemy ships, it often took years to decide who deserved the dividends. In the meantime, junior seamen were tempted to sign over their claims to a Navy Agent in exchange for goods and money paid out immediately. They could get new clothes, for example, and those who sold these were called slopsellers. If the sum they would get eventually was known, the Navy Agent could only deduct 2½% but if he was paying out in kind - new uniforms, jewellery etc - there was the profit from these goods to be considered as well.

Of the 174 licensed Navy Agents in 1809, no less than 66 were Jews, so Levi Samuel probably had friends in the community in the same business. That it could be highly lucrative was best illustrated by the £200 - £300 bond the Navy agent had to put up to get his licence. In today's money that is £11,000 - £16,000. In terms of average earnings you can multiply that by 10 again. If the Navy Agent committed any misdemeanours in paying out the prize money, or by overcharging the sailors for the work he did on their behalf, the licence bond was there to provide compensation.

Less commendable was the occupation of crimping. This involved a bounty from a ship's captain if you could find him some crew he needed. To get the men, the crimper would often find some likely candidates, get them drunk and then, effectively, kidnap them. They would wake up on the boat which was short-handed. It was a criminal offence to crimp Royal Navy men but it was lucrative for the crimper, whose ranks included, as we know from the records, a number of Jews at seaports around the country.

In a *History of Sunderland* published in 1819 the author described the Jewish community:

> The Jews residing in Sunderland and its neighbourhood meet for worship at a house at the bottom of Vine Street, formerly the property and residence of Lieut-Col. Lilburne. Difficult of access and in no way remarkable for its interior decoration, it forms a striking contrast to the grandeur and magnificence which once adorned the Jewish Temple at Jerusalem.

Vine Street was a considerable improvement as well on the room in Mallins Rig which was in use before its purchase, and the 1821 constitution of the Jewish community still survives. Perhaps the most remarkable element of it is the cost of becoming a full member, which was £2.10. Today, in terms of average earnings, that is £1,600, so it is not surprising that there were only six full members in all. David Jonassohn was one of them and he was the only member to sign in English. He was described in the document as David, son of Haver Jonathan SGL; the initials mean he was a Levite.

One other memento of those days which has survived is the pointer used to help read the passage from the pentateuch on the sabbath. It is silver, made in Newcastle and hallmarked 1817 though it was presented in 1820 and the inscription reads:

> These are the names of the men who gave money with a full heart for the pointer as a constant memory for them before G-d and may G-d shield them for ever.

There are eight names on the pointer. The constitution was constructed with equal attention to detail. The congregation decided that some old habits were past their sell-by date. The last day of Succot is the Rejoicing of the Law, Simchas Torah, when dancing and jollification are allowed in the synagogue to celebrate the occasion. Samuel Pepys, the Stuart diarist, attended a service at Bevis Marks London on that day and was shocked at what seemed to him extraordinary rowdy behaviour. The jollification was, however, now getting out of hand and part of the constitution was enacted to fine members half a guinea who threw things on Simchas Torah. If, however, such actions could be explained on such a happy occasion, what about those who threw things on Tisha b'Av, the second most solemn day in the Jewish calendar, commemorating the destruction of the Temple?

This custom, it was construed by those who did it, originated in the Book of Lamentations 3:53-56 which reads "They have cast stones at me....I called on thy name.... thou didst hear my voice." After due consideration, it was decided that it was unnecessary to continue acting out the casting of stones, however allegorical, and the half guinea fine was attached to this as well.

The community probably suffered in 1831 when a cholera epidemic which would kill 32,000 people nationaly, actually started in Sunderland. There were 215 deaths and Ayeres Quay must have been the scene of much mourning.

In 1834 the synagogue in Vine Street was destroyed in a major blaze which affected a number of the houses fronting the High Street. It was an ignominious end for Col. Lilburne's home. A few years later, in 1841, the Society for the Aged and the Sick was formed by the Sunderland community and this would develop into the Board of Guardians in 1886. By 1850 Myer Marks reported that he was the President, Secretary and minister of the Polish congregation but there was also a congregation of "Israelites" who met in the home of a Rabbi Jacob Joseph. To hold a full Jewish service, the only requirement is to have a minyan - 10 Jewish men present over the age of 13. You don't need a special building.

Jacob Joseph was another silversmith and jeweller who settled in Sunderland in 1790 and remained in harness until he died at 92 in 1861. He was described as a Rabbi and certainly is recorded as having discussed a technical point on a sefer torah (the scroll of the law) with the Chief Rabbi, Solomon Hirschell, in London. He was recruited in 1790 by Elizabeth Samuel who was a member of Abraham Samuel's family and looking for a suitable husband. She went to Amsterdam to interview him and when she persuaded the 21 year old Rabbi Joseph to come to Sunderland, they were married within two years. Besides his business career Rabbi Joseph was a Chazan/Shochet and he dominated the community until he died. He and his wife had no children but they were happily married for 60 years. He was dedicated to the congregation and served the community as their minister for the first 30 years without payment.

Rabbi Joseph also had a nephew, David, who obtained Hirschell's permission to act as a Shochet - the official slaughterer - in 1839. The shochet made it unnecessary to get the meat from Newcastle where, in 1832, it had been agreed that anybody from outside Newcastle would be charged ½p more per lb for their meat than the locals. The only exception was Sunderland where the additional cost would only be ¼p. Indeed, by 1862, there were two kosher butchers in Sunderland and they also provided meat for the communities in Hartlepool and Middlesborough. David Joseph took over from his father as the Sunderland minister, also retaining it as an Honorary post.

The Polish community was so firmly established by 1832 that they were the first Sunderland congregation to have a member elected to the Jewish Board of Deputies. Unfortunately, though, they couldn't afford the cost of sending him to the meetings in London. There were 76 seats in the Polish synagogue and only 34 had been sold. Worse, on the Saturday of census day in 1851 only 12 were to be found in shul. The Israelite congregation may have been smaller but they rallied 40-60 for the morning Sabbath service in Rabbi Joseph's house, which he put at their disposal as usual.

It was the Israelite community which had the original sifrei torahs, as Rabbi Joseph had removed them, with the encouragement of the original seat holders, when the communities split: "dissension having arisen in the greatly increased congregation owing to the great influx of foreigners." In 1856 it was estimated that, in total, there were about 250 Jews in Sunderland, but this number increased to 600 in 1876 and would reach 1,000 in 1905.

Sunderland grew further in importance as coal production expanded in the Durham area. It certainly wasn't a field of endeavour in which Jews had ever played much part but there was to be one mine - totally unique - in which a Sunderland Jew was a founder.

The company that owned the mine was Elliott & Jonassohn and it was formed in 1840. The Elliott was George Elliott (later Sir, an MP for Durham and a power in the mining land). Jonassohn is described as a merchant. Which probably meant that his family had started as pedlars, but had moved up a notch to shopkeeper. They might even have hired other Jews as their agents, visiting the neighbouring villages and the poorer parts of major local towns.

In 1840, Elliott was 26. He had started down the pit at the age of nine and had worked his way up. It isn't difficult to surmise that he could see the possibilities of making a fortune by owning a mine and Usworth, the one he had in mind, was only an open cast mine at the time. We can date open cast mining there from at least 1815, but open cast restricted the coal reserves which could be exploited and it might well have been sold for very little.

The question we will not be able to resolve is how Elliott and Jonassohn met. Jonassohn was born in 1795 and would probably have been reared abroad. He most likely came to Sunderland in 1813 because that was when he joined the local synagogue. He was 18 at the time and may well have come from Holland. Among other occupations, the early Jews serviced the port of Sunderland by selling goods at the dockside to incoming sailors. The navy preferred the salesmen to come on board as it meant the sailors wouldn't get off the ship - and be tempted to desert or fall into the hands of the crimpers. A lot of pictures of ports of the time include in the background a typical Jewish trader. They were the backbone of the original community - the tally men.

It would be a logical progression for Jonassohn to go from being a tally man to being a merchant. He would have learnt to understand commerce and Elliott probably would not. When they got together, Jonassohn was 45 and Elliott was 26, so the older man, knowledgeable about finance, would be the kind of partner that Elliot needed.

It obviously wasn't easy to raise the money because the shaft for the Usworth mine wasn't sunk until 1845 and mining only began in 1847. What neither Jonassohn nor Elliott possessed was a high degree of proficiency in mining engineering, but they joined forces with a Mr. Veiner, who provided that experience and also joined the Sunderland Jewish community.

Where did the money come from? There is no reason to think that Jonassohn could have paid for the shaft himself. There would eventually be three pits, the Frederick, Victorian and Wellington. The Sunderland Jewish community certainly couldn't have found the money. When the Polish congregation elected a member of the Board of Deputies which met in London, they had to write in 1841 to say that, again, they couldn't afford to pay for him to attend. They were mostly impoverished. Getting the necessary finance in five years could have been considered fast work.

Jonassohn did a great deal of good for both the Jewish and non-Jewish communities in Sunderland. He built a chapel and a church for his workers and, when his daughter got married, gave a princely 12.5p to every poor widow and senior citizen in the area. He also started the Usworth Colliery School which eventually had 400 pupils. All this generosity won him plaudits throughout the town.

Although he was happy to pay for the chapel and the church, he did not want to feel indebted in return to Christian benefactors. He was anxious to ensure that only Jewish contributions would be accepted for a new synagogue:

> He has no objection to publicity in the Jewish Chronicle so that Israelites in other towns may contribute, but has great objection to solicit the aid of Christians. He is quite sensible that assistance might be rendered by Christians, but is of opinion that Christians should not say that Jews could not build a synagogue without their subscription.

The mine originally employed 300 but that number expanded in the 19th century until it reached 1,200. It closed in the 1970s and, alas, during its 125 year history, 230 miners died in pit accidents. It is said in mining communities that this is part of the price of coal. In August 1850 the local paper commented, with approval, that the Jonasshohn daughters had opened a bazaar which was being held to raise money for the dependants of the victims of the latest explosion.

Certainly, Jonassohn had good relations with the non-Jewish dignitaries of the town. In 1843 the Corporation of Sunderland had petitioned Parliament to allow Jews to take a more suitable oath of allegiance if they were elected to Corporation office. A law agreeing to this was later approved and many of the Council attended the dinner Jonassohn gave in 1858 to mark the final passing of the even more important Oath Act which at last enabled Jews to be members of the House of Commons. This Act allowed them, when they were elected, to use an acceptable form of wording when taking the Oath of Allegiance .

For his part, Jonassohn had taken a leading part in the efforts made in Sunderland to support the British forces in the Crimean War. There was, of course, no conscription and so men had to be encouraged to volunteer. Jonassohn formed the Patriotic Club to raise money to pay a bounty to those who would go to fight. He also appealed for Sunderland men to man a gunboat, which was one of six being built in the shipyards on the Tyne to support the land army.

It was another reason why, throughout its 200 year history, there was always a very friendly relationship between the civic authorities of Sunderland and the Jewish community. The Jews were law abiding in all that really mattered, good examples for others in their strong family ties, charitable when they could afford to be - and often when they couldn't - and they would later produce more than their share of the professional men every town needs. They may have arrived as impoverished pedlars but they would go on to provide Sunderland with a great many doctors, distinguished lawyers, other assorted professionals and leading local politicians.

Jonassohn was a generous man to his own community. When a former synagogue minister died in Dublin, a subscription list was opened for his dependants and David Jonassohn sent £2. It was carefully reported in the *Jewish Chronicle* - D. Jones and Son - £2! Jonassohn's name has also come down to us because he was elected to serve on the Board of Deputies of British Jews in 1853 and this time the community had a member who could well afford the travelling expenses. Only now, Jonassohn was not allowed to take his seat. He had been married by David Woolf Marks, the minister of the West London Synagogue of British Jews. This is now the largest and most important Reform synagogue in Britain but when Jonassohn married, its services hardly differed from the Orthodox. The members were originally usually known as Seceders, rather than Reformers.

Nevertheless, the Board of Deputies had decided that a member of this breakaway congregation could not sit as a delegate and Jonassohn was a member of the synagogue in London as well as of the congregation in Sunderland. There was an enormous row and the President of the Board of Deputies, Sir Moses Montefiore, had to use his casting vote to decide the result of the motion to exclude Jonassohn. He used it to prevent Jonassohn taking his seat.

Jonassohn was not best pleased. He wrote to his community about the acknowledged and revered leader of the whole British Jewish community:

> Sir Moses Montefiore must, and will be held responsible for all the evils which may follow this act of monstrous injustice done to you. (The Sunderland community); and I consider him the more culpable possessing, as he did the confidence and grateful recollection of nearly the whole Jewish community, and taking the advantage of that position has by his vindictive spirit, inflicted great and lasting evils on the British Jewish community.

It was like attacking Queen Victoria, but the reaction of the vast majority of the existing Jewish community in Sunderland was, in fact, not favourable to Reform. This was to be the position of almost the whole Sunderland community throughout their existence. The members didn't argue, like many of the Reform, that the laws of the religion were old fashioned or should be changed. Rather than assuage any guilt by abolishing the laws, the members recognised that they should observe more of them, and hoped that the Almighty would excuse their shortcomings if they missed any.

There were a few who opted for the Reform way, which is to 'modernise' the religion, as they explain it, but the vast majority remained firmly Orthodox. Jonassohn had signed the constitution of the Sunderland community 30 years before, but when he joined the West London Synagogue his name was obliterated from the record of the signatories.

Sir Moses recognized that Orthodox Judaism was difficult to maintain. He wasn't even all that keen on Jews being allowed to sit in the House of Commons. His reasoning was, to take one example, that if they were seated as members, they might well, among other things, have to vote on Saturday and that would prevent them observing the sabbath. The breakaway congregation in London, the West London Synagogue of British Jews, aroused his deepest hostility. Montefiore knew that, in the past, breakaway movements which had started by only wishing to change comparatively minor aspects of the religion, had finished up advocating a pale imitation of the original faith.

Jonassohn was outraged that a man of his importance in the North East should be rejected. He put it down to Montefiore not wanting a competitive synagogue to his own in London, as defections from it might dissipate some of the income it normally received. This wasn't, in fact, Montefiore's motivation, though a drop in income for his Sephardi (of Spanish or Portuguese descent) synagogue was a factor when the West London synagogue was formed. Montefiore's rationale was that he was against the thinnest end of the wedge. He believed there was no room - and no need - for change. His attitude was typical of very Orthodox Jews. Throughout the life of the Beth Hamedresh, that thinking would always dominate their decisions. Jonassohn died in 1859, leaving the field clear for Elliott. He was deeply mourned by his fellow-congregants and his work force.

Jonassohn was buried in the cemetery of the West London Synagogue though an exception was obviously made for the raising of the pillar in the closed Ayeres Quay cemetery. The land for the new cemetery had been bought after an appeal had been made for funds; David Jonassohn gave £10 and a further 10 guineas (£10.50) came from the generous Rothschild family. In 1894 when more land was needed, the Bishopwearmouth Burial Board provided it free for the community.

As Sunderland had room in its cemetery, it was agreed in 1853 that it would accept burials from the members of the Newcastle congregation, whose cemetery had been closed by the local Board of Health. Until they found themselves some land for a new one, the Newcastle bodies went to Sunderland. After Ayeres Quay was itself declared full a few years later, new land was found in the Bishopwearmouth Cemetery where eventually there were three sections devoted only to Jewish burials. The first was used from 1856 - 1899, the second from 1899 - 1926 and the third from then on.

There had been a number of different communities by 1850 because the Landmannsschaften had different traditions and found it difficult to get on together. At this point, however, declining numbers made it sensible for all the congregations to join together. Finally, in 1857 the several communities decided to join forces, They formed a committee led by Aaron Moses Lotinga, a prominent ship broker, and took an advertisement in the Jewish Chronicle, which read:

> The Jewish community of Sunderland, at present amounting to 250 souls, have for the last 90 years (when the number was much smaller) worshipped in rooms under different congregational heads. They are now desirous of building a spacious synagogue and uniting the different congregations into one body, so that peace and unity may be established and the service of the Most High be conducted in perpetuity, and in a more decorous manner, in one body, than has heretofore under various congregations. They now appeal to their brethren to aid them in their good work.

This was a major fund-raising exercise and the Jewish Chronicle in 1861 congratulated them on their efforts:

> The congregation requires a synagogue. It is numerous enough to support one when it is established, but it is neither large nor rich enough to erect one entirely from its own means. It, therefore, as is customary in Israel in such cases, appeals to the pious zeal of sister congregations and their members. But it neither depends entirely upon this assistance nor fails to set the example. It most creditably puts its own shoulder to the wheel, and accordingly, we find that out of the £305 subscribed, £224 are

> contributed by a congregation numbering only 250, few of whom can be said to be in affluent circumstances.

It had taken three years to get the money together but once the contract was agreed, the building went up quickly. It wasn't just the synagogue, however. There were lots of individual items to obtain. One of the constituent parts of the new congregation would be the Polish Jews and they had a number of accoutrements which would be needed for the synagogue, plus two sifrei torah. (A scroll containing the first five books of the Bible). It was agreed to purchase all of these for £7.36p.

As a consequence of all the hard work and with the help of a particularly generous donation from Aaron Lotinga, a purpose-built synagogue was erected in Moor Street near the docks. In May 1861 the foundation stone was laid by Aaron Lotinga. Rev. David Joseph, the unpaid minister, conducted the service and read a prayer which had been especially written for the occasion by the Chief Rabbi. In handing over the silver trowel for the stone laying, Aaron Lotinga was told:

> Mindful of your indomitable exertions and the expense you have put yourself to raise subscriptions to build a proper place of worship, we consider this but an insignificant acknowledgement of our gratitude and esteem.

After the ceremony:

> A select party repaired to the home of Mr. Lotinga where an elegant entertainment was given, and kept up till a late hour.

and the synagogue was completed by December 1861. It was: "brick with stone dressing in the Italian style. It will be 25 feet high; 42 feet long; and 36 feet wide." It could seat 120 men and 70 women upstairs. "A battlement will surround the roof, in accordance with the injunction in Deuteronomy (chapter 22, verse 8.) "When thou buildest a new house, then thou shalt make a battlement for thy roof, that thou bring not blood upon thine house, if any man fall from thence." It was a biblical Health and Safety regulation. It was also in 1861 that Rabbi Jacob Joseph died at that splendid age of 93.

Before he died David Jonassohn had been prominent in the Appeal and in support of his wish to only have Jewish subscriptions, had offered to double any money raised from the Jewish community. If that promise was not honoured after his death, the family still made a very handsome £50 donation to the Building Fund.

In May 1862 the synagogue was consecrated by the Chief Rabbi, Nathan Marcus Adler and there was no way the community was going to allow this to be anything other than a major event in the town. The local paper reported:

> On Monday afternoon, the 5th May 1862, Mr. A.M.Lotinga, the President, accompanied by the executive committee, together with the Minister, Rev. Moses Woolf, proceeded to Leemside Station in five carriages to meet the Rev. Dr. N. M. Adler, who arrived at the above station at 7pm accompanied by his son, the Rev. Hermann Adler. They were conducted to the carriages in waiting, drawn by four horses and two postillions. They stayed at the Queens Hotel. The consecration service was conducted by Dr. N. M. Adler and a sumptuous dinner followed. On Wednesday, the Chief Rabbi and his son and the executive departed for Shields in a carriage drawn by four horses and postillion.

It must have been a fine sight and illustrated once more to the local population how seriously the Jews took their religion and in what high regard they held their spiritual leaders. Indeed, the locals must have considered it remarkable that, in order to observe the sabbath, almost all Jewish businesses in the town closed on the Festivals and on Saturday, which remained one of the main shopping days. On their doors was a sign which read "Closed from dusk on Friday to nightfall on Saturday". It was getting to be a long way from the days when the Jews kept their heads way below the parapet and took care to worship in anonymous buildings in back streets.

It was a great honour for the congregation that the Chief Rabbi also agreed to preside at a meeting but they were not all that happy at his suggestion that they should abolish the tariff for Aliyahs. Those were set prices for being allowed to take part in specific sections of services on the Sabbath and during Holy Days. The Chief Rabbi felt that these costs prevented the poor from getting their fair share of the honours. The practice continued, however, and the prices continued to range from 7½p to 50p.

Those who had originally come from different parts of Europe now settled down to live, somewhat awkwardly on occasions, as one community and it was agreed to pay £5 annually to help maintain the Chief Rabbi's office in London. Overflow services were soon needed on Yom Kippur when attendance was at its annual peak. Even so, the united congregation continued for nearly 30 years, though not always harmoniously. In 1868 the Minister, Rev. Hart advised the membership: "to make up their differences and stop their quarrels." It would not appear that this did much good as Rev. Hart resigned a year later. Sometimes there would be no minister at all for years.

Another area of great importance to the community was the religious education of the children, but here the results were not satisfactory. Financial support for the classes came from the London Society of Religious Education, through the Chief Rabbi's office, but only pressure from that source kept the classes going. In 1881 "Rev. I. A. Levy severed his connection with the school." The problem was normally that the parents weren't sufficiently committed to encourage their children to study. The classes were seen as a necessity but not as a field of study which the children could enjoy.

One problem was that it was very difficult to find a minister who could preach in English and run the cheder as well. When Rev. I. A. Levy was in office, the classes were subsidised by the London Society of Religious Education. They sent inspectors to check how the schools were performing and Sunderland invariably got low marks. Eventually, in 1881, Rev. Levy gave up the unequal struggle and only great pressure from the Chief Rabbi's office kept the classes in existence. He was admired as a preacher though. The *Sunderland Daily Post* in 1877 said he was "a popular preacher to his coreligionists, an active co-operator in all charitable and benevolent movements even outside his own community, and a warm hearted and well liked person of liberal thoughts."

When a new Secretary was appointed in 1871, the Chairman addressed the first meeting afterwards as a boxing referee talks to the fighters before the first round today. He told them it was: "his devout wish that the deliberations of the Committee be conducted with candour and fairness." As he didn't add "as before" one assumes that such a state of affairs had not always been possible in the past. The first Council had produced men who would serve the community all their lives, including Newman Richardson, who held different posts for the next 50 years, but synagogue politics would appear to be a disruptive element on many occasions in the future.

In their new synagogue, the Honorary Officers set about forming permanent committees for the benefit of the congregation. The first of these had been the Jewish Literary Society but it had disappeared after a few years. Also in 1869 the Sunderland

Hebrew Benevolent Society was formed under the Presidency of Newman Richardson, to help the poor members of the community. Even more permanent was the Chevra Kadisha which was organised properly in the same year. This society undertakes the duty of burying the dead. It prepares the bodies for burial, sits with the deceased and prays over the body until the time for internment and tries to make the burden of the mourners as acceptable as possible. Even in future years when the community split, the members of the Chevra Kadisha were drawn from both congregations and always worked well together.

The importance of the Cemetery in synagogue finances should not be underestimated. If land is bought for so much an acre and then sold at so much a square foot, the profits therefrom will pay a lot of bills. Item G of the Chevra Kedusha regulations reads:

> Before starting the work on the purification of the body, etc., a meeting is to be convened by the Warden, at which the amount to be paid to the Burial Society by the relatives of the deceased is to be decided. This is apart from the payment to be made to the Community.

Barnett Bernstein
Vanguard for Krottingen

As the importance of the port of Sunderland grew, it became a possible home for Jews seeking a better life. One of Sunderland's Jewish newcomers in the mid-19th century was Barnett Bernstein. He had lived in Krottingen in Lithuania but had been drafted into the Russian army at the age of 14. Eventually he was given leave to go home after 14 years service and immediately got help to flee the country. He finished up in West Hartlepool about 1859, because the price of a passage on a coal ship returning empty to the North East of England from the Baltic states, was very low indeed. The boat only managed 12 knots and the journey took 38 hours, but it had the great advantage that it was affordable.

When he got to West Hartlepool, Barnett Bernstein was taken by the Customs Officer to Abraham Cassell, a glazier and a fellow-Jew. Cassell took him in and provided him with the glazier's tools. One day Bernstein went to Sunderland to do a job. It took too long for him to get home that night. So he stayed and was so taken with the town that he decided to move there. From such a tiny event was to come a massive Krottingen influx into Sunderland, as Bernstein wrote glowing reports home about his prospects. He went on to do furniture repairs and finished his business life as a furniture manufacturer. Among those who emigrated from Krottingen in a list produced in 1869/70 were D. A. Olswang, Charles Gillis, Y. Pearlman and H. Berstein, whose descendants would still be in synagogue harness 100 years later.

It was to help immigrants like Barnett Bernstein that in 1874 the synagogue changed the name of the Society for the Aged and the Sick to the more all-encompassing Hebrew Benevolent Fund, later to be split into the Sunderland Board of Guardians and the Gemilas Hasodim. The SBOG gave out charity and the GH lent money at no interest to the newcomers to enable them to start a small business. If they were able to make a go of it, they would pay the money back.

After 1881 the influx of refugees from Russia became a flood as pogroms swept much of Eastern Europe as a result of the assassination of the Czar. The stories of terrible massacres moved the hearts of the non-Jews in Sunderland as well as the community and the Mayor started a fund for the Relief of Distressed Jews in Russia. As a token of thanks the congregation presented him with an Illuminated Address. The local paper reported:

> The addresses which are in the Hebrew language, with an English translation, are beautifully illuminated on vellum. Each is headed by a representation of the Shield of David, and concludes with the Blessing in Hebrew and in English. ...The Rev. H. P. Levy mentioned the fact that Mr. Wayman was the first to suggest the holding of a public meeting to protest against the Russian persecution of the Jews, and that he did so a week before the meeting held in London was announced.

The generosity that so many British people showed to Jewish refugees - total strangers from the other side of Europe - was remarkable. The London Mansion House Committee of the Fund for the Relief of Jewish Sufferers by Persecution in Russia raised no less than £82,000. (About £43 million today).

Anxious as everybody was to relieve distress, the burden of looking after a large number of penniless refugees on a long term basis was not tremendously attractive. In June 1882 there were 200 Russian Jews just off a boat, who were entertained to a substantial tea in Sunderland but then put on a train to Liverpool immediately afterwards. They could well have left with some of the food and clothing which the Lady Mayoress had been collecting for the newcomers. The charity was distributed by Rev. H. Levy who wrote to the West Hartlepool Steam Navigation Co. to thank them for their efforts on behalf of the refugee passengers.

Hospitality was not confined to Jews. When Moses Montefiore celebrated his 100th birthday in 1884, the minute book of the Sunderland community records:

> It was also unanimously resolved that considering the great distress now prevailing in this town, and knowing the universal philanthropy of the Venerable Baronet, irrespective of creed, the centenary shall be celebrated by this congregation providing a dinner for one thousand poor and necessitous children of this town...

Naturally, this was much appreciated locally and, in fact, about 1,200 were fed.

In 1886 Sunderland finally had a representative seated on the Board of Deputies. It was quite common for Jews living in London to represent provincial communities and the Sunderland congregation was very pleased when Simon, son of Sir John Simon, MP, the first Jewish judge, agreed to act on their behalf.

To an outsider, the Sunderland community would appear to have reached a form it would maintain for many years to come; similar to other provincial congregations, such as Edinburgh and Newcastle, Leeds and Manchester, Cardiff and Birmingham. There was no reason to expect that it would become over the years, a bastion of Orthodoxy in Britain, very different from the middle-of-the-road style of the existing Jewish community.

In 1881 the shipping company had bought 5,500 emigrants from the port of Hamburg, mostly not Jewish but seeking a better life abroad. Britain and America were the havens and Sunderland was particularly attractive to the Jews of Krottingen, that small town in Lithuania which we should now look at in greater depth.

Kretinga

Krottingen Market Day

Chapter 2
Krottingen

There is no way you can understand the Sunderland Beth Hamedresh unless you understand Krottingen in Lithuania. It's a small town, near a larger town called Memel and seven miles from the Baltic. Jews couldn't live in Memel until the 19th century because they were banned from making their homes in strategic ports. Krottingen was the centre of the import/export trade for the whole region, as it was only three miles from the border with Germany. In spite of the fact that it was hundreds of miles from Sunderland, a substantial proportion of the original Beth Hamedresh members came from Krottingen.

There had been Jews in the town since about 1640. The census of 1662 mentions two Jewish men and one Jewish woman. The Jews traded with Memel and some made amber jewellery as souvenirs from the stones washed up on the Baltic beaches. Some Jews were called Bernstein and the word Bernstein means amber in German. As in Sunderland, there were Jewish pedlars in Krottingen trying to get local villagers to buy something from their carts. There was also a Jewish dressmaker who made a good living looking after the needs of the few rich people in the area, who included the Graf, the local non-Jewish landowner. The vast majority of the Jews, however, were poverty stricken and scraped a living as best they could.

Describing the rabbi's house where he went for lessons as an infant, one eyewitness of the time wrote years later:

> Rabbi Asser's house consisted of one fairly large-sized room, where a Cheder was held and used as the living room for the family... there was also a small sized bedroom and a tiny kitchen. The rooms were sparsely furnished, the main one containing a large table and a backless form on each side and a chair at the top of the table, on which the rebbe sat when giving lessons. There was also a bookcase or shelves fixed to the wall for the Sephorim; and besides some plain wooden chairs and a few odd things, a small bedstead in the far corner of the room, for one or both of the children. The bedroom was also plainly furnished, containing two single beds, a chest of drawers and a few small articles. There was a complete absence of cupboards or wardrobes, all the clothes being hung on hooks fixed to the walls. Not unlike the majority of the houses in town, the floor boards were void of covering of any kind... The walls and ceilings were whitewashed, and usually renewed yearly, Erev Pesach.

The Old Homestead in Krottingen

The more affluent Jews might send their children to the cheder school with butter on their black bread, but most of the pupils would only have the plain bread and water for their lunch. A number of the town's children were crippled with rickets which comes from malnutrition. The diet of their teachers was hardly better. One head of a cheder was known for always having a bowl of broad beans for lunch with a glass of water. Only on one day a week, the sabbath, was a great effort made to improve the situation. The Jews would go without during the week so that they could make that single 24 hours memorable. Chollah would be baked instead of black bread, the sabbath candlesticks would be polished and lit, and the family would put on their best clothes. The sabbath day was very very special as an oasis in an unforgiving desert of existence.

For the 21st century Orthodox Jew, keeping to the Sabbath laws by not working on the holy day involves, among other perceived depradations, not watching television, not driving your car, very limited hot food, not going to football matches and not shopping. There are, of course, major alternative attractions to the day; quality time with the family, an opportunity to forget about business problems and a time to switch off and relax. The point is, though, that with the degree of affluence a considerable proportion of the British Jewish community now enjoy, the advantages and disadvantages make keeping the sabbath a decision to go without, rather than an unmitigated joy. It requires discipline rather than pure indulgence. Keeping the laws of Shabbot reverts to some extent to being a commandment rather than the one celebration in the week.

This wasn't true in Krottingen in the 19th century. There the Sabbath was all about advantages and what everybody dreamed of in Krottingen was the wherewithal to have another six sabbath days a week. At that time in Krottingen, for most people, it was a miserable life and there was also the draft for the army to make matters worse. Krottingen was under Russian occupation from 1795 till 1915 and the Jewish community had to provide more than its fair share of the young conscripts for Russian military service. When Nicholas I came to the throne in 1825 he devised a plan to convert the young Jews in his territories and by this means he hoped to eliminate Jewish communities in his empire. It was his way of dealing with the Jewish Problem.

So the Czar soon passed a law which made military service compulsory for almost all Jews from the age of 12 to 25, not for a few but for 25 years. The conscripts would be sent to military schools where they would be denied anything Jewish and subjected to a harsh conversion regime. If they accepted conversion, their lives would be easier. If they didn't, things would get steadily worse. By the time the system was abolished in 1855, almost 100,000 Jewish children had been dragooned into the army and the vast majority had died or disappeared.

In 1827 the Krottingen community were instructed that they must recruit 10 boys of 12 or upwards who would have to serve the 25 years and would be converted to Russian Orthodoxy, the state religion. Eldest sons were exempt, however, and Jewish families often pretended that other sons were really orphans they had adopted and they were given different surnames. If the conscripts didn't turn up for their medical examination before joining the forces, the family had to pay a hefty fine of 300 roubles. Often they went through the process of joining but then tried to flee the army camp to which they were sent. If they were successful, the objective was then to spirit them over the border to find refuge in another country.

Another terrible aspect of the conscription was that, through bribery or persuasion, it was possible to get your child excused, but this was not an option for poorer children. The community would often employ chappers, who were exactly like the crimpers kidnapping recruits for the British navy. There are even records of debates when the community agonised over whether to send a poor child or the child of the rabbi, or whether to send a religious child or one less observant. That such heart rendering decisions were necessary was the fault of the state.

Those unfortunate enough to be chosen had to serve in the army for up to those 25 years; they were Nicholyevsker Soldats. Being torn from their family homes, quite possibly for ever, was a shocking fate. A considerable number of the youngsters died before they even reached the far away outposts to which they were sent. The czars had all too often oppressed their Jewish communities and it was not surprising that the Jewish leader of the Polish uprising in 1794, Berek Yoselevitch, was born and brought up in Krottingen. He fled when the Poles were defeated but came back in 1806 to join the reorganised Polish army as a Lieutenant Colonel. He died in battle in 1809.

It could also be expected that nearly 100 years later, during the First World War, many Russian Jewish refugees in Britain would be unwilling to join up to fight alongside the nation's Russian allies. As the Rabbi says in *Fiddler on the Roof* when asked if there was a blessing for the Czar "May the Lord bless and keep the Czar - well away from me"! Czar Alexander II came to the throne in 1855 and continued to insist on compulsory military service for young men

Krottingen High Street

The Russian authorities also made life as difficult as possible for Jewish shopkeepers. To sell anything except food you needed a licence which cost an immense 1,000 roubles. For the most part, the shopkeepers in Krottingen pretended only to sell food and anything else was quickly removed from the shelves if an Inspector arrived from central government. This was to act illegally, but the difficulty with being law abiding in 19th century Krottingen if you were a Jew, was that obeying the law could lead to penury and starvation. As the Jews became accustomed - and resentful of - legislation which singled them out unfairly, there was a temptation to become their own judges on whether the law was really there to be obeyed without question. Where they finally arrived in Sunderland, there would be areas of British trading law which would create the same dilemma. It was like the exchange between the Professor and the Dustman in *Pygmalion*. "Have you no morals, man?" "Can't afford 'em guvnor."

Whilst there was a great deal of discriminatory taxation applied to the Jewish population, the non-Jews locally sometimes behaved far more generously. When Count Joseph Tyskiewicz celebrated his golden wedding in Krottingen, he provided money for eight poor Jewish children to be educated at the district school. Even kinder, there was no hospital in Krottingen, but the Graf had a resident doctor who he allowed to treat patients in the town without charge. The only home remedy at the time for a range of illnesses was a succession of cups of highly sweetened, milkless tea; the very limited cure-all of a hot drink.

In those days, however, diseases like smallpox, tuberculosis, diphtheria, cholera and typhoid were medically incurable and took a terrible toll on those who contracted them. From birth the baby was wrapped in a large bandage - swaddling clothes - for some months,, which was supposed to help prevent the infant getting rickets. The expectation of life at birth in England in 1870 was only 47 years and it would have certainly been lower in Krottingen.

Krottingen had a nickname. A lot of small Lithuanian towns did, like Dorbyaner's "pipkenikes", because there were so many pipe smokers. Krottingen's was "groiss-halters" which means snobs. So what did Krottingen have to be snobbish about? Admittedly, amidst so much poverty, you were likely to be looked upon with jealousy if you simply appeared plump and healthy, but the Jewish community considered itself truly rich in one singular way. In Krottingen they were proud of the fact that a lot of their members were experts on the Talmud and its later compilation, the Shulchan Aruch. Their mastery of the totality of Jewish law in those massive tomes made them famous and respected.

Wisdom, as is the Jewish way, was rated more highly than wealth.

To gain the knowledge, the men in the street studied; not just the rabbonim and synagogue officials. Often the community's wives would run tiny shops so that the men could have the time to hit the books together. If you didn't spend an hour or two every day working on the Talmud, you couldn't be considered observant. Far more Krottingen men studied in this way than you'd find in a Kollel, an organised institution for the purpose today. Often when a daughter got married, the young couple would live with her parents for a number of years. This was considered an acceptable alternative to a portion of her dowry. It was known as zein auf kest. In that way the husband would find it easier to study.

Everybody was, of course, shomrei shabbot, keeping the Sabbath in every minute detail. The original 4th commandment instructed the Jews to keep the sabbath holy. It enjoined them not to work on it. As the centuries progressed, however, decisions had to be made on what constituted work. So there are 39 areas of work which are covered in the rules as a result of detailed examination of the spirit and intentions of the original instructions.

The Jews also considered the teaching of their children to be of paramount importance, where the poor non-Jewish people in the town normally ignored education and sent their children to work when they were less than ten years old. In Britain in the 21st century young people who work hard at school in poor districts are often bullied. "Swotting" can easily be rubbished as abnormal behaviour. This is inconceivable in an Orthodox Jewish household where the abnormal behaviour would be if the child didn't study hard enough.

The children were sent to cheder, a Jewish school, at the age of five. They were allowed playtime and an hour off for lunch, but school hours were from 9 - 6. They would study the translation of the Pentateuch and the week's portion which would be read in synagogue next Saturday. Then they would move on to more advanced study; Rashi, the Mishnah and then the Gemorah, which they reached by the age of 10-12.

This was an A level programme in Jewish studies, way beyond the understanding of a majority of international Jewry even today. Yet the children, while taught translation, did not know how to speak Hebrew to each other. They learned to translate the Chumash, word-for-word, but the basics of Hebrew grammar were not considered important enough to spend time on. Most of the youngsters couldn't write Hebrew either. The lingua franca was Yiddish. One pupil remembered that, at the age of 10,

> "our class learned regularly the whole of the current week's sedra. We also did some translation of T'nach, commencing with Joshua, which I found to be very interesting and even thrilling at certain times."

Nobody considered the possibility of sending the children to non-Jewish schools, where they would have been in a minority and probably subject to a lot of bullying, simply because they were Jews. Non-Jewish schools were also often church foundations and the children might well have been exposed to efforts to convert them if they had attended. The pay of the teachers was minuscule, often as little as £1 a year per pupil.

So the Krottingens were proud of their Talmudic expertise and considered themselves superior to communities which did not possess an equal number of scholars. They sacrificed their material needs for the possession of the knowledge. Ignorance was considered true poverty; not living in poverty, as was the fate of the vast majority of them. Only that attitude had enabled the Jews to start again, time after time, maintaining the faith in countries to which they were forced to flee. We'll come across that attitude in a town called Gateshead in due course.

Although their Talmudic skill was a source of pride to the Krottingens, it was kept polished because of their devotion to religious practices. Judaism was a complete way of life and nothing was allowed to stand in the way of observing the many hundreds of mitzvoth involved. What is more, the community stood and fell together. Those in desperate need could always look to family and friends to try to help them.

Krottingen wasn't a big town in 1889; about 3,500 people. There were no pavements for pedestrians, though the main streets had cobbles. Otherwise, it was bare earth which in wet weather, made the roads a quagmire. "The streets were almost impassible unless you wore stievel, high legged boots." Almost all the buildings were constructed of wood, with highly inflammable straw roofs. Which didn't help when a fire started on the second day of the Festival of Shevuot that year and the whole place burned down in a high wind, bar a few houses and farms on the outskirts. It wasn't the first disaster of that kind by any means. A catastrophic fire had also occurred in 1855 and the town would burn down again in 1908. To make matters worse, there was also widespread famine between 1867 and 1871.

When the 1889 conflagration began, the Jewish community was about 35% of the total population. The natural result of the disaster was that the people finished up living in the street until they could rebuild their homes. Less than 5% had any insurance. The only other possible solution to their plight was to get out for good. There were many other excellent reasons for leaving Krottingen in 1889, apart from the effects of the fire. The economic prospects were dismal and the Russian government was still prejudiced against the Jews. As some members of the congregation had already emigrated to Sunderland, like Barnett Bernstein, to a lot of Krottingens it seemed sensible to try to follow them. After all the letters home, from people like Bernstein, had been very enthusiastic about the possibilities of a better life:

> They told of the plentiful supply of fresh water simply by the turning of a tap... instead of having to draw water from a brunnen, a deep well, in buckets and storing it in a tub in the house. And in place of candles or paraffin lamp... gas, an inflammable vapour, was used... we were also told about the sanitary conditions of the houses and of the well-equipped public baths... many of the better-off classes even had bathrooms built in their own homes... it was said that everyone in the country, rich and poor alike, had the choice of eating chollah all the week.

The reality might have been slightly different if you weren't rich enough to have gas lighting and internal plumbing. Nevertheless, over the years, about 50% of the Jewish families in Krottingen emigrated. It was, however, more than a physical departure. As one of them wrote many years later:

> This wasn't a simple matter, however, to one who was born and passed a great part of his life in Krottingen where his forebears had lived out their lives. It meant uprooting himself from his native town, go abroad to a strange land in search of a new life... a home and a livelihood for himself and his family. In the majority of cases, one was also devoid of any capital and, of course, entirely lacking a knowledge of the language of the country of his destination.

It took courage to go and it was a wrench to leave family and friends. The possibility, even the likelihood, was that you'd never see them again; a grandparent, a close school friend, a favourite cousin. From that point of view, the fire was a help because it made the alternative of staying even less attractive. To emigrate, however, also involved considerable trouble and expense in getting the necessary permission from the state. The few prominent Jews in the town helped those who wanted to go without the hassle.

> (He) called for me in a trap and we drove to about 10 or 15 minutes walk from the... frontier. Then, on dismounting from the trap, we walked slowly along hand in hand, as if we were just having a leisurely stroll together... on reaching the frontier, the sentry standing there, who evidently knew my escort very well, and no doubt received substantial 'tips' from him, slightly raised his hand to his hat... and we continued our stroll onto German soil.

It was illegal emigration and that was how you got out. A considerable number of Krottingen Jews were gone within two or three weeks of the fire. The cost of the passage by boat to Sunderland, 4th class, remained very low. The common Jewish process when you arrived in a foreign country at the time, was to find someone you knew in the town, or had been recommended to, and they would take you in until you could get settled down.

This was invariably the way it worked. Partially, the high level of cooperation was based on the fact that no Jew ever knew when he might turn from being the provider to being the supplicant. Some who befriended poor children in Krottingen and afterwards emigrated to Sunderland, were rewarded by the hospitality they then received when they too emigrated, from those they had originally looked after. In Krottingen also there were a few, quite substantial, Jewish farms in the countryside and they took in the old, the sick and the children from the fire for several weeks, while the families tried to sort out their shattered lives.

The memories and traditions of Krottingen remained clear in the minds of the newcomers to Sunderland. They were still impoverished but they were heirs to a rich tradition. It had been their custom in Krottingen to study the massive Babylonian Talmud from start to finish, page by page, taking about a quarter of a century to complete. When they eventually completed the mammoth task they would have a celebration - and then start again. They left Krottingen and, as soon as they reached Sunderland, they simply began once more from where they had left off. The Blatt, as it was called, was first completed in Sunderland in 1902 and so must have been started in about 1880 in Krottingen.

The Dutch and German born Jews in Sunderland were in a substantial majority and they considered themselves a cut above the Lithuanians - or got a kick out of pretending to be so. The Krottingens soon found they were going to be treated by the resident Sunderland Hebrew Congregation as second class citizens. They had to sit at the back of the synagogue some distance from the best seats because they couldn't afford better, but they could still take comfort in the fact that they knew more about the prayers than the older established worshippers. If their knowledge of English was weak, if their dress was shabby and their appreciation of English culture was pretty well non-existent, they were still well educated in Jewish studies.

As far as their secular education was concerned, a class was formed with the express purpose of "teaching the newcomers the 3 R's." As early as 1890 there existed a Sunderland Jewish Mutual Improvement Society. The Victorians were keen on self-help as a way of escaping deprivation and this fitted in well with the attitude of the emigrants.

The Litvaks found that the resident Hebrew Congregation members were often not well versed in the Talmud at all. Here at last was a battlefield where they could fight for their self-respect. If the Hebrew Congregation was more prosperous - and that was only to a very limited extent - if they had been settled in Sunderland longer and knew the rules of the secular game better, they were still vulnerable to criticism on their standards of Jewish observance and knowledge. That, therefore, was the battlefield the newcomers would choose, on which to compete.

This is not to say that the newcomers were anything but sincerely genuine in their Orthodoxy. They would have looked askance at the Englisher shul members for not studying the Talmud every day. Their full name for the alternative congregation was Der Englishe Chayers which, roughly translated, means the pompous, would-be English gentlemen. There are less attractive translations. In their turn, the original Hebrew congregation members called the newcomers the Greeners, which implied that they were ignorant, naive peasants. One-upmanship was soon alive and well and living in Sunderland.

Even more would the newcomers have been disconcerted that the existing community only met for services on Friday evenings, on the sabbath and for the festivals. There were no weekday morning, afternoon and evening services. This would have been unthinkable in Krottingen but the problem, of course, was finding 10 men over 13 years old who would turn out in any weather to make up a minyan. Without a minyan there are important prayers you can't say. This number the Englisher shul couldn't manage, so no midweek services. The Krottingens could collect the quorum without difficulty and they continuously kept up a very high standard of observance in all the other multifarious areas as well. This takes a great deal of discipline, faith and learning.

It is only when you start to study other small Jewish provincial communities at the time that the glaring differences between the general standards and the Krottingens is thrown into sharp relief. Provincial comunities were withering and dying, like Falmouth, Dover and Bath. It was impossible to get a minyan for a Sabbath morning service in Oxford and many other towns. Daily religious study would have been considered totally impossible because there would have been no support for it. Certainly, there were very frum communities in London and in one or two other major cities, but for a small town like Sunderland, the commitment of the Krottingens was like comparing the England cricket team with a village green side.

Along with all this, though, there was also the hidden agenda for the Krottingens of retaining their self-respect in an alien environment. From the point of view of the men of Krottingen, however, inferiority was not an option. It goes against the Jewish grain anyway. The newcomers could do even better than produce a quorum for the three daily services. After all, their religious enemies in other faiths had been trying unsuccessfully to relegate Judaism to the ranks of inferior religions for centuries. Dealing with problems, just involving other Jews, was much easier. The immigrants might have had to put up with disdain from the more established Englisher shul members while they found their feet, but they knew a revolt was inevitable. It was just a question of a matter of time. There would be likely to be a small defection at the beginning but if it followed the usual Chareidi pattern, it would grow steadily.

The Englisher shul members would feel they had done their duty by the newcomers. It was their synagogue, built with their hard earned money and owing its traditions to the Dutch, German and Polish immigrants who had come to Sunderland in years gone by. They would have expected the Litvaks to have recognized this, to have been suitably grateful for the support they had been given by the congregation, and to docilely take up their positions at the back of the synagogue, deferring to their betters.

CROTTINGEN RELIEF FUND.

DEAR SIR,

We beg to draw your kind attention to the accompanying letter from the Rev. A. A. Green to the Jewish Press, and venture to hope that it may appeal to your sympathy and assistance. The smallest donations will be thankfully received and may be addressed to Mr. Green, Treasurer to the Fund.

Yours obediently,

ISRAEL JACOBS,
B. BERNSTEIN,
SOL. GALLEWSKI,
M. SHERGEI,
D. A. OLSWANG, } Committee.
ISRAEL HARRIS,
CHARLES GILLES,
JOS. PEARLMAN,

THE DISTRESS AT CROTTINGEN

TO THE EDITOR OF THE "JEWISH CHRONICLE."

SIR,—May I ask you kindly to allow me to draw attention to the appeal which has been made in your advertisement columns, in the hope that what I am able to say about the extent of the trouble, and the intention of the Relief Fund, may help a cause, the merits of which have been brought recently under my immediate notice. The natives of Crottingen who are in England are not very many, and they are nearly all resident in Sunderland. When intelligence was received that their native town had been completely destroyed by fire, and that nearly 2,000 people were homeless, they inaugnrated a Relief Fund, in furtherence of which they they asked my assistance. This I was enabled to give without any hesitation, because their own respectability was a guarantee for the truth of the statements which had reached them from their relatives, and because I am in a position to know that, before appealing elsewhere, they themselves had subscribed to the extent of their ability. From the first, due recognition was given to all the difficulties attending the transmission of money to Russia and its proper application. In view of these I went to Russia the week before last charged with the duty of enquiring fully into what had happened, and for the purpose of estimating the assistance required, and arranging for its propor application. I found that the distress and destitution had been in no way exaggerated. Crottingen lies in a valley off the main road near the Russian frontier, about ten English miles from Memel. The pretty picture made by its white walls, when seen in the distance, was rudely broken by the discovery that they were walls alone, the desolate wrecks of former habitations. The ruin is complete. It was impossible for me to distinguish where the streets had once been. Charred timbers, and a few walls here and there, alone marked where once had been the homes and marts of the people. Numbers were quite homeless, content to sleep in the open air if they could but procure temporary shelter for their wives and children, for their aged and sick ; to accommodate these latter sheds had been hastily made. I question whether some of the boxes where three families are lodging ought to be considered fit habitation for three horses. The few houses which are left are more than overcrowded, and my own sensation on breathing the atmosphere inside them prepared me for the fears expressed by the doctor of the town that, to the existing evils, the addition of pestilence might be expected. I was careful to make independent enquiries as to the extent of local assistance. In Memel, the nearest town, an unsectarian relief committee has collected 4,000 marks. Of this sum, a great part has been expended in forwardiug food and clothing for the relief of present necessities. The chances of adequate assistance in Russia are minimised by the rival claims of no less than nine other towns farther in the interior where fires have recently taken place. Assistance, to be of any value, must reach the people while wood is cheap, and while the summer weather permits the work of reconstruction. If help is delayed until the rainy season sets in there is little hope that the people will be able to remain where they are, and they may be driven by absolute necessity to add by their presence to the existing burdens of their brethren elsewhere. The rebuilding of the Synagogue—or, at least, the Beth Hamidrash—before the advent of the new year seems to be indispensable to the possibility of keeping the community together. In these circumstances their friends here feel reluctantly compelled to make the present appeal. In endorsing it I venture to hope that what I have myself seen, and the undertaking I am able to give as to the administration of the fund in the interests of donors and recipients by the Memel Committee, will recommend the case alike to foreign Jews in England who can form an adequate idea of the existing distress and to others who, without their experience, can sympathise with the sufferers and share the concern of their friends living in our midst.

Yours obediently,

A. A. GREEN.

3, Salem Avenue, Sunderland,
July 21st, 1889.

The Krotingen Appeal Letter

The arrival of the considerable number of very Orthodox Jews after the unexpected fire in Krottingen had indeed been expertly taken in its stride by the Sunderland community. After all, of the 1,000 Jews in the town, it is estimated that 500 had connections with Krottingen. It also did not create a situation for which there was no precedent. Looking after Jewish refugees from one calamity or another had been necessary for those communities who were unaffected for thousands of years. The correct procedures were quite clearly established and the Sunderland community followed them.

First of all, there was a widespread appeal for funds to rebuild the shattered Jewish community. The Krottingen Relief Fund numbered among its organisers many members of families who would continue to serve the Sunderland community for many years in the future. Among them were Israel Jacobs, Barnett Bernstein, Solomon Gallewski, David Olswang, Israel Harris, Charles Gillis and Joseph Pearlman. The Sunderland congregation contributed generously but took the precaution of asking its minister, Rev. Aaron Green, to take the funds personally to the town. They wanted to make sure that the money did the most good and was not stolen in some way by the authorities. Rev. Green was appalled by the destruction he found and, when he returned, he spearheaded further fund raising efforts through the *Jewish Chronicle*:

> The distress and destitution had in no way been exaggerated; the ruin is complete... it was impossible for me to distinguish where the streets had once been, charred timbers and a few walls, here and there, alone marked where once the homes of the people had been...the men were content to sleep in the open air if they could procure temporary shelter for their wives and children, for the aged and the sick; to accommodate these latter, sheds had been hastily made... the few houses on the outskirts of the town, which escaped destruction, are more than overcrowded.

It was a powerful appeal and it was followed by another in 1891 when a further effort was made to help the Jews in the town. The published list of contributors who responded included 50p from Chief Rabbi Hermann Adler, 50p from Haham Gaster and 25p from Dayan Spiers. A lot of money was raised and this by the British Jewish community for the Jews of a congregation in Lithuania; it was the typical reaction Jews had traditionally offered.

Aaron Green was only 28 when he came to Sunderland from Sheffield and he was destined to be one of the most famous ministers of the Hampstead Synagogue in London.

It was understandable that he would want to move on to a fashionable community, but his attitude contrasted with many of the future Beth Hamedresh ministers, who, having found a congregation with their own strictly Orthodox views, were happy to remain where they felt at home. Rabbonim Bloch and Hurwitz, for instance would move on, furthering their careers, but father and son Rabbinowitz, Rabbonim Babad and Zahn would die in office.

As far as Rev. Green was concerned, "He was not... happy in his duties in the provinces. He resented the restrictions inherent in the work of a Provincial Minister." The point was that he was far from the seat of the Chief Rabbi's power in London. By contrast, the Beth Hamedresh ministers would much prefer to run their own shows far away from central control. While he was at Sunderland, Rev. Green was certainly committed to his congregation and was remembered for the night schools he organised to teach secular subjects to immigrant children.

As for the refugees, the newcomers were following in the footsteps of Barnett Bernstein and they were made welcome. The synagogue members saw to it that they had somewhere to live and were fed. It might be only a spare attic but it was a secure base. The father of a family or the eldest son would often come first. Then when he had made sufficient money and had found the rest of the family somewhere to live, he would send back for the rest of his kin. It might take a couple of years. A social worker was once complaining to a Jew about families with three generations of unemployment in her town. The Jew explained the correct method to adopt to solve the problem. The social worker tried to make the Jew understand the problem. "It's alright for you," she said "You've got 2,000 years experience"!

The financial position of the Krottingen immigrants depended on their status in Lithuania and what they had been able to rescue from the fire. Some, naturally, could adjust more easily than others and a few families were quite comfortably off. They were very much the exception, though, and for the vast majority the question was how to manage to earn a living when you didn't even speak any English?

The simple answer that you should get a job with a company in need of more staff, didn't work for a Krottingen. Such an organisation would have to be prepared to give you every Friday afternoon and Saturday off, so that you could go to synagogue. You would need all the Festivals off as well and for many of the immigrants, at least that one hour a day to study the Talmud. At a time when an early 20th century Shop Act would *restrict* the hours of work to 12 hours a day from Monday to Friday and 14 on Saturday, this was a list of demands which would receive short shrift from the vast majority of prospective Jewish, not to mention non-Jewish, employers. However, the solution to the problem of how the immigrants *would* set out to support themselves in some other way, followed a long tradition as well. The able- bodied would not want to live on charity. That wasn't the Jewish way. They would want to borrow some money and set up in business on their own.

The existing community in Sunderland provided the money. It was recognized that it was only a loan, but it enabled the newcomers to buy some goods which they could sell on at a higher price than they paid for them. In theory and often in practice, they then paid back the initial loan for which they would not have been charged interest. Orthodox Jews can't charge other Jews interest, according to the din. The polite description for the occupation, which so many of the newcomers adopted, was a Credit Draper. They were more commonly known as tally men. The English surname for such traders is Chapman. They were pedlars. They sold on credit to people who couldn't afford to buy the goods in any other way. So much deposit and so much a week.

The tally men were the forerunners of the Mail Order industry and from those tiny beginnings were created some great Jewish companies in the 20th century, like Great Universal Stores. The way it worked was that you would go to a wholesaler who would sell you some goods on credit. If they did add interest, it would be included in the total price they charged. They normally gave the tally men a 15% reduction on the normal price. The wholesaler would probably be a Jew who had started in exactly the same way as you had now, but had prospered sufficiently to come off the road and open a warehouse.

The newcomers would get a cart and hawk their wares round the villages and the poorer districts of the towns. You would go from house to house, knocking on the doors; you would be known as a Klapper. Jewish immigrant pedlars were to be found all over the country. Indeed, the caricature of the Jew as a pedlar in Britain had been current since the early 18th century. The rates of interest charged were high. As moneylenders in mediaeval times, before the expulsion, Jewish interest rates could reach 80% a year. One prominent retailer during the Slump had started his working life as a pedlar in the Welsh valleys. He thrived sufficiently to have furniture shops which offered Hire

Purchase terms in the 1920s. In the middle of the Depression in the 1930s he went on record as saying "the day profits fall below 200% we'll all be ruined!" He was talking about the mark-up on goods but, admittedly, he also had to pay for rent and staff.

The Krottingen tally men had to pay for neither and their profits were very much lower, but that was the means by which many of them tried to build or rebuild their fortunes. Typically, the purchaser would pay the money back, with the interest, in 20 weeks, at so many pennies a week. The pedlar could then also repay the initial loan. Indeed, on many occasions, the money would be offered as a gift. The Loan Society provided the wherewithal to start climbing out of the gutter.

Door-to-door selling is a tough profession but it was a little easier in those days because it often saved the householder from making a long journey to the shops. It also enabled the poor to pay for goods they couldn't have afforded if they had to settle up for them all in one go; there were no credit cards. For a penny or two a week, over a comparatively short period of time, you could indulge yourself. As a householder could see what was on offer in the pack on the pedlar's back, the salesman didn't have to speak much English. One Sunderland tally man was said to have a total English vocabulary of three words: "one sponge, one shilling". (5p). There was also the perfectly genuine advantage of the tally man that it enabled wives to do their shopping without having their husbands in tow; the working man in those days would consider it effeminate to accompany his wife shopping. He might occasionally do so, but he usually didn't like it.

The pedlar could work his own hours and his religious commitments could be fulfilled. He would attend the morning service in the synagogue and then catch the 8.30 train to the outskirts of the town, with his assortment of wash leathers, needles, ribbons, lace, sponges, toys, window glass or whatever else might be attractive to a buyer. On a larger scale there was a considerable demand for gas mantles to take advantage of the new invention. One immigrant recalled:

> I don't remember what kind of goods he traded in, but I believe it was some cheap pictures, in the sale of which, by peddling, a number of the new immigrants were occupied. These pictures were gilt-framed oleographs of New Testament subjects and were supplied by the local picture framer, Yankele Freedman. They were hawked from door to door and it was rather a quaint sight to see these travellers, some with beards, walking through the streets with pictures of Mary and Joseph, "The Last Supper" and other subjects, suspended with string, and dangling from their shoulders.

There were problems, of course, if you had a young son and wanted him to be a tally man. The first was that he needed a licence and he could only get one when he was seventeen. The second was that half price tickets on the buses to the outskirts of the town ended when he was thirteen. The third was that he was expected to attend school until he was thirteen. If you were a youngster, at different ages, there was a choice of three laws to break when you went out to work.

There was little time for school for an immigrant male child. From the age of about 12 or even younger, he would be sent out to become a pedlar. He would do so without a licence and was subject to being arrested and charged in court for the offence. If he was that young, the magistrates would let him off with a caution, but the fear of the law, as it had been enforced in Lithuania, made being hauled up before the magistrates a scary experience. It took time for the immigrant to realise that England wasn't run like a Russian province. As one immigrant recalled:

> I was very much impressed by the considerate action of the police officials, in setting free the 'culprit' before the fine was paid. This made me realise the vast difference there existed between the humane treatment of offenders of the law by the English police and the harsh, and often cruel, manner which the slightest offence by a Jew was dealt with by the Russian authorities.

There should have been a moral dilemma here. A problem of how to square the circle. On the one hand the child was taught that every law in the Talmud needed to be observed in detail. It was expected that there would be a constant effort to improve the level of observance and breaking the laws was severely frowned on. For example, to be a member of the community, as we've seen, every applicant was expected to keep all the laws concerning the Sabbath.

Yet, at the same time, the knowledge that your young son was breaking the laws of the country you were living in, that he could finish up with a criminal record, had to be accepted if there were to be any chance of making both ends meet while still keeping to the laws of the Talmud.

What justification could be offered if the child recognized two different standards were being applied? The most common one was that the laws of the country had not been laid down with your consent. Exactly the same as the avoidance of the tax on running anything other than a food shop in Krottingen. Therefore, the argument went, the law could be ignored and you were prepared to take the unfair consequences. In countries like Russia where the treatment of Jews was discriminatory and often vicious, this argument carried a lot of weight. How, though, could you apply the attitude you could justify in Russia to a far more liberal Britain? Only by instilling a belief that what had happened in Russia - and in many other countries - could happen in Britain as well. Therefore, it was justifiable to take whatever precautions were necessary to be prepared for such a calamity. If you could earn enough money, you could more easily emigrate again in an emergency.

There was very thin evidence that it was even slightly possible that there could be widespread official anti-Semitism in Britain. Gangs in the poorest parts of Sunderland might shout catcalls and use their fists on the child pedlars on occasions. The old Jew, so recognizable in his sabbath clothes, might be subject to anti-Semitic remarks in the street. That was really all. The perception of the reaction of the ignorant to the unknown was summed up at the time in a classic cartoon in the humorous magazine, Punch. Two workmen digging up a road are looking at a stranger on the other side of the street. The caption reads "Oos 'e?" His friend replies "Looks like a stranger" and his companion adopts the characteristic approach to such situations "'eave a 'alf a brick at 'im"! Notice, one brick, no beatings and no state aid for violence. Very different from Russia.

Admittedly, because of the very large number of Jewish refugees who had entered the country since the pogroms started in Russia after the assassination of the Czar in 1881, there was a desire among many native Brits for the passing of an Aliens Act to reduce the influx. That eventually happened in 1905. There would even occur the sole - and very minor - pogrom in the 250 years of post-Restoration British history, in Tredegar in 1911, which the authorities put down with immediate effect and everybody swore wasn't anti-Semitism anyway. Nevertheless, the Krottingen newcomers knew they were foreigners and their experiences back home in Lithuania were not reassuring.

The Lithuanian Jews were known as Litvaks and Chaim Bermant, for many years the celebrated observer of Jewish life in Britain, summed up their viewpoint as he saw it: "Now Litvaks....are, by tradition, the most easy-going of Jews, never indeed, questioning the law, but always adapting it to suit their circumstances." It was true but, of course, the point was that the Krottingen Litvaks were starting from a much higher level of observance than the Jews who belonged to the United Synagogue.

There were many kinds of pedlars and tally men. One method of scrambling for a living was to become a glazier. This involved carrying quantities of glass on your back and looking out for houses with broken windows. With the amount of petty vandalism to be found in the poorest sections of town, there was a lot of work available if the slum family could afford the pane of glass.

There were also pedlars who carried small bolts of cloth and clothing material. The bus conductors were accustomed to finding room for such passengers and the youngest Jews would travel to the furthest parts of the town where the likelihood of bumping into a policeman without possessing a pedlar's licence, was less likely.

Naturally, most of the children were initially anxious about knocking on strange doors, felt demeaned by rejection, were embarrassed by not speaking the language and scared about the possibility of being abused and even attacked by bunches of non-Jewish kids. It was a very hard life, but if you learned the trade, you could help the family survive, for most of the money you earned went into the family financial pot. You might get pocket money, but that was all. The older you were, the more you would probably be able to contribute, and this would continue while you lived at home until you got married. Even after that, helping elderly parents who were too old to work or were suffering from debilitating illnesses, was often necessary.

Although they spoke little or no English, it was perfectly easy to converse in Yiddish within their own Jewish community. Yiddish was spoken by Ashkenazi Jews; a mixture of German, Hebrew and several other tongues. It was consistently used for speeches and sermons long after the Krottingens had settled in Britain. It still is in many very Orthodox communities. On the other hand, getting the people of Sunderland to understand the tally men meant the pedlars learning English, which the vast majority would set out to do.

Being a pedlar was not a high status occupation. They were often looked down upon as foreign, common and poor by those who had come before, but it was a way of surviving. The concept was explained by Chief Rabbi Jakobovits a hundred years later, when he was asked by the most senior clerics in the country to join with them in protesting against what was perceived as a lack of government support for the poor, during Prime Minister Margaret Thatcher's time.

Rabbi Jakobovits replied that he regretted that he couldn't support the Church leaders because of this different Jewish approach to the problem; the Jewish way was to help the impoverished to make some money and get out of the poverty trap, not to wait for a government to take on the responsibility.

The Prime Minister was delighted with this approach and Rabbi Jakobovits became the first Chief Rabbi to be elevated to the House of Lords. In fairness, starting from scratch, the same approach by the Church of England would be an absolutely massive logistical nightmare.

For the emigrants, amidst the poverty of their lives and the squalor of the infrastructure of their homes, often without plumbing or indoor sanitation, there shone the same one weekly occasion when all would be forgotten for a magic day; the sabbath. Just like in Krottingen, what little money there was would be saved for a good meal on Shabbot. On a Saturday morning, among all the neighbours in their shabby, threadbare clothes and cloth caps, there would set out for synagogue a resplendent figure. Clad in a frock coat with a top hat, the Jew would walk to synagogue to join the rest of the community in prayer. The locals got used to it. It was true that in the Englisher shul the emigrants would be tolerated rather than welcomed. He wouldn't get the honours of opening the ark or being called up to help with the reading of the weekly segment of the pentateuch. Nevertheless, he would look the part.

Krottingen remained dear to the hearts of the emigrant community. One of the most loved and respected spiritual leaders in the town was Rabbi Shemuel Yitzhak Hurwitz, known as the Rebbele (the under-rabbi), and in the mid-1890s it was decided to raise a collection for him on a permanent basis. The Krottingens each gave ½p a week and the money was sent to Lithuania twice a year. The rabbi would immediately give half of it to the poor and this kindly generosity continued until he died. There were other calls on the benevolence of the community as well. Some of the emigrants were absolutely poverty stricken and could be in real danger of starving to death in a world where there was no unemployment or family benefits. The mothers and children would be reduced to begging from door-to-door and would be given coppers, a hot drink or a meal to help them survive another day.

On the other hand, the first signs of the professional Jews who would support Sunderland in future years were appearing on the horizon. In 1894 Hermann Wolfe got 14 passes in the preliminary examinations for membership of the Pharmaceutical Society of Great Britain.

He might well have been a pupil of Hyman Levy, who was a schoolmaster in the community. Also in 1894, to mark the fact that he had been diligently teaching the children for eight years, he was presented with "a framed address, Kiddush cup, and a purse of gold." The latter might have been something of an exaggeration, but it was a charming way of describing the results of a collection.

The non-Krottingen Jews in Sunderland had a genuine dilemma. How to get the newcomers to assimilate to the Jewish approach in Britain. From the point of view of the members of the longer established Sunderland Hebrew Congregation, the important thing was to behave like other Jewish congregations in Britain. The result was that the level of observance was, generally, low by Orthodox standards, even if they all had Jewish mothers and were, therefore, halachically Jewish. Most immigrants would eventually adapt. A lot of the Krottingen Jews were made of sterner stuff.

It seems highly likely that there are a very large number of small towns in Lithuania which have left little impression on history. The Jews of Krottingen made sure that their town would occupy an honoured seat at any assembly of historic Jewish centres. The Beth Hamedresh members always remembered Krottingen but the nickname of the community was now Krottingen Upon Wear.

Chapter 3
Founding the Beth Hamedresh

Things were peaceful in 1889. The Queen's Golden Jubilee had been celebrated two years before with great enthusiasm and in 1888 1,000 poor children in Sunderland were given a free dinner as a memorial to the passing of Sir Moses Montefiore, one of the truly great figures in 19th century Jewish history in Britain. There were nearly 50 Jewish tradesmen now operating in the town, though not a single professional.

The time came when Rosh Hashonah was to be celebrated. The morning service had been concluded - it goes on for more than five hours - and the congregation had gone home till the afternoon service started. Towards the end of the interval a Krottingen immigrant mounted the raised section from which the prayers were led and started singing psalms. Berel Nosen Franks was a mountain of a man and he was watched by a number of his Krottingen compatriots, who were delighted to see the Lithuanian custom maintained in its normal form.

When, however, an Honorary Officer of the synagogue arrived, he was appalled. Nobody had given this man permission to mount the dais and say prayers. That was a responsibility which belonged solely to the elected Honorary Officers of the synagogue. He abruptly and publicly told Franks to stop and come down from the dais. Everybody was furious; those who supported the Honorary Officer and those who wanted the singing of the psalms to continue.

For Franks it was a public humiliation. He did stop, but he also walked out of the synagogue, followed by a number of his supporters. They went at the invitation of one of the worshippers, Wolfe Jacobson, to his home and continued with the psalms. At that point it became obvious that there would be considerable support for starting a separate synagogue and that was the trigger for the breakaway community to come into being in 1890.

The home of Wolfe Jacobson soon became too small for those who wanted to worship there and so they first moved to the home of Charles Gillis and then found their first permanent home in the aptly named Zion Street, calling themselves the Chevra Torah. Within their ranks they encompassed both those who supported the Chevra Tehillim - those who wanted to perpetuate the custom of singing the psalms - and the Chevra Gemara - those who regularly studied the Gemara.

Now this latter group had its roots deep in the Krottingen practice of studying the Gemara every day. One of the emigrants to Sunderland was Charles Cohen - known as Reb Chatze because he did have semichah - and Reb Chatze it was who had started the Chevra Gemara to continue the Blatt which would become one of the distinguishing achievements of the Sunderland Beth Hamedresh. He was, in his youth, the teacher to the children of Reb Elinka Levinson who was the premier citizen of Krottingen and a descendent of the Vilna Gaon.

Gershon Levy, like so many other members of the new Beth Hamedresh, had been born on the continent. This was in 1859 and he only reached Sunderland when he was forty years old. By profession he was a grocer. It was just the arrival of another small shopkeeper and talmudic scholar, but a quick glance round the Sunderland community convinced Levy that if he didn't do something about it, talmudic scholars in Sunderland were likely to become an endangered species. His knowledgeable compatriots were getting older and there didn't appear to be much in the way of educated youngsters to take their place.

So Gershon Levy decided to start a Gemara class for the boys in the town, just as Chatze Cohen had started a Chevra Gemara for the adults to study the volumes. Gershon Levy's classes took the boys to the next level which was Chatze Cohen's Blatt. Rev. Kaplan, who was also the Chazan and Shochet, was put in charge of the teaching. From then on, the Gemara was part of the adult study of many members and was taught at the Beth Hamedresh Cheder. Where the normal ambition in the country's chedorim was to get the pupils to at least learn to read their prayers in Hebrew and, hopefully, to have some idea of what they were saying, Levy aimed stratospherically higher.

If the Beth Hamedresh Cheder was going to have a Gemara class, they were really going to take their studies seriously. There is nothing elementary about Gemara, which is a commentary on, and a supplement to the Mishnah. The Mishnah contains the core of the Oral Law and was prepared for publication in Tiberias and Jerusalem 1,500 years before. It is a giant compilation and you can easily study it all your life without mastering it all. It was a substantial intellectual challenge for the boys. From those pupils would come a lot of the students who would go on to Yeshiva, for even deeper study, in the future.

Reb Chatze Cohen
Founder of the Chevra Gemara

Gershon Levy
Founder of the Gemara Classes

Chatze Cohen was typical of those Jews who have two very different persona in life. In commercial life he was a tally man, who also took orders for coal on behalf of a wholesaler. He spoke no English and could not be described by any yardstick as a success in business. Indeed in his latter years, the family supported him. However, in the circles of the Sunderland Jewish community he portrayed a very different picture. Always immaculately turned out in morning dress, with a top hat and a furled umbrella, he was an object of awe for his talmudic learning. He was married twice, fathered 22 children and some of his descendants would go on to run Sunderland for many years. Two Labour leaders of the Council, Sir Jack Cohen and Charles Slater, plus Lt. Col. Mordaunt Cohen, for some years the leader of the Conservative party, would be powers in the Sunderland land.

Chatze Cohen's Chevra Gemara would study every day - the Blatt Shiur - and to these sessions in the future would come a total mixture of the congregation - doctors, lawyers, businessmen, pedlars and students - all attending in order to study every day. There has to be inspirational and firm leadership for this kind of innovation and Charles Slater, Chatze Cohen's great grandson and a very competitive leader of the Sunderland Labour Party many years later, commented dryly "it seems that my great grandfather was somewhat querulous, argumentative and obstreperous and I can't think who might take after him!"

The Blatt was conducted every day before the evening service and while the expert who conducted it (the magid shiur) might change over the years, the work continued. For successive periods of 26 years the whole of the Babylonian Talmud was examined and studied. Four complete studies would be completed in the history of the congregation. There would be a small celebration - a siyyum - when they completed studying each of the 36 volumes, and a big party when they completed the whole. The discussions which began in Yiddish, only changed to English after many years.

Chatze Cohen left Krottingen for Sunderland before the fire and, as a youngster, he had devoted himself wholeheartedly to study. By the time he was 16 he had learned the greater part of the Talmud and mastered Poskim, the responsa of famous rabbis to queries, which eventually led to authoritative decisions on Jewish law. He never joined the Moor Street synagogue, preferring to form his own minyan. Within his own community, besides conducting the blatt, he gave very fine sermons and at the end of his life, when he was about 80, he published a volume of them.

The foundation of the Beth Hamedresh had been triggered by the expulsion of the congregant who wanted to recite the psalms on that Rosh Hashonah some years ago. The custom of saying them continued in the new congregation. They were also said with fervour and zeal on many special occasions - when someone was ill, recovered from illness, and when remembering the dead. The psalms chosen when someone was mourning a parent were such that the name of the deceased was spelt out. The general practice of saying the Tehillim continued on Sabbath afternoons between the afternoon and evening services. During the month of Ellul, before the high Holydays, the whole of the Book of Psalms was recited, five at each morning service. Compared to almost all of the other British Jewish provincial conmunities, the level of application was as outstanding as it was rare.

In 1891 the new congregation was just beginning to settle down when there was a major distraction; what was to be their attitude towards Choveve Zion, the movement which was intent on increasing the amount of agricultural development in the Holy Land by Jewish settlers? Should they support it or should they concentrate on matters nearer home? That year the case for Choveve Zion was put to them by a travelling speaker called Chaim Zundel Maccoby, or as he was familiarly known, the Kaminitzer Maggid.

Chaim Zundel Maccoby the Kaminitzer Maggid and a great advocate of Zionism

For two or three hours the renowned speaker made the case for supporting the Jews in the Holy Land. Although the deroshah was in the Englisher shul, many members of the new congregation came along to listen to the great man. As he pointed out, though, there was one class of Jews who did not support him. He described the various type of occupant of the cheaper seats in the synagogue and eventually reached the empty pews which were normally occupied by the richest members of the community.

They were empty for the same reason that Zionism would in the future have its work cut out to appeal to the resident British community. It went right against the grain. The official policy, promulgated by generations of Honorary Officers over the centuries, was to make it absolutely clear to their fellow citizens and the government that the Jews considered themselves, first and foremost, citizens of the United Kingdom. They feared that to support settlements in the Holy Land might give the impression that they had two loyalties; one to Britain and the other to what would become half a century later, the State of Israel.

There might be enthusiasm for Choveve Zion among the immigrants; their umbilical cord to Britain was a much later growth. Many of them had thought they were coming to America anyway - or were in transit to the New World. It was mostly out of politeness that the audience for the Kaminitzer Maggid agreed to form a local branch of the society, to raise money for the cause. It didn't last very long.

The Maggid himself went on to be the Rav of the Federation of Synagogues, a combination of small, very Orthodox congregations in London. As such, however, he decided he wasn't in favour of Choveve Zion after all and even spoke against Zionism when it appeared under Theodore Herzl's banner. The Maggid's son, however, would decide to settle down in Sunderland.

There was another attempt to gain the support of the Sunderland community in 1893 and this time the Zionist speaker was Colonel Albert Goldsmid, who although he was Jewish, didn't know it until he was in his teens. There was an enthusiastic reception for his talk, but again little happened thereafter. It was the same with the first Zionist Congress and Herzl's visit to Britain to gather support. He raised few waves in the North East, though he did achieve one very considerable change in attitude after the first congress. Where previously the concentration had been on creating agricultural settlements in Palestine, now it was recognized that political action would be needed as well.

The new immigrants were by now settling down well in Sunderland though economic conditions in the town were badly affected by "panic in the mining and engineering trades" in 1892. Not only did the Board of Guardians have to help out an increasing number of members of the community, but it also had to start a national appeal to try to raise additional funds from benefactors in other parts of the country.

The official Sunderland bodies were careful to avoid stirring up any feelings of animosity towards either foreigners or Jews. It was Rev. Green who attacked the tally men and Jewish hire purchase furniture companies in 1893, after he had left the community for London. He also protested against the practice of recovering bad debts in the County Court, feeling that all such actions reflected badly on the Jewish community.

Rev. Green's letter in the Jewish Chronicle to this effect, produced a storm of protest in the next week's issue and the point was strongly made that none of the non-Jewish organisations had complained. This was explained in a letter from a Sunderland non-Jewish journalist who wrote that:

> If local journalists refrain from exceedingly "unfriendly references" to certain County Court cases it is because they feel it would be unwise and unjust to say that which, though true, would be calculated to excite prejudice against the great mass of Jews who are fair dealing and upright.

Compare such an attitude to anything of a similar nature in Lithuania, and the large numbers of immigrants becomes even more understandable. Indeed, by 1894 Zion Street had become too small for the new community and they decided to move to larger premises in Villiers Street North, down by the docks. The new building would be able to seat 200 men and 70 women, which would leave plenty of room for the community to grow in size. The Englishe shul made one last despairing effort to bring them back into the fold in 1895. It was a bullying approach, however, rather than any attempt to compromise. J.S.Levy, the Secretary of the shul wrote to Charles Gillis as representing the new community, and said:

> I am directed by the Executive Council to inform you that at a meeting held on Sunday last, it was resolved that this congregation withdraws its permission to hold minyan (services) away from the synagogue and that Rule 83 be enforced.

Rabbi I S Bloch
The first Rabbi of the Beth Hamedresh

It was not uncommon for a synagogue to have a rule preventing alternative services to those held in the synagogue. It made it more difficult to get the 10 men needed for the full service if there was more than one service at the same time. If there was an attempt to form a new community, this would inevitably weaken the old one. But the Beth Hamedresh was far beyond being brought back into line by now. All the Hebrew Congregation could do was deprive the old members who had defected from the privileges of being members. It was a declaration of war and the Hebrew Congregation would do their best to undermine the Beth Hamedresh for a number of years to come.

The original families in the Englisher shul had come to Sunderland from Holland and Poland and had mostly drifted into the middle-of-the-road religious behaviour of the rest of the British Jewish community. There would always be Englisher shul families who disliked their children fraternising with those of the Beth Hamedresh. There were two reasons for this; first the innate snobbishness of those who felt Krottingens were foreign and common. Second, the possibility that their children would be influenced by those of the Beth Hamedresh in their level of religious observance.

What the Englisher shul members feared was the type of conversation where their children asked them why their family didn't observe some of the mitzvot like their Beth Hamedresh friends. Since there was no excuse and the Englisher shul parents didn't want to be equally observant, it was felt better that the children shouldn't be exposed to such influences. It might not happen, but many felt it was better to be safe than sorry. No matter how long the two communities lived side by side, there would often be an element of this thinking which kept them apart.

The Beth Hamedresh congregation now went further. They hired themselves their own rabbi - 29 year old Rabbi Shmaryahu Yitzchak Bloch. Rabbi Bloch came from Krottingen and married a Krottingen girl, Rachel Rokeah. He came from a family of rabbonim, his grandfather being Reb Aaron who was the senior shochet in Krottingen. He studied under Rabbi Yizele Petersburger, who was a student of Rabbi Yisroel Lipkin, better known as the famous Israel Salanter. The family could even trace its ancestry to the Vilna Gaon (Rabbi Elijah ben Shlomo Zalman, 1720-1797) - and in rabbinic circles you can't do much better than that. His rabbinic pedigree had been impeccable and he, presumably, took on the role of Gemara Maggid, to conduct the study periods.

Rabbi Bloch's exercise of the skills of a communal rabbi was another matter and the 1901 minutes suggest that he was often at loggerheads with a number of members of the community. One cause of contention was likely to be the question of Zionism which split the community. Bloch, when later a minister in Birmingham, attended the Zionist Congress as a delegate, but most of the leaders of the general Sunderland congregation did not support the movement. Things got so bad that it was decided to withhold his salary and that situation continued for a number of months. Today Rabbi Bloch would have had an unanswerable case if he had gone to an Industrial Tribunal on a plea of constructive dismissal, but such legislation was many years away and the Beth Din would even now be considered a more appropriate court in which to settle the dispute. Rabbi Bloch served the Beth Hamedresh for eight years and then accepted the call from the Jewish community in Birmingham.

When Bloch was unavailable, the Blatt could be taken by other knowledgeable members of the congregation. Where the Beth Hamedresh had a surfeit of experts, most provincial communities at the time would have given their eye teeth for a Talmudically educated member.

By 1900 the Jewish congregation of Sunderland had increased again substantially. The cheap sea route from Lithuania and Germany to Sunderland remained a great attraction. The Beth Hamedresh community, as a consequence, had outgrown its premises once again. The *Jewish Chronicle* reported: "Notwithstanding a Beth Hamedresh having been built in another part of the town, the accommodation for worshippers was totally inadequate." So it was decided to knock down an old building in Villiers Street and put up a new synagogue.

The contract was given to local architects, M & I.R. Milburn. The price agreed for both the new synagogue and a substantial mikvah was £1,500. It would be paid for by raising the seat prices and by going out to solicit donations. £157 was raised in 1897. It was hard going but the work started in October 1898 and a mortgage of £650 was obtained to tide the congregation over. The new synagogue was built without a warden's box. All were to be considered equal in the eyes of the Almighty. It would have electric light, though.

Villiers Street South Synagogue
The Second Beth Hamedresh Synagogue

Built 1899 – extended 1921, Sold 1937

In 1893 the records had showed that there had been 49 Jewish tradesmen in Sunderland and no professionals. In a Jewish population of 600 in all, there were nine pawnbrokers. For a congregation which consisted mostly of poor tally men, trying to eke out a living selling in the neighbouring villages, the building of the new synagogue was a fine achievement. It would be a distinguished centre for the new community, though it was not used for weddings. In those days the ceremonies were at the homes of the parents, often in the open air, with the Reception in a local hall.

It was agreed to ask Sir Francis Montefiore to open the new synagogue complex when the time came. Of all the eminent Sir Moses Montefiore's descendants, Sir Francis was the most acceptable. Although the congregation had started life as a breakaway from the Englisher synagogue, many of the Greeners continued to have cordial relations with those they had worshipped with for a long time in the old synagogue. They could be related to each other as well. In the future some would serve on committees for both congregations. From the beginning, for instance, there was only one chevra kedushah for both synagogues There was only one cemetery as well. In 1892 when the Sunderland Hebrew Benevolent Society changed its name to the Board of Guardians, this body also had the support of both communities.

Naturally, the Hebrew Congregation had its own criticisms of the Beth Hamedresh. One was that the congregation lacked decorum. It is, of course, true that nobody talks in a church service except to repeat the prayers. In a Jewish sabbath service, which usually goes on for two and a half hours, there is usually a lot of conversation. Both the Englishe shul members and the Greeners congregation might be equally guilty but as one North East leader put it: "In the Beth Hamedresh everybody dovened (prayed) but nobody listened." If the chazan was conducting the service, the ideal was to sing with him in unison, but there is nothing in the law to prevent you going at your own speed.

The atmosphere between the Honorary Officers of both communities was less friendly. There were many reasons for this. The Beth Hamedresh members were mostly recent immigrants, speaking Yiddish and looking to Lithuania for any spiritual guidance they might need. In the choice of a rabbi, they would consult Lithuanian authorities, like the famous Rabbi Yitzchock Elchonan Spektor of Kovno. The Hebrew Congregation in Sunderland had left the continent far behind and was affiliated to the British United Synagogue and the Chief Rabbi. The Chief Rabbi, Hermann Adler, was naturally going to support the Hebrew Congregation because of its affiliation to him and because he was trying to discourage any separatist movements among the newcomers from the pogroms, which had raged in Eastern Europe from the early 1880s.

These refugees had totally transformed the demographics of the British Jewish community. Where this had numbered some 35,000 in 1880, it would be more like 300,000 in 1914 and the difference was the refugees and their families. They placed impossible burdens on the old community because of their need for financial support for the predominantly poor immigrants.

They also changed the image of the community from "Englishmen of the Jewish persuasion" to Orthodox Jews from the Continent who found themselves in Britain. They stuck to a foreign language, Yiddish, rather than English. Their Orthodoxy was an irritant to the old community who, before they arrived, had been able to kid themselves that a more nominal observance of the laws was acceptable.

In defence of the Chief Rabbi's position, the possibility existed that the flood of newcomers might have the effect of altering the traditional British tolerance of its Jewish community. The need was to resist the passing of an Aliens Act, not only because it would prevent additional Jewish refugees from reaching Britain's normally hospitable shores, but also because it would be recognized as, primarily, an anti-Jewish piece of legislation and potentially sour relations. Adler wrote to many influential rabbonim on the continent to ask them to tell their flocks that Britain was not a land flowing with milk and honey and that the streets were not paved with gold. Those he asked to help spread the word that they shouldn't come included Rabbi Spektor.

It got worse, though. The Chief Rabbi's father had had to face the development of movements in the provinces anxious to give their local rabbis more authority. There had, for example, been a running battle for some years with Manchester in the 1850s. It had been resolved with the Chief Rabbi still wielding full authority, but the trouble could break out again. Whether it was the left wing of the new Reform movement or the right wing of the very Orthodox immigrants, the Chief Rabbi's position was under some threat. Those who supported him in the provinces by accepting his jurisdiction were going to find him on their side in any dispute with more Orthodox newcomers. So for a number of years the Chief Rabbi refused to recognize that the Sunderland Beth Hamedresh was a properly constituted Jewish community.

The reports he received on the community could well have been biased but there was precedent in the North East for refusal to recognize a community. In 1867 there had been an effort to form a second congregation in South Shields and Adler's father, Chief Rabbi Nathan Marcus Adler, had written "the funds of your synagogue are small enough and ought certainly not to be diminished by the establishment of separate synagogues.". There had also been the split in Sunderland itself between the original settlers and the Polish immigrants.

Why did this matter? What was so important about being recognized by the Chief Rabbi? Two main things; only the Chief Rabbi had the right to allow a community to authorise weddings. And only the Chief Rabbi could licence a shochet, the ritual slaughterer. He would do neither unless a community recognized his jurisdiction. Here the members of the Beth Hamedresh had a problem too. They were unaccustomed in their homeland to having any rabbinic authority except their own rabbi. The concept of a Chief Rabbi was unknown to them. It was regarded as an eccentricity of the British community.

The Beth Hamedresh members wanted their traditional arrangements. They wanted their religious practices to remain safely in their own hands. Particularly was this so as they did not trust the Chief Rabbi and the United Synagogue to create a culture of sufficiently rigourous observance and in this they were right. The United Synagogue may not have officially set the bar lower, but most members were not expected to clear it.

On the other hand, the Beth Hamedresh did not want to continue to have to go to the local Registrar's office to get their weddings legalised. The alternative was to go, cap-in-hand, to the Engishe shul for a certificate, but both involved a loss of face; the Registry Office involved the introduction of the state and the Englisher shul meant asking a favour of the other community. There was another issue; the Beth Hamedresh did not want any question raised in the wider community about the proficiency of their shochet. There were advantages to accepting the Chief Rabbi's jurisdiction, just as they perceived disadvantages. It would also have been remembered that when the Hebrew Congregation wanted a new minister in 1888, the Chief Rabbi had offered to support them with a subsidy from his Provincial Ministers Salary Augmentation Fund. The Beth Hamedresh could use help of that kind.

The Greeners set out to solve their problems. First they wanted their shochet approved by the Chief Rabbi. They wrote for support to the Englisher shul, as Hermann Adler had said he would not see the candidate for the position of Shochet unless the approach came from the Englisher Shul.

> It was unanimously decided by the Trustees and Committee to beg you to consent to our sending our Mr. Kaplan to London to be examined by Dr. Adler on his competence as a shochet....in view of your intimation that Dr. Adler would receive Mr. Kaplan....we would abide by Dr. Adler's decision to the full if this would lead to a Union of Shechitah.

The last thing the Honorary Officers of the Englisher shul wanted was the legitimisation of the Beth Hamedresh. They resented the implication that a more Orthodox synagogue was needed because they weren't keeping up a high enough standard. The Beth Hamedresh members made no bones about their doubts on the subject and it was deeply insulting to the Englisher shul members, even if it was justified. Whatever help the Beth Hamedresh sought for many years, the English Shul tried to resist. With the question of shechitah they tried to make conditions. They wanted all the butchers selling kosher meat to be approved by their synagogue alone and they wanted an agreement from the Beth Hamedresh that they wouldn't appoint any of their own. They only offered one fifth of the profits from the operation to go to the Beth Hamedresh, and they wanted the Beth Hamedresh's Mr. Kaplan to be under their sole authority.

The Beth Hamedresh reacted with indignation:

> ...I am instructed to inform you that we are of the opinion that you do not comprehend our motive in approaching you in this matter and we again wish to put it clearly before you that our sole aim and object in these negotiations are to establish peace and harmony in our midst, and as you are aware that the Shechitah question is the main obstacle to this desirable change, we are agreeable to remove same. But your reply and conditions seem to imply that we are in a helpless plight and appealing to you to extricate us from same. If these are the facts, then I am instructed to refute same, and to inform you that our Beth Hamedresh has never been, as it is now, in so good a position.

The Beth Hamedresh suggested one shechitah board for Sunderland with five representatives from the Hebrew Congregation and two from theirs. They also asked for a quarter of the profits rather than a fifth. To some extent the Beth Hamedresh were bluffing, because their financial position was not anything like as rosy as they had stated..

A small congregation was trying to pay for a Rabbi, the Talmud Torah - where the children received their Jewish education - a mikvah for ritual purification, and a shochet. Furthermore, times were hard and the tally men had difficulty in paying their synagogue dues. The congregation even had difficulty finding the £2 a week for the rabbi's salary.

In March 1902 the Hebrew Congregation replied that they would see if a constitution and rules could be drawn up for a combined shechitah board and suggested four members from their shul and two from the Beth Hamedresh. If this didn't work, the Hebrew congregation still wanted sole authority to licence the butchers. The Beth Hamedresh agreed to the meeting but again rejected the idea that they should hand over authority for licensing the butchers to the other side.

The meeting went well but an unforeseen event occurred which threatened to sour relations between the two communities in a big way. The Treasurer of the Hebrew Congregation took it upon himself, without official consultation, to bolster his appeal for support for the Hebrew Congregation Building Fund by attacking the conditions at the Beth Hamedresh mikvah. The Treasurer's widely distributed report stated that the mikvah was unsanitary, and added for good measure that several wives of the Englisher shul members had become ill from using it. He denounced it as "unfit for a human being to enter during the summer" and said it was draughty and dangerous to health.

Now, if you're starting a new Orthodox Jewish community, there are some things which take absolute priority. They include a cemetery, a sefer torah - and a mikvah. A synagogue comes after those. So the mikvah, a ritual bath to allow the members to set a high standard of hygiene and purification, was a fixture which, if you attacked its administration, was striking at the heart of the community. The secretary of the Beth Hamedresh went ballistic.

> ...this abusive libel has been published after you have built a Mikvah in opposition to ours, it is clear that the only motive for this defamatory libel is to cause us to suffer both morally and financially.

The Treasurer might have got away with it, but the Beth Hamedresh mikvah was quite new and had been approved by the Corporation and sanitary authorities. The sanitary authorities had declared it satisfactory and the Hebrew Congregation knew very well that you can't beat City Hall. They retracted very fast. They wrote that their President had known nothing about the report and disclaimed any responsibility. As the Treasurer was writing in his official capacity, the disclaimer was difficult to sustain. The Beth Hamedresh pressed home its rare advantage and coupled the dispute over the mikvah with the shechitah board.

> ...we are of opinion that you have not given this serious affair any consideration... and whereas we have not received any notification from you in regard to the Schechitah Board scheme, we assume that your Council cannot agree to same.

They threatened to appoint a second shochet without further discussion. Not surprisingly, things were patched up with dispatch and the shechitah committee drew up and submitted rules by May 7th 1902. These were adopted unanimously, the shochet went to London and was duly granted his certificate by Hermann Adler, though, irritatingly, this was not sent to the Beth Hamedresh because the Chief Rabbi still didn't recognize it as an official community. The Beth Hamedresh received it via the Englisher Shul Honorary Officers.

Another opportunity for co-operation came up when Edward VII was due to be crowned in June 1902. The Hebrew Congregation invited the Beth Hamedresh to their thanksgiving service. The Beth Hamedresh turned down the invitation on the grounds that they were having a service of their own. Both would have found the service premature, as Edward VII was operated on for appendicitis on the eve of the coronation and the ceremony was delayed until August.

It is over 100 years since the Beth Hamedresh and the Hebrew Congregation clashed over these issues. The minutes of the proceedings of the two synagogue bodies which are available to us give the decisions reached but no clues to the way the discussions went. The question, therefore, is who led the opposition to the Beth Hamedresh? It was unlikely, for example, to be Simon Olswang, who would serve as Treasurer of the Hebrew Congregation in 1903 and 1904 and President of the congregation in 1905, 1906 and 1907. He would have been on the Board of Management of the synagogue in the years of dispute, but he was also a member of the Council of the Beth Hamedresh and he had come from Krottingen in 1871. Surely, he would have voted to help his friends and tried to find a compromise.

Who would have been powerful enough to ensure that the Beth Hamedresh received little co-operation and, on occasions, downright opposition? The likeliest candidate is Alderman Newman Richardson, who was born in Poland but by this time could be said to have come from an old Sunderland Jewish family.

Richardson served as the President of the Hebrew Congregation during the arguments. We know for certain he was a Warden in 1898, 1899 and 1904, President in 1900 and 1901, Treasurer in 1908, 1909 and 1914 and Vice President and Treasurer in 1915. He paid the largest subscription for a seat among the synagogue members and in 1901 gave a very generous £25 to the shul for two stained glass windows in memory of his son. He was elected a Sunderland town councillor in 1894, made an alderman in 1915 and turned down the opportunity of becoming the mayor of the town. The reason he made known was that he thought it inappropriate for someone to be mayor who had even a slight foreign accent, which was the case with him.

There is no doubt, though, that Richardson would have been a popular choice. He was well known for his generosity in providing a first class Christmas dinner for the poor children in the East End of the town. It was just that, with his Edward VII beard, Richardson was trying, as was the Chief Rabbi, Hermann Adler, to make the Jewish community more English, less obviously an ethnic minority. To this end, in the United Synagogue, the senior clerics were called ministers, they weren't encouraged to have semicha and they wore dog collars as part of their clerical dress, like vicars.

With the aim of anglicising the community so apparently deeply engrained in Richardson's outlook, the Beth Hamedresh represented an entirely alternative viewpoint. The attitude of the United Synagogue towards its ministers was anathema to the Greeners. Furthermore, the Krottingens often had strong foreign accents and they had rabbonim who led their flock rather than followed meekly in the footsteps of the Honorary Officers. For the members of the Beth Hamedresh, the requirements of the Talmud also took precedence over fitting seamlessly into the way of life of the citizens of Sunderland.

Certainly, they were peaceful and law abiding, but they did not seek municipal office, which they would have been unlikely to obtain anyway. They were everything that Richardson didn't want of his community and, in this, he was also mirroring the attitude of the Chief Rabbi. Hermann Adler, for example, condemned Yiddish, but that remained the lingua franca of the Beth Hamedresh. He would, privately, also have been irked that the Beth Hamedresh should consult eminent rabbis in Eastern Europe about future candidates for their pulpit, rather than himself.

If Richardson had asked the Chief Rabbi's help to try to stifle the development of the Beth Hamedresh as a separate congregation, he would have found a ready ear. And in a small town, if your President was an Alderman, he would know how to lead his committees and would have their respect. Members might not agree with his views but they would feel abashed at trying to argue against his wishes. In public, Richardson did not publicise his feelings. In 1903 he even opened the new Talmud Torah building the Beth Hamedresh needed to accommodate its growing membership. He would doubtless have been present at the service in the Beth Hamedresh to mark the occasion, at which the next minister, Rabbi Hurwitz, "delivered" an impressive initial address. Nevertheless, Richardson's viewpoint was antipathetical to that of the Krottingens.

Certainly, 1904 saw problems within the Hebrew Congregation as well. In April the Council considered the resignation of 23 members, defeated candidates and their supporters, who wanted to secede and start their own shul. In May the Chief Rabbi presided over a meeting to try to resolve this obviously serious problem. It was only with difficulty that Hermann Adler even secured approval, before he began the meeting, that his eventual ruling would be binding.

To try to resolve the dispute, Adler asked Richardson to resign, which he agreed to do, although the Treasurer indignantly refused to follow suit. Once Richardson had resigned, the dissenters said they were happy to withdraw their opposition to the present state of affairs. Now the row obviously had somethings to do with the finances of the synagogue because the Treasurer insisted at the meeting that he wouldn't resign because his books were all in order. That so many should be threatening to secede, however, would suggest that those who were members of both the Beth Hamedresh and the Hebrew Congregation might have been happy to have an excuse to attack the Honorary Officers if they were orchestrating the opposition to the Greeners.

Certainly, the opposition to the Beth Hamedresh's requests now started to fade away. This could well have been because a Krottingen, Simon Olswang became the President in 1905/6/7. As he sat on the council of the Beth Hamedresh, he would have understood, far more readily than Richardson, where they were coming from. He might also have softened Richardson's approach when the two men became mishpocha; Louie Richardson marrying Henry Olswang.

Of course, not all the Beth Hamedresh members had actually come from Krottingen. In 1899 there arrived from Verballen in Lithuania a family called Pearlman. The mother was a widow and there were three boys, Leibish, Joseph and Shlomo. Leibish eventually emigrated to America but Joseph and Shlomo became pillars of the Beth Hamedresh congregation. They were very different as businessmen. Both started as tally men, but where Joseph thrived, Shlomo found it very hard going. In the synagogue, they both worked hard for the community. Shlomo's particular interest was in the Talmud Torah (The Hebrew school for children). He devoted himself to its work for very many years and, as a consequence, was affectionately known eventually as Rebbe Pearlman, even though he didn't have semicha.

The importance of the Talmud Torah to the community as a whole cannot be overestimated. In the Church of England the nearest equivalent to a Talmud Torah would be the Sunday School and most Jewish denominations also hold classes on Sunday mornings, which are often well supported, and on an evening or two a week, which are not. In Orthodox communities the Talmud Torah is considered the lifeline, the umbilical cord, which keeps the child within the Jewish fold and ensures there will be Jews in the future. It is felt that only by lengthy and continuous study at the Talmud Torah will the child learns the important tenets of Judaism and their value. It gives the youngsters the facts, so that if they consider giving up the religion as adults, at least they will know what they are giving up.

The curriculum is extensive, the child makes real sacrifices in terms of playtime, and the teachers are crucial to the success of the whole exercise. Shlomo Pearlman believed all this to be true and he set out to do far more than his part, to inspire and educate the children in his care in Jewish studies. At the time methods of teaching were harsher than they are today. Many teachers would punish the children physically for infractions, but Shlomo Pearlman was a gentle man and treated his pupils with kindness. He was first class at his job, for which he was paid a pittance, and which made demands on him which adversely affected his business life. He had to be at the school at 5 o'clock on every weekday evening to start the classes, which took place after the secular studies of the child's day. It cut short his time on the road as a tally man and it would put additional pressure on his own family to support him when he ran short of funds.

Joseph Pearlman
One of the most generous supporters

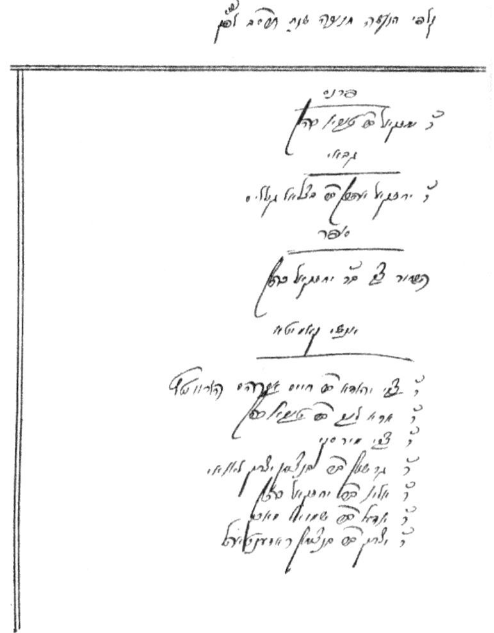

Officers of the Chevra Gemara 1902

By contrast, Joseph put in the hours to build his business. He was a tally man for over 25 years and eventually four of his sons joined him in the enterprise. Shlomo studied bookkeeping and worked for him in that area.

In the years after the First World War, economic conditions in the North East led to the General Strike of 1926. When the workers struck, their incomes stopped. They couldn't pay the tally man his weekly instalment and he had the legal right to repossess the goods. Joseph Pearlman was a good man; he got his wealthy brother-in-law, Abe Merskey, to negotiate with the banks to tide him over when his receipts dropped, and then allowed the families on strike extended credit until they could pay. All strikes end eventually and Joseph Pearlman got almost all his money eventually. He also got a very large amount of gratitude from those he had helped in such difficult times.

As a result, Joseph was able to expand his business, move into running furniture shops and he was able to give his brother, Shlomo, a permanent job as a bookkeeper, which kept the wolf from the door. Shlomo's son went one better than a bookkeeper and became an accountant. Leibish, in America, died young from the effects of being gassed on the Western Front, as part of the American forces in the Great War. As he was unmarried, he left his estate to his family back in England. The life insurance made a welcome addition to Shlomo's funds. The Slump did not affect Joseph's business much, as very few people in the Durham villages would have lost money on the stock market.

One death at this time was very much regretted. This was the passing of Isidore Isaacs in 1901 at the early age of 36. Isaacs was remembered by the community for his fine rendering of the Haftorah, the passage from outside the first five books of the bible, which he always sang on the first day of the festival of Shevuot. To the townsfolk, however, he was a young man who had become one of Sunderland's leading solicitors through sheer ability and hard work.

At the time, one of the most powerful and militant groups of workers was the Durham Miners Association, but amidst the socialist rhetoric and the battle for better conditions and pay in the mines, it was Isadore Isaacs they looked to for legal advice. He was said to have "an infinite capacity for taking pains" and was much respected in legal circles for his strict adherence to Orthodox Judaism. Indeed he became a great friend of Canon Greenwell who was the Chairman of the Magistrates in Durham and Isaacs negotiated many improvements for the miners without antagonising the owners; a very considerable achievement.

The decade ended with the finances of the Beth Hamedresh still a cause for concern. In 1910 it was decided to charge all the members ½p a week to eliminate an overspend for the previous year of £50. To put such a figure in context, it had been possible to insure the building against burglary for a premium of 25p a year.

One of the contentious questions which remained was whether to have a choir or not. On the one hand, the melodies would sound more impressive if sung by good voices. On the other hand, the choristers might ask to be paid if they were professional singers, and the sound of their voices could distract a worshipper from saying his prayers. He might be going faster or slower than the choir and most members wanted to maintain their independence in this, as in all other matters. The compromise in 1909 was to have a choir, but only on the Yomin Naroim, the High Holy Days.

There was one other route to respectability in both the Jewish and the wider community in Sunderland; that was to become a Freemason. In Lithuania, a Catholic country, Freemasonry was not welcome. Freemasons take an oath not to divulge their secrets and Catholicism holds that everything has to be confessed to the priest. There is no such problem with Judaism and Jews have been members of the craft for hundreds of years.

Sometimes Jews were members of lodges with a mostly Christian membership and sometimes they started lodges of their own where the membership was, primarily Jewish. In Sunderland in 1899 Julius Jacobs became the Worshipful Master of the Phoenix Lodge, which was very likely one of the latter, as the meal after the meeting was Kosher. The Phoenix could well have been a reference to the recreation of the Krottingen community in a new country.

As any respectable man can become a Freemason, the opportunity to belong enabled immigrants to mix socially with leading figures in the town or the Jewish community. It served as some counterbalance to the discord that often soured relations the between the two Sunderland synagogues.

Beth Hamedresh, Mowbray Road

Chapter 4
The Hirsch Hurwitz Years

With the departure of Rabbi Bloch to Birmingham, looking for a replacement took a fair amount of time. Joseph Pearlman was put in charge of the search, together with Hirsche Cohen and he found candidates all over Europe. When the Beth Hamedresh advertised, there were applications from experienced rabbonim, many of whom would become eminent, like the future Dayan Hillman, who was not selected. There were in all over 50 candidates, which would be remarkable for any pulpit today. It was eventually decided to ask the Kovno and Slobodka rabbonim to give an opinion on the final shortlist of two. The experts both strongly recommended Rabbi Hirsch Hurwitz of Casadora in Lithuania who had been appointed to his first community when he was only 21.

The Beth Hamedresh didn't want to make the appointment appear a decision by a few people on a committee, so they called a meeting of the whole Sunderland Jewish community to consider the subject. Even members of the Englisher Shul were invited and many of them accepted. There was a large gathering in November 1902 and it was unanimously agreed to invite Rabbi Hurwitz to be a candidate.

Which meant that he wouldn't be appointed until he had preached in the synagogue and met the good and the great. He was sent £5 for his journey, arrived in good order and duly made a very favourable impression. It wasn't, in fact, easy to find the £2 a week which was to be his salary, but the Zionist committee was prepared to make up any shortfall so long as the appointment was approved by the Chief Rabbi. This was a sensible precaution as negotiations were now at a quite advanced stage for the Chief Rabbi to recognize the Beth Hamedresh as a community in its own right. Rabbi Hurwitz was approved unanimously and moved to Sunderland with his wife, Hannah.

This was not, however, before there was another row with the Englisher Shul. It came about because, initially, the Beth Hamedresh had not consulted the Chief Rabbi about a suitable candidate. Hermann Adler might well have had a number of worthy ministers he would have liked to recommend for promotion but nobody asked him. So the Beth Hamedresh probably thought it a sound idea to cover their backs with a joint recommendation to him for confirmation of the appointment from the two Sunderland communities. That would also guarantee his salary from the Zionist committee.

Rabbi H Hurwitz
A towering influence in the development of the Beth Hamedresh

The Secretary, David Gillis, wrote to the Englisher Shul at length. He explained that the whole community had been invited to consider the applicants and had chosen Rabbi Hurwitz. He went on:

> We have...unanimously decided not to take final steps before submitting the matter to you and respectfully ask you to cooperate with us and to lend us at least your moral support. Our aim and object....merely to strengthen and maintain the peace and goodwill amongst us. The members of our Beth Hamedresh do fully recognize the power vested by law in the Ecclesiastical Authority of Anglo-Jewry, headed by the Very Rev. The Chief Rabbi, Dr. Adler, under whose jurisdiction we desire to place ourselves...

Would the Hebrew Congregation endorse the choice of Rabbi Hurwitz? All their members had been invited by the Beth Hamedresh to the selection meeting, so they had been consulted. The Honorary Officers still found cause for offence. They took umbrage at the fact that the Honorary Officers hadn't been consulted as leaders of their community, but merely as members of their synagogue. As a result, the Hebrew Congregation sent back a short and dusty answer: "Re your letter of the 3rd inst., which was considered at this afternoon's Council meeting, the following resolution was carried, viz., that this Council are not prepared to co-operate in the election of a Rav."It was pure pique. The Beth Hamedresh shrugged their collective shoulders and went ahead anyway.

Relationships were going to improve, though. As a historian of the community, Arnold Levy, Gershon Levy's son, wrote 50 years later.

> With the advent of Rabbi Hurwitz, a complete change in the atmosphere of the Beth Hamedresh took place. Through the Rav's forceful, optimistic and progressive leadership, the Beth Hamedresh regained its self-respect. It was no more the "step child" of the community, though it still lacked recognition by the Chief Rabbinate.

Insofar as the community's self-respect was perceived to be firmly based on their superior level of Orthodoxy, the need to regain it probably refers more to the number of occasions on which the community had been rebuffed by the older congregation. It was typical of the greater Orthodoxy of the Beth Hamedresh, vis a vis the Englisher Shul, that, soon after Rabbi Hurwitz's arrival, there was a Siyyum Hagodol of Shas, to mark the conclusion of the study of the Babylonian Talmud which had started back in Krottingen. It was a formidable achievement, like a rambling club climbing Mount Everest.

Looking at the next generation to carry on the good work, Rabbi Hurwitz also won approval in the year of his appointment for the opening of a Yeshivah, which established from the beginning of his ministry that the Beth Hamedresh would be setting the highest talmudic standards for the Sunderland community. It was customary for small Jewish provincial communities to struggle to get a Minyan during the week. Starting a Yeshiva was the difference between a GCSE and a Ph.d. The Yeshiva was strongly supported by Gershon Levy and it proved possible to draw all but two of the students from local families. The exceptions came from Leeds.

From the beginning the whole Sunderland community had been concerned about the future supply of good candidates for their pulpits. The Englisher Shul had nine ministers between 1862 and 1897, not all of whom had worked out well. In 1890 a letter had been written to Hermann Adler, asking him that "the students trained as Jews' College should be qualified to obtain semicha". The Chief Rabbi had replied that "he would be gratified if they could be" but 21 years later when the current Englisher Shul rabbi, Salis Daiches, raised the question again, there had been very little progress.

By 1903 the Zionist movement was starting to find a little more support in the community and the Simchas Torah aliyahs were donated to the Zionist National Fund. When Rabbi Bloch left, Rabbi Hurwitz, turned out to be even more supportive of the Zionist cause. Hurwitz did not set out initially to convert the congregation to Zionism but he made his own position clear. At the time, if you raised enough money, you could send a delegate to the Zionist Congress and the Sunderland community raised enough to send two to what would be the 6th Zionist Congress in Basle in August of that year. Rabbi Hurwitz was invited to be one of them. Israel Jacobs was another and Isaac Cohen attended as an official reporter for the *Sunderland Echo*!

The English delegation to the 1903 Zionist Congress Basel
Showing Rabbis Hurwitz and Bloch (back row 2nd and 3rd from left)
Seated: (4th from left) Israel Jacobs, Israel Zangwill, Theo Herzl, Herzl's Mother. Rose Lipman, Annie Jacobs (far right)

There were a number of causes célèbres to give the proceedings at the Congress even more urgency. One had been a horrific massacre at Kishinev in Romania, where 47 Jews were killed and nearly 600 wounded by a mob rioting on a false rumour that the Jews had killed a boy. The true culprits were identified but too late. Another outrage was the ongoing Dreyfus affair which threw doubt on the impartiality of the French government and its relations with its Jewish community. The discussions at the Congress also centred round the possibility of the British government offering the Jews a National Home in Uganda.

Rabbi Hurwitz had voted for the creation of an investigative committee to go into the question, and said he had an open mind on the subject. Strategically, it is often a good idea to let a proposal of which you disapprove get talked out, and only intervene if it appears to be gaining agreement. As an Orthodox rabbi, Hurwitz would have wanted the Promised Land to be the National Home and not some African enclave, far from the Western World where most of the Jews lived at the time.

Rabbi Hurwitz did say at the end of his speech to the Sunderland community that they should have "faith in the ultimate achievement of our aims, the rehabilitation of the Jewish people in Eretz Yisrael". The actual vote at the congress was 295 in favour of accepting the British offer, 175 against and 99 abstentions. Herzl died before the next conference and the Uganda proposal died with him.

What was really needed to get the Sunderland community to work hard for the Zionist cause was someone with the personality and drive to inspire others to rally round. It was a young lady from South Shields, Annie Jacobs, who stepped into the breach for a few years. She had also been a delegate at the 6th Congress and it was her determination which led to the formation of the Sunderland and South Shields Ladies' Zionist Association. She made sure of the support she needed by persuading Newman Richardson's wife to become its President. Zionism in Sunderland became fashionable. Annie Jacobs was quite content to be the Secretary, an officer who does most of the work and who can relatively easily become indispensable.

Progress was considerable. The Ladies' Society became affiliated to the English Zionist Federation, Annie Jacobs attended its Annual Conference and then the 7th Zionist Congress in Basle. The cloud on the horizon, though, is always easy to forecast when a lady was a key figure in those days. Annie Jacobs got married a year or so later, moved to

Newcastle with her husband and the Association started to decline from then on, until it was revitalized in the 1930s.

The rabbi continued to provide support though and when Rabbi Samuel Daiches took over at the Englisher Shul in 1905, he was a Zionist as well. There was even a visit from a power in the English Zionist Federation land, the Haham, Moses Gaster. An inspiring speaker and a man who disliked the idea of Uganda intensely, Gaster drew an enormous crowd in Sunderland and got them to approve the choice of the Holy Land for the National Home by acclamation.

The fact remained that the mere idea seemed very far fetched in those early days of the century. The impossibility of getting the Turks to hand over the Holy Land was quite obvious. Another objection came up again and again; what was the point, the Zionist critics asked, of seeking an impossible dream, when part of the cost would be to undermine the claim of the community to only be loyal to King and Country?

Another ongoing problem existed for years. At the beginning, when traditionally the British and the Germans had been allies, the German speaking origins of the founder of Zionism, Theodor Herzl, were unimportant. When, up to the early 1930s, the official language of the Zionist Congress remained German, it made a perceived alliance between British Zionists and the former First World War enemy an even greater embarrassment for its Jewish opponents in Britain.

It had been significant that when Theodore Herzl first came to London to drum up support a few years before he died, the only communal leader who would chair his meeting was Haham Gaster. Just as the richer members of the Sunderland community would not support the Kaminitzer Maggid, so the Cousinhood in London, almost to a man, would not support Herzl. Furthermore, although Rabbis Hurwitz, Samuel and Salis Daiches and Gaster were all for Zionism, the Chief Rabbi, Hermann Adler, was not.

Hermann Adler's position was very understandable. What he was fighting to avoid was the introduction of the Aliens Act which would limit the number of Jews who could escape the pogroms and discrimination in Europe. The pressure to pass such an act was growing on the government and the bill would be motivated by a specific desire to reduce the number of Jewish immigrants. If its proponents could point to a joint loyalty in the Jews, part to the Holy Land and only part to Britain, it would be a substantial plank in their argument for restricted immigration. In which case those Krottingens, for example, who still wanted to emigrate to Sunderland would be among those likely to suffer first. Adler wanted the battle for a National Home to be placed firmly on the back burner.

The Beth Hamedresh was continuing to attract new members and around 100 had joined by 1903. The Talmud Torah was also thriving with more than 100 children attending the classes and four teachers looking after them. A separate building was needed and was found in 1902 in Meaburn Street.

The Hebrew Congregation had decided in November 1903 not to continue with their opposition to the acceptance of the Beth Hamedresh as a proper community by the Chief Rabbi. Subject to agreeing to certain conditions, Hermann Adler now agreed that the congregation should be officially recognized and be granted a certificate to register marriages. Charles Gillis would be appointed as the first Marriage Secretary. He was followed by Joseph Pearlman and then, perhaps uniquely in Anglo-Jewry, he was succeeded by his son, Mottie Pearlman, and finally his grandson, Meyer Pearlman, the family giving over 75 years service in the office.

In spite of this newly supportive attitude by the Hebrew Congregation, the perceived need for the Beth Hamedresh to divorce itself from the other synagogue in the eyes of the general British Jewish public, remained a constant. Already, in 1904, the Beth Hamedresh wanted to send a representative to the Board of Deputies where the Englisher Shul already had a delegate. They wrote to the Board to justify their application:

> Our congregation was established in 1888; the reasons of our having formed ourselves in a separate Congregation were: 1. That the other Congregation had not enough accommodation for the whole of the Jewish community in Sunderland. 2. That in our opinion the other Congregation was not conducted in such an Orthodox manner as we desired and it became essential in the interests of peace to form ourselves in a separate Congregation where we could conduct our services in the manner most sacred to us and we have over 100 members and we have built a suitable place of worship.

It seems unlikely that the Englisher Shul would not have been made aware of the contents of the letter by some friend at the Board of Deputies. They could not have been best pleased to find that while, for their part, they had withdrawn their opposition to the appointment of a Greener Shul Marriage Secretary, the Beth Hamedresh was still criticising their level of Orthodoxy in public.

The congregation's application for its own representative at the Board of Deputies was considered and it was agreed that Elkan Adler, the Chief Rabbi's brother, should act in that role for them. A Jewish pukka sahib, Elkan Adler was to represent the Beth Hamedresh for many years. He didn't always agree with the stance they wanted him to take on a number of matters, but he loyally reflected their views.

It was interesting that the Beth Hamedresh had said the congregation was founded in 1888, rather than 1889 when the row erupted over saying the psalms on Rosh Hashonah and the walk-out occurred. The latter incident certainly did trigger the forming of the new congregation, but perhaps it was considered a less respectable cause than a decision for some of them to study the Talmud together in the previous year.

On January 10th 1904 the Annual General Meeting of the Beth Hamedresh considered the terms laid down by the Chief Rabbi for permitting the community to have its own Marriage Secretary. They were simple enough; if they wanted their own Secretary, then the form of worship and religious services, and all matters concerning their religious administration had to be under the supervision and control of the Chief Rabbi. Furthermore, nobody could be appointed, either as preacher or reader - effectively, Rabbi and Chazan - without the agreement of the Chief Rabbi. Nor could anybody conduct a religious service or preach without permission of the Chief Rabbi.

The attendees voted to accept these conditions which, if they had been observed, would have reduced the influence of their Krottingen tradition to a considerable extent. The congregation, however, recognized the reality of the situation. The Chief Rabbi was the only official permitted by the government to appoint Marriage Secretaries for Jewish communities. If they wanted to give up relying on Registry Offices to confirm that their marriages were legal, then that was the price they had to pay. It was possible to go to court for a separate certificate, on the grounds that the Chief Rabbi was withholding it unreasonably. This was, however, an expensive process for a small shul. The 1904 minutes set down "The Beth Hamedresh was a congregation under the jurisdiction of the Chief Rabbi."

In approving the Chief Rabbi's condition, however, the problems of possible conflict between the traditions of London and Krottingen were brushed over with a nod and a wink. It would be time enough to worry about them if difficulties came up at some time - in what everybody hoped - would be the long distance future. If they did, the traditions of the community might well outweigh a promise given under some duress.

The early 1900s had seen more massacres of whole Jewish communities in Russia. The members of the Beth Hamedresh did their best to raise money for any survivors but there was a general feeling in the country that the funds should not be used to enable them to emigrate to Britain.

Indeed, the records of the Beth Hamedresh in 1905 record that a letter was received from London stating that funds which had been collected in aid of the victims of massacres in Russia were not to be used to help the destitute refugees come to England. The monies collected by the Beth Hamedresh were, as a consequence, held in abeyance for further clarification.

The attempts by Jewish authorities to discourage Jewish refugees from coming to Britain did not influence the authorities sufficiently. The Conservative Balfour government was facing defeat in the election of 1906 and one of their last bills, to try to regain some popularity, was the final passing of the Aliens Act. It had been on the cards for many years and there was now enough support in Parliament to get it passed.

In mitigation of what we would now consider a racist measure, if you wanted to avoid the restrictions of the Aliens Act, the exceptions to the rule were substantial. Factually, if you were healthy and had the offer of a job, you would probably be given an entry permit. The number of Jewish migrants between 1906 and the outbreak of the war in 1914 continued to be substantial and the Jewish population in Sunderland continued to grow, as it did in many other cities.

In 1904 the annual income of the Beth Hamedresh had reached £490 and in 1905 yet another effort was made to create a joint Shechitah Board with the Englisher Shul, but they replied that they still considered the timing "inappropriate". They might well have still been smarting at the criticism of their standards of observance in the letter sent by the Beth Hamedresh to the Board of Deputies. There was one other administrative change emerging from the proceedings of the Beth Hamedresh, when it was agreed to invite the treasurer of the Chevra Tehillim to join the Beth Hamedresh main council.

It was in May 1904 that the Chief Rabbi, Hermann Adler, visited Sunderland to mark the 42nd anniversary of the opening of the Englisher Shul. On Shabbot he preached to the Hebrew Congregation and on the Sunday evening he went to the Beth Hamedresh and spoke there as well. The differences in his addresses were significant. At the Hebrew Congregation he spoke of the passing of the second reading of the Aliens Immigration Act by parliament.

Although this was, indeed, a measure to restrict the number of Jewish immigrants, the Chief Rabbi vehemently rejected any such idea, saying it would be a "flagrant injustice" to suggest it. The Hebrew Congregation, by implication, would be expected to know that the government would never pass an anti-semitic measure. It just wasn't true, but Chief Rabbis are expected to be part of the British establishment and support the elected government. This role they always carry out conscientiously and it stands the community in good stead.

By contrast, when he spoke at the Beth Hamedresh, the Chief Rabbi's sermon was half in English and half in Yiddish. His message was not an appeal to Englishmen to trust their government. It was an appeal to a congregation which had originated overseas to adopt "English modes of life." Adler would have realised that to suggest to men from a province in Russia that a government was never going to be anti-semitic would probably be considered a joke in poor taste. They had never known a government like that. Rabbi Hurwitz offered a hearty vote of thanks to the Chief Rabbi; his mere presence contributed to giving credibility to the official status of the community.

The attacks on Jewish communities in Eastern Europe continued unabated and although they posed no threat whatsoever to the Beth Hamedresh, the congregation was intensely concerned to try to help their overseas brethren, particularly those suffering from the Russian government's indifference to their plight. In 1905 there was a meeting in Brussels of various Jewish groupings, but all that could be agreed upon was to set up an International Jewish organization. This the Beth Hamedresh supported enthusiastically and called on their representative on the Board of Deputies, Elkan Adler, to put forward their views. This Adler did, though his own degree of enthusiasm for the idea was unlikely to be great. The fact was that, if the Jewish community in Britain had any problems, the Board of Deputies was their conduit to the government and the system had worked perfectly well for 150 years.

The last thing the Board of Deputies wanted was to hand over their excellent relations to a foreign body to negotiate on their behalf. They put up every argument they could devise against the plan. The problem of travelling times to meetings, the need for ample advance notice of meetings and agendas, the additional expense, and who to allow to join such an organisation in the first place, were just some of the obstacles raised. In March 1906 the Board of Deputies committee, set up to examine the proposal, unanimously agreed not to recommend it. Even today, the Board of Deputies remains the organization which officially reflects the views of the British community.

By 1906 the Beth Hamedresh congregation had grown sufficiently to enable it to have two Shacherith (morning services) at 7 o'clock and 8 o'clock. The 7 o'clock service was for those who had to get to work early or had to travel to their destinations, like the tally men. The 8 o'clock service was for those with a slightly more leisurely way of life

This decision to have two services may seem of little import, but one of the problems facing any number of Jewish congregations is to get one group of 10 men together on a cold morning to make up a quorum for the full service. To have the luxury of two services was not only a tribute to the devout nature of the congregation. It was also an indication of just how many of them could be regularly relied on. Because to be sure to have 10 present, you would be well advised to have at least 15, if not 20, who could normally be available, in case anyone dropped out. A lot of provincial communities at this time had abandoned morning, afternoon and evening services. The Beth Hamedresh held all of them all the time.

In addition to the necessary congregants, during the course of the year there were certain appurtenances needed. One of these was an Ethrog, which grows on a Citron tree and was symbolic of the harvest and used in the Succot service in the Autumn. Today, in many Orthodox congregations, you will find dozens of Ethrogim, bought by the members for their own use. In 1906 the Beth Hamedresh bought two, which could be used in turn by the whole congregation. They cost two guineas each, which in today's money is no less than £850 - each! Admittedly, an Ethrog cannot be used unless it is totally without blemish, but even so, the profit margin for the retailer would appear considerable. Succot wouldn't be Succot without the Ethrog and the shaking of a bound combination of cuttings from trees which grew in the Holy Land, called the Lulav. When members were ill or unable to attend the synagogue the Shammas (the beadle), would take the Lulav and Ethrog to each of their homes to enable them to carry out the commandment.

It was necessary for the Honorary Officers to try to keep the synagogue finances in some sort of balance and still make allowances for the financial difficulties of the congregation. When Rabbi Hurwitz received an offer from the community in Leeds in 1910, he left the Beth Hamedresh with much regret on both sides, but he wasn't replaced until 1913.

While the forms of service in the Beth Hamedresh coincided, in all the major details with that of any other Orthodox community, there were differences. For instance, it is customary to light a candle and say special prayers on the anniversary of the death of a parent or sibling. There was, however, another exceptional element in the Beth Hamedresh for those who were ovelim (had recently lost a close relative) or had Yahrzeit (were mourners on the specific day.) Where it is normal to say the appropriate prayers from your seat in the synagogue, in the Beth Hamedresh, the mourner would often go to the Oran Hakodesh where the Torah scrolls are kept and recite them there. There is also a time in the service, after the Oleinu prayer when mourners say the Kaddish prayer again and in the Beth Hamedresh this opportunity was reserved exclusively for the one who had lost a parent. At the Beth Hamedresh the mourner would attend services on the Hebrew date of the passing, on three occasions during the day to say Kaddish.

It became customary that after the morning service when a member had yahrzeit, remembering the death of a close relative on that day, there would be whisky and cakes provided by the family, and cigarettes would also be distributed. As they took the cigarettes many of the congregation would wish the mourner the traditional benediction "long life". An anomaly in the light of today's knowledge of the harmful effects of tobacco. In those days when most people smoked, there was a problem for them on the festivals that no fire could be created and so no match could be struck, To overcome this, candles were lit in an anteroom before festivals to allow members to light their cigarettes.

Adon Alom was only sung at the beginning of the service on Rosh Hashanah and Yom Kippur. The prayer, Lecho Dodi, on Friday night was sung with the congregation standing, where it was more normal not to do so. There was also a special Selichos book kept called K'minhag Littae - the Lithuanian minhag - the way they did it in Lithuania. Just to make sure the old customs weren't forgotten.

Unmarried men did not wear a tallith in the synagogue. If they were called up, they borrowed one. (Deuteronomy 22 - 12.13.) Their eligibility as potential husbands was, thereby, seen by the ladies in the gallery. Another custom seldom seen except in communities like the Beth Hamedresh, was that of wearing tephilin on the intermediate days of the festivals.

During the year there are five megillot - books of the Bible which are only read once a year. Such as the Book of Esther on Purim and the book of Ruth on Shevuot. These are usually read from the appropriate prayer book, but in the Beth Hamedresh there were proper scrolls kept for each separate book and it was from these that the reader sang.

Every organization likes to have a rule book. The rules of the Beth Hamedresh were formulated over a considerable period of time and printed in 1908. There were 56 regulations and they were acceptably comprehensive. Many of them, of course, they had in common with other congregations, like the neighbouring Hebrew Congregation.

It was established at the outset that only Orthodox Jews could be members and they had to be elected by secret ballot. There was no blackballing though; if you had a majority of one on the vote, you were accepted. However, to qualify as Orthodox, this not only meant that you had to be born of a Jewish mother, but if you were married, it had to be to a halachically Jewish woman. If you married outside the faith, it was a free country, but you would not be accepted and, if you were already a member, you would immediately lose all your rights and privileges of membership.

The synagogue was identified as being under the supervision of the Chief Rabbi and the Rabbi of the congregation. Only four years after the agreement to recognize the Chief Rabbi's sole jurisdiction, he had become Joint Head with the rabbi. In future, though, the role of the Chief Rabbi was very seldom a factor. The pecking order of supervision which linked the Chief Rabbi with the local rabbi was, however, also significant for another reason. The order of importance in the Chief Rabbi's synagogues would instead have probably placed the lay officers ahead of the minister. The order would have been Chief Rabbi, Honorary Officers and then rabbi. In the Beth Hamedresh the rabbi took on a much more senior role. The truth was also that the congregation had never stopped looking to Eastern European practice for its spiritual guidance.

The example that the Beth Hamedresh would set in running their own affairs was a signal to another community - Gateshead - that such a decision was viable. That the Chief Rabbi in London might regret such a decision but, if the congregation set high enough standards of observance, he would not take any drastic action to rock the boat.

There was a generous membership of the Council. It would consist of the elected President, the Treasurer, nine registered members and the Beth Hamedresh trustees. Cabals were to be avoided. The way a synagogue is run depends very much on the personalities of the Honorary Officers, the support they have in the community and their relationship with the Rabbi. So the rules of the Beth Hamedresh were a very desirable foundation for judging the work - and sometimes the intrigues - of the membership and, sometimes, the cliques. A quorum for AGMs was set at seven members of the Council and 20 members.

Those who formulated the rules were anxious to avoid a cabal being able to be self-perpetuating in exercising power in the community. The by-laws stipulated that no member could be both President and Treasurer in the same year. The two offices couldn't be held by a father and son, by two brothers, or by a father-in-law and his son-in-law. This did not, however, prevent father and son acting as President and Secretary, and the Gillis family would fill both offices for many years. One strange rule was that if two candidates in an election finished up with the same number of votes, then the two names went back into the hat and the first one to be pulled out was declared the winner.

The President's right to spend money without authority was restricted to items of up to only £2. He would remain an unelected member of the Council for a year after he stopped being President, but would then have to seek re-election if he wanted to remain an officer. The Council was instructed to meet at least once a month and was designated the arbitrator if there were disputes between the President and the Treasurer, on the one side, and individual members on the other. This careful balancing act was complicated, however, by the rule that all pronouncements on behalf of the congregation had to be cleared with the President. If that rule was rigourously applied, the President was given the power of veto over anything he didn't like.

Drawing up constitutions is a perilous etymological game and while the rules were obeyed, it did not prevent a few families from becoming pre-eminent in the community. The truth is that those who put in the most work over a long period are likely to finish up running the organisation.

The Beth Hamedresh was never going to be a rich community. The demands on its income were not only going to have to cover the upkeep of the synagogue and the payment of the officials. The congregation would also try to support both local and international Jewish charities and to help those members who fell on hard times. The question, therefore, was always how to raise more money.

One method they used, like many other synagogues at the time, was based on the giving of honours during sabbath and festival services. It was the custom that if a member was called up to the reading of the law, then a donation would be offered. This would also cover such occasions, among others, as naming a new-born child, or on the anniversary of the death of a parent, a forthcoming marriage or a recovery from ill health. The donations were traditionally announced in continental denominations. So pennies were Bas, a shilling (5p) was a Dinar and a crown (25p) was a Keser. A guinea (£1.05), however, was still a guinea. The system is called shnodering and it was in use for a very long time indeed.

On the High Holydays, just to be called up was a distinction and over the New Year and Yom Kippur, the honours would actually be auctioned. This resulted in substantial sums being raised but, eventually, at one New Year service, one aliyah (honour) resulted in a bid of no less than five guineas (£5.25). This was immensely generous but the feeling among the congregation was that the donor might not be financially able to honour his pledge. As the whispers grew, the congregant became very angry and shouted out "You don't trust me for the money. Well, there it is." And he pulled the donation from his pocket and placed it on the table. There was an appalled hush. It is strictly forbidden to carry money on a sabbath or festival.

The result was that it was agreed that the honours would never be auctioned again, except on Simchas Torah at the end of the festival of Sukkot. That was to keep the tradition alive and the honours which were auctioned included the Chosan Torah and the Chosan Bereshith; the two men called up respectively for the reading of the last portion of the book of Deuteronomy and the beginning of the book of Genesis, which are said on that day. Though the auctions brought generous bids, the honours were actually always given to the rabbis.

The members were, of course, the primary source of the funds needed to run the synagogue. If you were a month in arrears in paying your seat rental, you lost your vote. If you were 12 months in arrears you lost all your privileges. You would, however, have two months grace to pay up before that took effect. Widows only paid half the normal seat rental. Additional funds might be obtained by fining members 12½p if they used unbecoming language at a meeting. If you did it three times, you were expelled.

There was a larger fine if you avoided being called up during a service to get out of making the customary donation which came with the honour. You were expected to shnoder 2½p on the Sabbath, and 5p on a Festival, so it was economically very sensible to accept the honour without, for instance, pleading a call of nature at the crucial time. The fine for avoiding being called up was 52½p and if you refused any other honour, the fine was still a thumping 25p. If you were called before the Council and didn't show up, that incurred a fine of at least 12½p.

Another fine was imposed on a a bridegroom who did not come to the synagogue on the sabbath before his wedding. His presence ensured that of his family and, therefore, considerable extra donations when they were given honours. So his absence was costly to the community, and the fine for absence was 52½p again. The total synagogue costs for the wedding, including the Ketubah, the wedding certificate, was set at £2.10p, though the Council was given the power to reduce this to £1.05 if there was a poor family involved.

In Judaism a rabbi is not needed to conduct a wedding. Two witnesses, unrelated to the betrothed, are the only essentials, to be able to say that the event was conducted according to the rules. The Beth Hamedresh nevertheless wanted to keep the marriages of its members in-house and so it ruled that, within the community, this right was confined to the appointed officials. If any other member conducted a marriage ceremony, he would lose all his privileges. The income from marriages had to be protected.

Although all the elected members gave their service to the community absolutely free, there were several offices where you could be fined for not turning up. Every meeting you missed as President or Treasurer cost you 50p and the Secretary or a member of the Council 25p.

Another Krottingen tradition was the custom of writing ethical wills. A will was not just about the distribution of the deceased's estate. It would be comprehensive enough to include such instructions as how to continue the family business and an admonition to treat the widow with the greatest respect. How to deal with his seat in shul, never to have an argument over a kaddish, which charities to continue to support and to remain good Jews with a kosher home. A multitude of details would be covered.

As far as the paid officials were concerned, Rev. Kaplan had resigned as Shochet and Chazan in 1905. His departure was, however, short-lived and he soon reapplied for the position and was welcomed back into the fold. Then in 1907 the position became vacant again and this time the job went to Rev. Barnett. His qualifications did not, however, include those of a porger or Mohel. Porging an animal after shechitah completes the kashrut. Becoming a mohel is a task where the slightest error is a great deal more serious, As these qualifications are of extreme importance to any community, Rev. Barnett was soon replaced by Rev. Warrantz of Mushnick, Russia who had all the right skills.

Rabbi Hurwitz said "Mr. Warrantz (he was, in fact, a properly qualified rabbi) was a a perfect and qualified man, and (Hurwitz) expressed himself that the six years he had been in Sunderland he had always hoped and wished to have such a shochet and now he was pleased we had such a candidate and he hoped he would be unanimously accepted". Which he was and stayed with the community for the next nearly 40 years. He was kindly and quiet and he was very learned.

With or without the involvement of the Chief Rabbi, the appointment of Rabbi Hurwitz had been a great success. In 1910, after Hurwitz had been in post for seven years, Dayan Hyamson had visited the Cheder to assess the quality of the Jewish education the children were getting. "He would not hesitate to say that the standard attained by them (the children) was the highest ever reached by any school attached to a synagogue in the United Kingdom".

The explanation, of course, was that Rabbi Hurwitz was setting Eastern European standards of education, unlike the normal English approach, and the congregation parents made sure their children did not play truant. In the Englisher shul the example of Rabbi Hurwitz's scholarly eminence may have been the reason why they recruited two ministers in the decade who were substantially superior to any ministers they had employed before.

They were the Daiches brothers, who were born in Vilna and educated at Leipzig University in Germany. Samuel, who was the older, came to the congregation in 1905 and when he left to become a lecturer at Jews' College, he was replaced in 1908 by his younger brother, Salis. Both had Semicha and PhDs, with Samuel's thesis being on Scottish philosophers and Salis' on Assyrian and Babylonian antiquities. Samuel had graduated magna cum laude and both were serious intellectuals. Salis had taken a pulpit in Hull when Samuel came to Sunderland but left after a few years:

> Although his three years ministry in Hull was highly successful, Dr. Daiches found it impossible to continue his activity in that city on account of the peculiar conditions that prevailed in that community.

No further details are available! In Sunderland both got on very well with Hirsch Hurwitz and would be invited to preach in the Beth Hamedresh on occasions like the second day of Passover.

The early years of the century were very difficult for many members of the Beth Hamedresh. The problem was an unusual one for the times; inflation. If the Retail Price Index was 100 in 1837, it had declined to 74 forty years later. The reason was a major drop in the price of food, due to the importation of cheap North American wheat and other agricultural products.

The situation changed with the Boer War. It was a very expensive conflict. It went on for several years and it had to be paid for. At the end, the Boers were defeated but there was still substantial inflation in Britain to upset the economic apple cart. As a consequence, money was short for most families and the tally men found making a living even more difficult. Which accounted for the payment of their synagogue dues falling into arrears.

The year 1909 would be long remembered by the congregation for the most distressing of reasons. Hermann Cohen, a son of Chatze Cohen, had been prominent in its councils even as a young man. He had served as President but now, at the age of 41, he was robbed and murdered by a burglar. The killer was never caught and the horror of the event cast a pall over the community. Two silver breast plates for sifrei torah were donated in his memory.

Although the congregation had grown, the effects of inflation and a general economic downturn produced a deficit in 1910 when the Treasurer announced the financial results for the year. It was, therefore, resolved to obtain a bank loan of £50 and to pay it off by charging all the members a penny (½p) a week more. In addition the best seats in the synagogue were going to cost 10p a week extra, the next best 7½p, and 5p and 2½p would be added to the cost of those who sat at the back.

Herman Cohen
A former president, murdered at 41

Wolf Jacobson
Who offered the Chevra Tehillim a home

What had started as an uneasy relationship between the Beth Hamedresh and the Hebrew Congregation still continued to simmer, even if, on the surface, there was now accord. In July 1909 the Englishe Shul sent a letter to the Greeners which any outsider would consider generous and complimentary. It was signed by 23 members of the congregation and it read:

> We the undersigned members of the Sunderland Hebrew Congregation, hereby petition the Council to contribute a sum of £26 per annum towards Rabbi Hurwitz on the ground that Rabbi Hurwitz renders useful work to some members of our Congregation. That such services are also rendered by him to those who are neither members of this Congregation nor of the Beth Hamedresh. We trust you will see your way to grant this Petition, for the benefit of the Congregation, and the general Community.

After a lengthy discussion the Beth Hamedresh said "no". Presumably, they did not wish to be beholden in any way to the Hebrew Congregation. They must have feared that this would be a way of influencing Rabbi Hurwitz and might have felt they were being offered charity. Assuming that the members of the Hebrew Congregation only acted with the best in intentions, the refusal must have been resented.

In other ways, though, the two congregations did work together and sometimes the organization to whom they didn't want to be under an obligation, was the state. In 1902 the council had opened a new Workhouse infirmary. A Workhouse was where the council dumped local people who were too old, too sick or too penniless to survive without some form of aid. They were dreadful institutions, because it was the intention of the councils to try to discourage people from going to the Workhouse, as that involved keeping them at the cost of the ratepayers.

At the opening "Alderman Forbes said that the Jews were a great example to all Churches in the country. During the 27 years he had been Guardian, he had never known a Jew or Jewess to make application for relief." This proud record was temporarily ended in September 1907 when the *Jewish Chronicle* reported that "For the first time in its history, a Jew has been admitted into the Workhouse at Sunderland." No later than the following week, the *JC* had a follow-up story.

> In reference to the report in last issue that a Jew has been admitted into the Workhouse - Mr. Simon Olswang, Treasurer of the Hebrew Board of Guardians, wishes to say that the executive of the Board immediately took charge of the inmate and sent him, according to his desire, to his relations in Liverpool. The Board has asked the Municipal Board to inform them of any application for relief or admittance by any co-religionist, so that they can deal with them.

The Board of Guardians was, of course, jointly run by the two congregations. To an outsider it may seem an act of charity on their behalf far beyond the norm. After all the Workhouse was full of nominal Christians. Why such a different attitude towards one poor wretch? When you have allowed for compassion and generosity, there were other considerations. Not, necessarily, in any order, or applicable to only one congregation.

There was the din, the law, that laid down the correct procedure in such cases. There was the reputation of the community as one which would not be a burden on the state. That mattered after the Aliens Act when Jewish immigration was curtailed, partly on the grounds that the immigrants could, indeed, become a cost to the country. There was also the resentment at the idea of coming under any obligation to a local authority. The Jews were a proud people. Poor or even impoverished, they wanted to be as good as their neighbours. They also felt that the destitute reflected on the whole community.

That it proved the Jews were not as good as their non-Jewish neighbours; snobbery, fear, resentment and the demands of Jewish law were all factors which emerged in cases like these.

In 1911 the coronation of George V was a less important event to the Beth Hamedresh than the resignation of its famous rabbi, Hirsch Hurwitz. The year also marked, however, the recreation of a 19th century institution which would help bind the whole Sunderland Jewish community together for many years; Sol Novinski started up the Jewish Literary and Social Circle again. It only had 30 members when it was originally formed but by 1936 it would have 150. It had its own premises and the building contained a library and rooms for meetings. The Circle put on plays, held dances and concerts, organised essay writing and arranged public speaking contests. It became the social centre for both old and young and many a happy marriage saw its beginnings within its walls.

Chapter 5
The Rabbinowitz Years

The fame of Rabbi Hurwitz as a scholar and as an able communal rabbi guaranteed that he would receive offers from other communities. As the Beth Hamedresh had difficulty in paying the £2 a week salary he had originally been awarded, Rabbi Hurwitz had little option but to look elsewhere if he was to maintain a reasonable standard of living for his family.

When a group of synagogues needed a Rabbi for their community in Leeds. This became the catalyst for Hurwitz leaving Sunderland. Whilst his resignation was much regretted, it was fully understood why he was going. The Federation, from whom the offer came, was to the right of the United Synagogue so that its standards of yiddishkeit were very similar to the practices in the Beth Hamedresh.

It was agreed that the rabbi would leave for Leeds on a weekday and a large delegation of the Leeds community gathered at Leeds station to welcome him. One of its members had actually boarded the train at Harrogate in order to be the first to welcome the rabbi - and to try to ensure that when he took up his office he would continue to buy his chickens from the members' firm, as had his predecessor! The rabbi referred him to Mrs. Hurwitz as the decision maker in this matter!!

Leeds at the time was famous for its tailoring and a large number of the synagogue members worked for tailoring companies or ran their own little tailoring businesses. They turned up at the bench in their working clothes on the morning of his arrival and then they all took the time off to welcome him at the station and go on to the installation in the synagogue. For such occasions they covered their heads in the usual way and a large crowd of Jewish tailors met the rabbi wearing their Sabbath top hats. When a sea of silk hats on Leeds station greeted the new incumbent, it was somewhat to the surprise of the non-Jewish travellers.

The welcoming committee would have said that it was the correct mark of respect for the Almighty and their new minister and the opinions of the non-Jews were not their concern. When you see a Jew going to synagogue in Golders Green today wearing 18th century Polish nobleman's dress. It is considered that exactly the same principle applies. As there was some dissension between the various Leeds synagogues, none of the other city rabbis attended Rabbi Hurwitz's installation, which meant that they missed his initial sermon which lasted an hour and a half!

Rabbi Hurwitz remained a highly respected figure in the north of England until he died, but he did not eventually take up the most senior ministry in Leeds. He didn't think his English was good enough to preach in the language the congregation wanted and consequently he debarred himself. Instead he accepted the pulpit of a small Leeds synagogue, the Chevra Tehillim, the Psalms of David congregation, and served it faithfully for 35 years. In addition, he was appointed Leeds Ab Beth Din, to preside over the court.

Replacing Rabbi Hurwitz was never going to be easy. He had been an inspiring leader and simply to find the money to pay the next incumbent was going to be hard enough, without the problem of finding a rabbi of equal calibre who would take the post. Certainly, there was no hope of continuing the yeshiva without him, and that pioneer of the yeshivas which would emerge in the North East in the years to come, closed down.

It was customary to wait a suitable period of time before appointing a new rabbi, particularly if the incumbent had died in office. It was not only a mark of respect but a sensible precaution; if you appointed the wrong man, you were likely to be stuck with him for a long period of years. Logically, the Beth Hamedresh should have then turned to the Chief Rabbi in London for help. They had promised to do so as a condition of being granted the right to have their own Marriage Secretary and their own Shochet only a few years before.

Looking to London, however, remained unattractive for many of the Krottingen families. They much preferred the option of asking the advice of distinguished Russian rabbis, and when Hermann Adler died in July 1911 there wasn't a Chief Rabbi to appeal to anyway. Even the Hebrew Congregation, always loyal to the Chief Rabbi, made the case for greater independence. In 1912 the minister, Salis Daiches, had attacked the idea that everything had to be run from London, holding publicly that the provinces could take care of themselves. Almost as a mark of his independence, Daiches had gone as a delegate to the 10th Zionist Congress. There was a conference held on the traditional structure in London, but there were no major changes as a result.

פסק דין.

זה הסכסוך שנולד בין חברי ביהכ"נ דזהר סטמפורדהיל לרגל שאלת הרבנות פה ושבגלל זה התפלגו ונחלקו ביניהם עד אשר והרבה מהחברים רצו להתרחק מביהכ"נ ולעשות להם חבורה בפני עצמה, הנה ואחרי ששני הצדדים הסכימו לבוא לפני בי"ד לפשר ולתווך ביניהם בכדי להחזיק השלום והאחדות, ובאו אתנו אחרי ששמענו את הטענות והתביעות מצד האחד של ושניה, פסק הבי"ד ע"פ דרך התורה והיושר, ואלה התנאים שעליהם לקיים בלי שום סירוב ואיחור.

א) על ועד ביהכ"נ לסלק מתוך הועד זה והרבה תמורתו חברים חדשים שיהיו להם זכות כמו אנשי הועד שנבחרו מתוך הקהל ע"י אסיפה כללית. ואלה המה החברים החדשים: ר' יחזקאל כהן, ר' גרשון לוי, ר' שרגא כהן, ור' יעקב חיים כהן. ואלה [illegible] מתוך הועד בכדי להכניס על אשר הועד [illegible] בשנה הבאה [illegible] נבחר לחבר הועד.

ב) ואלה החברים החדשים שנוספו כעת להועד ישבו בהועד בלי שום בחירה מהקהל, רק על משך שנה אחת, הגם עד כמו בחירת הועד החדש ע"י אסיפה כללית שתהי' אי"ה בשנת תרצ"ב הבעל"ט.

ג) על הועד וכן גם על הקהל מוטל החובה לבלי לשנות באופן וסדר בחירת רב לדרוש [illegible] שהוחלט ביניהם באסיפה כללית, הוא לבלי לבחור שום רב כל זמן שלא תבוא אלו הסכמת הרבנים הגאונים ברוסיא שיהיה פה לשאול ולענות. ואך כי אופן וסדר בחירה כזאת היא היותר נעלה [illegible] לקבלת רב חדש, [illegible] אנשי הועד לדעת את הבחירה, [illegible] הדבר בלי שום [illegible]. וגם הקהל לא יוכל לקבלו לרב, [illegible] כל זמן שלא תבואו הסכמת הרבנים ברוסיא [illegible] להתנהג בסטמפורדהיל לא יותר משני שבתות, [illegible] לדרוש את הדור.

ד) הרה"ג ר' מנחם [illegible] [illegible] הסכמות לדעת על הבחירה, [illegible] הרבנים הגאונים על הבחירה [illegible] הרב.

ה) [illegible] זכות הרב הנבחר יהי' [illegible] הרב [illegible] וכן [illegible] זכות להרב הנבחר לקבל את משרת הרבנות [illegible].

ו) זכות הסמכות לקחת חוק [illegible] הועד [illegible] כי השינוי בהנהגת ביהכ"נ יגרום ח"ו [illegible] ביהכ"נ.

ז) גם [illegible] הדבר [illegible] של הועד [illegible] בין החתונות ובין [illegible]. יען כי שינוי גם בדבר הזה יגרום ח"ו [illegible] הבתים.

[illegible] חבורו [illegible]: [illegible]. [illegible] גם להקהל [illegible] יהי' [illegible] השלום והאחדות [illegible] התורה והעבודה ותשלום בשלומותם.

והנה [illegible], כי השלום והאחדות [illegible] ובאו [illegible] באנו על החתום היום יום ג' לסדר, [illegible] כ"ו שבט שנת תרצ"ב לפ"ק.

נאום [illegible] סטמפורדהיל

נאום ישראל יעקב בהרב ר' אברהם הכהן יפה נ"י חופק מאנטשעסטער

P'Sak Din

Another subject which arose in the interregnum between Chief Rabbis was a suggestion that there be formed an International Association of Jews loyal to the Torah who would try to alleviate anti-Semitic outbreaks around the world. The Hungarian delegate at a conference to discuss this suggested that only Orthodox Jews be acceptable as members. This was opposed by Salis Daiches who wanted everybody to be allowed to join, but the whole concept came to nothing as national bodies wanted to retain their independence of each other; not much change there then.

The political manoeuvrings which led to the appointment of Chief Rabbi Hertz in 1913 meant that any London authority had little time or interest in what was going on in a Beth Hamedresh in the North East. Equally, the Beth Hamedresh liked neither candidate for the Chief Rabbi vacancy and withheld its vote from both of them.

This, however, did not make life any easier for the Beth Hamedresh members. During the interregnum the ministerial responsibilities devolved onto Rev. Warrantz. Although he was referred to as such, Warrantz did, of course, have semichah and was entitled to the title of Rabbi. Perhaps the title of Rabbi in the Beth Hamedresh at the time implied an authority which the congregation didn't wish to offer him. Another word which had negative overtones in those days, oddly enough from our present-day viewpoint, was Jew. Its meaning in the dictionary gave examples of many aspects on antisocial behaviour. It was for that reason that the Englisher Shul had taken the title of the Hebrew Congregation rather than the Jewish Congregation.

It is, perhaps, significant that, today, on the island of Rhodes in Greece, there is a memorial to those who died in the Holocaust. It is a pretty garden but it is called the Square of the Hebrew Martyrs. The word 'Jew' still seems to stick in the throat but then the behaviour of the Greeks towards their Jewish citizens in modern times was seldom beyond reproach.

The alternative claims of various candidates for the vacant post led to such heated arguments that there were threats of secession. There were two main candidates for the vacant pulpit; Rabbi Mendel Behrmann and Rabbi David Rabbinowitz. Rabbi Behrmann started with the advantage that he had family in Sunderland. In order to avoid yet another split in the community, the Beth Hamedresh reached an agreement to ask a number of eminent rabbonim, not connected with the synagogue or the Chief Rabbi's office, to give them a ruling. It was a distinguished group who considered the arguments and handed down their P'sak Din in 1913. It was couched in terms like Queen's Regulations. They said:

> Regarding the differences that have arisen between the members of the Beth Hamedresh of the town of Sunderland concerning the question of the Rabbonus, through which a quarrel has spread amongst them, so much so that certain members have desired to break away and form a community of their own. Since the two factions have agreed to rely on us to compromise and mediate for the sake of peace and unity, we have declared the following after having heard the claims and complaints of each side - a P'sak Din according to the Torah and equity. The following conditions must be abided by without any reluctance or refusal.
>
> 1. The committee of the Beth Hamedresh must co-opt a further four new members who shall have the same rights as the other members of the committee who have been elected by the general body at the general election. And these are the new members. Rabbi Y. Cohen, Rabbi G. Levy, Rabbi Shmerye Cohen and Rabbi Isaac Cohen. The last mentioned should receive a letter requesting his willingness to join the committee as a measure of appeasement for having his letter written the previous year ignored when he was elected member of the committee.
> 2. These new members who have been co-opted at this time to the committee shall remain on the committee (without having been voted by the general body) for a period of one year only, i.e. until the next General Election in the year 5674 (1913/1914).

Having provided the committee with umpires who couldn't be removed until the final decision on a new rabbi had been reached, the Beth Din went on, totally ignoring the Office of the Chief Rabbi in London:

> 3. It is the duty of the committee and indeed the entire community not to change the form on order of the election of a rov from that which was decided by them at the General Meeting, i.e. not to elect a rov so long as there does not arrive an approval from the Rabbonim and the Geonim of Russia to whom they had turned for advice, since this is the best and most acceptable method of electing a new rov, and the town of Sunderland will be outstanding in worthiness compared to others, Therefore, if the Rov of the town of Mottella shall come to Sunderland at the calling of the committee to stand for election, and during the course of his stay shall not come an approval from the Rabbonim, then it is up to him to leave the town without any claim or complaint and also the community cannot elect him as Rov even if he satisfied all of them, so long as there does not come to him the approval of the Rabbonim of Russia and for this matter he should remain in Sunderland not more than a fortnight, after which time he must leave the town.

It was a blanket statement of the ultimate authority of the eminent rabbonim in Russia but what had happened to the agreement between the Beth Hamedresh and the British Chief Rabbi? Nothing was heard from London and once the community had got away with this categoric denial of the Chief Rabbi's authority, it was not likely that they would abide by it, or even seek it, again.

The P'sak Din held that all the candidates could stand but the successful one must have a majority of 10 over the next highest. If there were 50 voters, the successful rov must have 30 votes. It might have avoided such disputes happening again if a small clique were appointed who were the only ones who could deal with spiritual matters. The Beth Din would have none of this:

> We also do not agree to the suggestion put to us to form a separate committee to deal with spiritual matters and that they alone shall deal with those issues, but rather that matters shall stand as heretofore and that the entire committee shall deal with all things, be they spiritual or temporal, for any change even in these instances can only cause jealousy and enmity and a diffusing and weakening of the strength of the Beth Hamedresh.

It wasn't just that every member was as good as every other, but that the setting up of oligarchies was not the official Jewish way; unfortunately, it has happened time and time again but the rabbonim still frown upon it.

The appointment was finally made of Rabbi David Rabbinowitz. He came from a long line of rabbonim, his father being Rabbi Gedaliah Romanower. Rabbi Gadaliah married and had ten children. Horrifically, his wife, Yehudit, lost her husband and all her children, except David, in just one week when cholera raged through the house. She agreed to have David sent away for his education and he got his semicha from the Vilna Kollel. Known by the anglicised name of David Rabbinowitz, his name at home had been Rabbi Dovidal Romandower. He was a disciple of Rabbi Israel Salanter, who had formulated the concept of Musser as part of the semicha curriculum. The core importance of this spiritual adjunct would be particularly seen after the Second World War.

Rabbi David Rabbinowitz
Served the community from 1913 - 1924

By the time he was 22 David Rabbinowitz was the Rabbi of Mohilev in Russia. He married, lost four children in his turn to Cholera and, after the 1906 pogroms, came to England to serve in communities in Liverpool, Grimsby and London. For six years he was the rabbi of the Cannon Street Synagogue in the City and he was widely respected. Rabbinowitz was profoundly learned - he was said to know the whole Bible by heart - and he carried out his duties with exemplary zeal, according to contemporary accounts. Rabbinowitz was said - somewhat inappropriately - to have lived the life of a saint.

Rabbi David Rabbinowitz and family

The Council noted, with regret, that there was little chance of getting financial support from the Chief Rabbi's Provincial Ministers' Salaries Augmentation Scheme. They might also have been sorry they had turned down the Hebrew Congregation's offer of financial support to Rabbi Hurwitz. It could have created a precedent for the richer congregation to support future Beth Hamedresh rabbi, but then it was the perceived danger of indebtedness to the Englishe Shul which had led them to turn down the offer in the first place. There were, of course, other men who had semicha but chose, for the most part, to follow secular careers.

There were men like Rabbi Richenberg, who took the Blatt when David Rabbinowitz was ill. He was only the shammas, the beadle, at the synagogue, but he was that learned. They might have earned a living as tally men but they retained their dignity. One day a congregant tried to attract his attention by calling out "Shammos". The rabbi ignored him. The congregant tried again and complained that the rabbi wasn't paying him any attention. Rabbi Richenberg replied "You know my name. When I want to speak to you, do I call you Bal H'Agola?" A Bal H'Agola is a menial horse and cart driver. Chazan Warrantz also remained as Chazan and supported the team.

If the community had been at loggerheads over the appointment of Hurwitz's replacement, the same did not apply to their social lives or to their relations with the Hebrew Congregation. There may have been no radio or television in 1911 but there was no shortage of Jewish societies in Sunderland to offer enjoyable alternatives.

The *Jewish Chronicle* listed the Hachnosas Orachim Society, (the Welcoming Committee) the Chevra Tehillim Society, and the Gemiluth Chasodim Society. Then there was the Ladies Guild, the Hebrew Literary and Debating Society, the Jewish Social and Literary Club, the Jewish Women's League, the Hebrew Order of Druids, the Zionist Association and the Mount Pisgah Beacon of the Order of Ancient Maccabeans. Organisations to take care of good works were in no way neglected either, and these were in the capable hands of the Hebrew Board of Guardians, the Hebrew Benefit Society, the Hebrew Ladies Benevolent Society and, of course, the Chevra Kadisha.

It is often said that if you have three MPs in Israel you could form four political parties; Jews like to belong and run associations. The Englisher Shul and the Greeners were now mixing harmoniously and were firing on all cylinders.

When the First World War broke out many traditional attitudes had to be re-examined. For example, Germany had been the traditional ally of Britain for 200 years. The Kings of the House of Hanover were also Kings of England. It was the Prussian Marshall Blücher whose army tipped the balance in Wellington's favour at Waterloo. Prince Albert was from the German house of Saxe Coburg and a friend from university days of

Chief Rabbi Nathan Marcus Adler. Now, after so many years of close alliance, anything German was suddenly anathema.

This meant that if you had a German name, it was a good time to change it. Prince Louis of Battenberg had to give up his position as First Sea Lord because of his German ancestry and the family name was changed to Mountbatten. The Saxe Coburgs became Windsors. At the outbreak of war, the local JPs in Sunderland refused to accept Jews as Special Constables and asked those who had already received their papers, to return them. The reason was not Anti-Semitism; it was anti-German - but that did not stop complaints flooding into the *Jewish Chronicle* from the Jews who had been rejected.

Among those who were outraged at the discrimination was the proprietor of the Sunderland Echo, ex-MP Samuel Storey. He pointed out in the paper that those who had been refused were either British born or naturalised. Furthermore, even if they had foreign names, they did not have German or Austrian parents. The Krottingens, of course, were from Russia. Storey objected: "If Jews can be in the army, can also be officers in the army, can gain the Victoria Cross or die for the country, how can they be considered unfit to be Special Constables in a town in which they are citizens and well-known men." The Board of Deputies also protested.

The Beth Hamedresh members were more likely to be affected as they were the recent arrivals and hadn't changed their names. They also had another problem though when it came to the need to defend their new country; they had to accept that the hated Russians, cause of the pogroms in Lithuania, were now their allies. Most bit the bullet and did their duty, but it was a hard pill to swallow.

The community offered the Talmud Torah building as a temporary hospital for the wounded coming home from France. A Jewish Women's Sewing Circle settled down to produce warm clothing for the troops. All 11 Jewish furniture manufacturers in the town offered to send beds and equipment where it was needed. Captain Miller, a Sunderland veteran of the Boer War, hurried home from India to join the colours. Everybody agreed that the maximum support must be given to the National Relief Fund to help pay for the war.

War is no respecter of religious observances. Wars do not stop for Shabbot or even - as was learned in 1973 - for Yom Kippur, when the Egyptians attacked Israel on that day. One question, therefore, was what action could be taken to differentiate the holy days from the norm. In the Second World War, Rabbi Rabbinowitz's son, Rabbi Moshe Rabbinowitz, told one of the recruits, Mordaunt Cohen, that on Shabbot he should carry his rifle in the wrong hand to show he wasn't working! His father might well have made a similar comment.

At the beginning of the First World War Britain had the smallest European army among the great powers. Even so, there was no move to introduce conscription. Initially, to join up was considered to be the mark of the patriot and, by October, 16 Sunderland Jews had enlisted. From the pulpit, Rabbi Daiches in the Hebrew Congregation synagogue appealed to the young members to do their duty. Another appeal was for financial support for the Belgian Jewish community who had fled the country when it was invaded. The Belgian Jewish Relief Fund benefited from the usual enthusiastic response.

Among those who decided to fight for king and country was Private Issy Jackson. He was hit by shrapnel in May 1915 and died of his wounds. Jackson had been educated at the local Bede grammar school and it was generally true that the better the school, the more likely it was that their pupils would join up. By June 1916 Driver Mark Freeman was on sick leave at home in Sunderland and was able to report that 60 Sunderland Jews were in the forces. In October of that year Private Charles Letzky was killed in action.

In October 1916 Sergeant George Jacobs was awarded the Distinguished Conduct Medal just before he was killed. Corporal Sydney Asher was recommended for a commission just before he, too, was killed. Joe Gillis, a member of the Beth Hamedresh died as well. A Memorial Service was held for the men and Brigadier General English who attended took the opportunity to say "It was the Jews who, by their defence of Jerusalem against the Romans, taught the world how to fight for an ideal."

In 1917 Lance Corporal Myer Gallewski was awarded the Military Medal for gallantry but was killed at the front before he could receive the award. He was one of those who had volunteered at the outbreak of the war when he was only 16. Lionel Bernstein, Reuben Hyman and Private S. Lipman were also killed that year. Lipman had been wounded twice in the Gallipoli campaign but recovered sufficiently to return to the fighting in France. The casualty lists were appalling, In one day at the Battle of the Somme there were around 40,000 dead and wounded on the British side. It was not surprising that Reuben Bloomburg promised publicly that if he survived the war, he would stand throughout the Yom Kippur service. This wasn't that exceptional among the congregation, but the service does last 12 hours!

In all, 16 Sunderland Jewish military were killed in action and many more were wounded. At a memorial service for four of them in 1916, Rabbi Salis Daiches had said: "With their blood they had paid the debt of gratitude which the Jewish race owed to this country and which had provided a haven of refuge." Where young men had joined up at the outbreak of the war, conscription brought an influx of the older men as well. Many went into the Russian Labour Corps which was attached to the Northumberland Fusiliers.

To join up and take your chances was one thing. There was work to be done on the Home Front as well though. Money was raised for the Jewish victims of the war in Russia and for the relief of Polish Jews. One Jew in Sunderland, who had been born in Galicia, was interned at the Lancaster Concentration Camp. He was only released when Rabbi Daiches appealed to the Home Office. At the time a concentration camp did not have the infamous connotations it was to acquire in the Second World War. The British had first coined the term in the Boer War when Boer families were herded together to prevent their younger members becoming guerrillas. Disease carried off a large number of them.

In 1915 the Sunderland community also mourned the death of a non-combatant; Rabbi Israel Levy who had served the Sunderland congregation from 1870 - 1881. Rabbi Levy had been trained for the ministry by Chief Rabbi Solomon Herschell who had held that office from 1802 - 1842. He was known as a great wit and a fine talmudic scholar who had held the congregation together. As early as 1847 when he had a pulpit in Manchester, he gave his sermons in English, which was very unusual. He lived to be 91 but towards the end of his life he went blind, though this did not prevent him preaching, as he always spoke ex tempore. His last post was in Hull and when he passed away, Rabbi Daiches commented "when he ended his career....he was one of the least known, most poorly paid synagogue officials in the country. But he never complained." You have to be pretty dedicated to be a working rabbi.

When he was in Sunderland it was said that Rabbi Levy made the weekly sermon an indispensable part of the Shabbot morning service. It would have been unusual because most ministers gave very few sermons in the course of the year. It was remembered that on one Kol Nidre night the electricity failed in the synagogue. The moon, however, shone through the windows onto the pulpit: "It was then he looked more than ever a true 'Messenger of the Lord.' "

The Talmud Torah was very highly regarded and in 1915 the examiners proclaimed themselves "delighted with the proficiency displayed" by those who attended. The Beth Hamedresh congregation continued to flourish and when the opportunity came to buy additional land adjoining the synagogue in 1916, they found the money to do so. They also benefited from Mr. B. Smith giving them "a massive set of silver and gilt breast plates (for a sefer torah) in memory of his wife and an engraved silver pointer in memory of his son, Moses." A handsome gift from the synagogue came when Mr. Rick retired as President of the Talmud Torah in 1917 and was presented with a "gold Albert and watch." An Albert was a watch chain. The mortgage of £850 was also paid off, with all the money being donated locally, except £25 which came from the ever-generous Rothschilds

The war raged on and the allied cause was not gaining the upper hand. More and more the key to possible future success was seen in terms of getting the United States to come in on the allied side. As, however, there were millions of Americans whose ancestry was German or Austrian, the need for persuasive argument was paramount. The British government took the view that if they could win over the Jewish community in America - violently anti-Russian, and often of German or Austrian extraction - the Jewish leaders would have an influence with the American government.

David Lloyd-George, whose law firm had represented the infant Zionist movement in England in Herzl's time, thought that promising the Jews a National Home if the allied side was successful would be very popular. The leaders of the British Jews were horrified at the idea; they considered a movement to create a National Home for the Jews would throw suspicion on the commitment of the community towards the United Kingdom. The head of the Board of Deputies and the head of the unelected but powerful Anglo-Jewish Association, took it upon themselves to write to The Times to say that the community didn't support the idea.

They probably did reflect the views of the majority of the Jews in Britain at the time. Membership of the Zionist Federation was small, the idea of retaking the Holy Land seemed far fetched and few would have wanted to live in Palestine, to go on Aliyah. The two leaders, however, had made one enormous miscalculation; they had forgotten to consult with the members of their organizations. Indeed, at a meeting of the Board of Deputies a short time before the letter was sent to The Times, the subject wasn't even raised.

The response of Sunderland was typical of the provincial communities who eventually voted against a motion of confidence in the Chairman of the Board of Deputies. The words of a motion passed by the two congregations in Sunderland were identical. The members of the Beth Hamedresh:

> records its emphatic protest against the statements made in that letter, against the unauthorised use made of the names of the parent organizations which had not been consulted, and against the attempt made to mislead the general public with reference to the Zionist objects and the aspirations of the mass of the Jewish people.

Of these complaints, by far the most important was the lack of discussion. The provinces were seriously proud. By a narrow majority the Chairman of the Board of Deputies lost the vote of confidence in June and resigned. In all, 32 of the 36 deputies representing provincial communities voted against the Chairman, including Professor Dr. A Buchler for the Beth Hamedresh and Israel Jacobs for the Hebrew Congregation. The government issued the Balfour Declaration.

It was also in 1917 that the Czar was overthrown in Russia. The Sunderland Echo quoted the Morning Post as saying that their Russian correspondent believed that the Leninist revolutionaries were Jews of German origin. Rabbi Daiches indignantly denied it and the newspaper retracted. There were, in fact, a number of Jews in the Leninist high command but, in view of the appalling treatment the Jews in Russia had received for well over a hundred years, it would have been surprising if that hadn't been the case.

Unfortunately within a few years of joining the Beth Hamedresh, the rabbi, David Rabbinowitz, fell ill and for a number of years was unable to carry out his duties. Rabbi Daiches represented the community in official circles. David Rabbinowitz was still ill in 1919 but the situation was made far worse for him when his devoted wife, Leah, died in the Sunderland Fever hospital in the February of that year. After the Great War ended there was a flu pandemic throughout the world which probably killed more people than died in the war itself. Unfortunately, at the time, there were no anti-viral drugs and young and old succumbed. The rabbi and his wife had been married for 45 years and the community rallied round to do its best for the widower.

The war may have ended but when Rabbi Daiches left the Englisher shul in 1919, another, if very minor conflict by comparison, erupted. The whole of the Englisher Shul Council and the Secretary resigned and the members had to settle their differences and elect a new one. If the Beth Hamedresh seemed to have fewer outbreaks of serious discord within its ranks, it might well have been due to the firm grip on communal affairs that a few of the founding families maintained over the congregation. The recurrent names of Cohen, Gillis and Pearlman served on over the years, financially unrewarded, but content that their Lithuanian tradition was being correctly upheld. On a happier note, Sol Novinski and Gertie Macgrill reorganised the Literary Circle after the war and joined up with the Zionists to create the Sunderland Zionist Association.

Inscription of Reb Chatze Cohen in a presentation
Might well have spoken better Hebrew than English

As the synagogue extension was being built, the Festival services were held at the Victoria Hall. The new Villiers Street was completed in 1921 and opened by Sir Stuart Samuel, who was the son of the great Jewish philanthropist, Samuel Montagu MP, later Lord Swaythling. Swaythling had founded the Federation of Synagogues, primarily in the East End of London, at the end of the 19th century and the Federation was well to the right of the United Synagogue. The Beth Hamedresh parnass at the time did not have a perfect command of English aristocratic nomenclature and seniority - he wasn't the first to have the problem. In presenting a gold key to the Guest of Honour, he addressed him in Ivrit as "My Lord King, Sir Stuart, Esquire. I hereby present to you a...." and dried up. Rabbi Hurwitz, who had arrived from Leeds to lend lustre to the proceedings, prompted him by handing over the key.

David Rabbinowitz's successor was always likely to be his son, Rabbi Moshe Rabbinowitz. He came from Russia where he had been the Chief Rabbi of Orel Russia. It was said of Moshe Rabbinowitz that he never had to open a book when he was teaching. He knew everything by heart. Even if this was a slight exaggeration, there was no doubt that Rabbinowitz was a mighty talmudic brain and the rabbis at the Sunderland Hebrew congregation in his time would have been, talmudically, far less able.

It wasn't that they were poor scholars, just that Rabbinowitz set such exceptionally high standards. Moshe Rabbinowitz was also the ideal candidate because he could look after his father who suffered a stroke in 1922. Moshe Rabbinowitz was already 42 when he lost his mother and was not sorry to have an excellent reason for leaving a country where 250,000 Jews had perished in pogroms during the civil war between the Soviets and the supporters of the former Czar.

During 1923 he had come to visit his father. He stood in for his father in the synagogue, delivered all his lectures and took the daily Blatt. Overall, he made a very good impression. When the Annual General Meeting took place, 87 of the congregation attended to vote unanimously to adopt him as their rav. It was agreed to provide a pension for Rabbi David, to give his son £50 to bring his family over from Russia, and another £50 to buy him a house. The succession had taken place smoothly and the new rabbi was delighted with the post. It gave him the immense pleasure, for example, of being able to get an ethrog and lulav at Succot, a purchase which was impossible in Russia. On every Succot thereafter, the Rabbi could be seen holding the plants and the fruit close to him throughout the service.

That potential crisis having been avoided, in 1924 only 60 attended the AGM where the new rabbi's salary was approved, providing he attended the Talmud Torah three times a week. The congregation was still deeply concerned that the Jewish education of the children should receive the top priority. The Talmud Torah might be losing money, but it was doing a vital job.

Rabbi M E Rabbinowitz
He knew the books by heart

Eventually, after a very long and painful illness, David Rabbinowitz died in 1924 at the age of 63. He had married again after his first wife died - rabbis are always supposed to be married - and the congregation made the necessary financial arrangements for his widow. There was also the problem in 1924 that one of the Beth Hamedresh officials had retired. The possibility that a replacement might be found in Britain seemed remote to the congregation, who decided and preferred to advertise in the appropriate media in Kovno. The position of Chazan cum Shochet cum Mohel was offered at a salary of £6 a week.

As all of this should have been done through the Chief Rabbi's office in London and with his approval, the new Chief Rabbi, Joseph Hertz, must have been informed, if only because he was going to find out anyway. Nevertheless, it was still to Kovno, rather than Kings Lynn or Kingston that the Beth Hamedresh looked for its new minister.

When, in 1926, there was a proposal to make a charitable contribution towards placing the Chief Rabbi's name in the Zionist Golden Book, it was approved by the Council by only one vote. There was a much better response in 1927 for the Appeal Fund to help those who had suffered in an earthquake which had caused a great deal of damage in Palestine. The General Strike of 1926 made life particularly difficult for the Beth Hamedresh tally man, as we've seen with Joseph Pearlman. As a little practical help is worth a ton of pity, the Council arranged to set up an Emergency Loan Fund. Twenty members of the congregation each guaranteed a £50 overdraft provided by Lloyds Bank.

As a result Lloyds agreed to loan up to £1,000 to the Loan Fund. Those members in need could borrow from £20 - £100 and pay it back by instalments until December 15th 1928. Whatever remained outstanding would be repaid to the bank by the guarantors. So if the bank lent £1,000 but had only been repaid £900, the 20 guarantors would be liable for £5 each. The guarantors charged no interest; it was simply a generous move to help their brethren. Those who needed it could borrow money from the fund and pay it back when conditions improved. The preamble to the announcement of the Emergency Loan Fund said:

> the object of the same being to assist business people who are members or the wives of members of the Sunderland Beth Hamedresh and who may find themselves financially embarrassed on account of the recent coal strike.

Meanwhile, the British mandate in Palestine was still hard to administer. Moshe Rabbinowitz was not an enthusiastic Zionist himself, though he would oppose the White Paper the government eventually came up with to reduce the number of Jewish refugees who could go to live in Palestine in the 1930s. His wife, Chaya, was an enthusiastic Zionist. It was said that Zionism was the only thing they ever quarrelled about and eventually Chaya's nephew became the President of Israel, Ephraim Katzir. The Rabbinowitz family were invited to the inauguration.

For a few years Rabbi Moshe Rabbinowitz's opposite number at the Hebrew Congregation was Rabbi Dr. Alec Silverstone, who was only 27 when he was invited to minister to the community. Dr. Silverstone spent most of his working life in Southport, to which he moved in 1927. Whilst never nationally famous in his Southport community, it would be a mistake to underestimate the knowledge and ability of men like Silverstone. He had obtained his semicha from the Manchester Yeshiva and, at almost the same time, had completed his studies for a Ph. D. from Manchester University. He might have been seen as less eminent than Rabbi Rabbinowitz but he was very bright.

It is very important that the authorisation of a conversion is certified by a rabbi whose authority is generally accepted. Thus conversions under the auspices of the Chief Rabbi present no problem. At this time in Britain, however, it was much less centralized and provincial rabbis would take it upon themselves to make decisions. The process was to form a Beth Din with three rabbis officiating and for that body to take the responsibility of approving the recommendation to convert an applicant. If and when the situation arose, Rabbi Rabbinowitz had no hesitation about converting whoever he considered a properly qualified candidate. Even more so, as one of the Cohen family wrote in his memoirs:

> Rabbi Silverstone was famous for performing conversions. In one day he converted six women who married members of the congregation who later became quite prominent in the community.

It was only when the London Beth Din acquired Dayan Abramsky that the great sage asked all the British rabbis to stop acting on their own. But then Abramsky had a fully justified reputation for talmudic brilliance. In a court case he was asked by the judge who was the greatest talmudic expert in the country. He answered that he was. When the judge mildly rebuked him for his apparent lack of modesty, Rabbi Abramsky agreed with the judge, but pointed out that he was on oath and thus had to tell the truth.

At the Beth Din he tightened up the rules in other ways as well. He declared that the hind quarters of an animal were not kosher because it was such a skilled process to make them so. Most of the shochtim were not up to the task. This aggravated the butchers who now had more meat on the carcass they couldn't sell. Again, an argument could rage about overweening authorities in London or provincial communities trying to bypass London. The position on conversion is, however, slightly more complicated than this.

A convert from another religion might want to marry a Jew in an Orthodox synagogue anywhere in the world. If their conversion document wasn't accepted because the authority who had granted it was not known to the community far away, it would cause unnecessary complications. It was far better that the granting authority had an international reputation.

Just before the death of David Rabbinowitz, Rabbi Bloch had died in 1923. He had laid the foundations of ministerial practice during the early years of the Beth Hamedresh and if it wasn't for good founders, progress would always be that much slower. He may have ruffled many feathers but he had laid down the law correctly.

The Beth Hamedresh suffered an even more grievous loss when Chatze Cohen died in 1926 in his 84th year. He had led the Blatt Shiur for 30 years, was held almost in reverence by the community but remained a very modest man. Although few members of the Beth Hamedresh deserved greater eulogies at their passing, Chatze Cohen left strict instructions that there should be none at his funeral. Although he had fathered those 22 children - many notable - his life had involved considerable sadness as well. As his obituary in the *Jewish Chronicle* pointed out "Though he suffered innumerable sorrows throughout his long and active life, he remained steadfast in his Judaism. To thrive, every community needs a Chatze Cohen. The Beth Hamedresh were fortunate to have a string of them over very many years.

Chatze Cohen's grandchildren remembered with affection his custom of walking to their homes on Rosh Hashonah to bless them, and his great pride in all his family. On the front of his house there was a name plate which read C.H.Cohen & Sons. In his later years he mellowed, becoming very slightly less strict but, overall, continued to set the standard by which the rest of the community would compare their own performance. The contribution the family would make to local government in Sunderland began in

1929 when Jack Cohen was elected to the Council and combined his civic duties with the office of Secretary of the Beth Hamedresh.

Moshe Rabbinowitz was to prove an able successor to his father, though they had different personalities. Moshe was easily roused and when he was roused, he was irascible. Although he was soon known for his kindness, he did tend to be excitable and the calm of the Beth Hamedresh was often disturbed by his eruptions. He was particularly hard on those members of the congregation who didn't conform to the religious principles of the Beth Hamedresh. One key point was the commandment strictly to keep the sabbath day holy, Shmirat Shabbot. Rabbi Rabbinowitz's view was that if you worked at your business on Saturday afternoon, then you should be deprived of your membership.

The dilemma for those members who were in the retail furniture trade, was that most of their business was done on Saturday. Non-Jewish husbands and wives were only able to shop together at the weekends and buying furniture was a major expense for their households. They wanted to make the decisions together and that meant looking at the furniture available on that day. It would not be putting it too strongly to say that, at the time, a furniture shop which was closed on Saturday was unlikely to be commercially viable.

There was only one approved way out if you had a non-Jewish partner. Then you could have a Heter Iska drawn up, a document which specifically awarded all the profits for opening on Shabbot to the non-Jew. Of course, the tally men, if they were employed by a Jewish company and chose to work on the sabbath, that was up to them. Neither solution was likely to remain a secret and "the neighbours will talk"!

The inevitable result would be that a number of members in such occupations would leave the community and join the Englisher shul which had a more lenient viewpoint. This did not concern Rabbi Rabbinowitz who would treat them in an offhand manner even if they stayed in the community.

It is easy to make a judgement that Moshe Rabbinowitz was unnecessarily obdurate, but it would be from the view of members of a congregation who had no personal knowledge of the sacrifices that his former congregants had made to observe the mitzvot. Moshe Rabbinowitz had served in a Russia where hundreds of thousands of Jews had been massacred in the bloody aftermath of the Revolution. He had fought to maintain traditional Jewish practices in the face of a government that was determined to destroy organised religion in their country.

He had seen the sacrifices his congregants were prepared to make, laying down their lives for the sake of their beliefs. The contrast with those members of the Beth Hamedresh who wanted to sell furniture on Shabbot was stark in the extreme. He had a strong case for believing that to treat them in an offhand manner was to be generous to a fault. He would have recognized, however, that Britain was not Russia and would fervently hope that it never would be.

Even so, the Beth Hamedresh congregation never missed an opportunity to emphasise the importance of their heritage. In the 1920s the prayer for the Royal Family was always said in Hebrew and the sermons were always in Yiddish. In the Englisher shul both were in English. The net result of the approach of Rabbi Rabbinowitz was a strengthening of the performance of the mitzvot by the congregation, but one where those who were not inclined to follow his instructions, often left for the less stringent Hebrew Congregation.

It has been well said that Jews find it easier to survive oppression than toleration. Toleration often led to an increase in the percentage of young people marrying out as people from different cultures came to mix more easily. In 1925 the Beth Hamedresh announced:

> The committee place on record their disapproval of intermarriage, which is so much prevalent in this town, and decided not to grant any facilities to further this obnoxious practice....also a copy of the resolution be sent to the Beth Din.

It was a pious hope that a resolution of condemnation would have much effect. Those who married out knew very well the reaction of their families and the community.

There were also many instances, however, where Rabbinowitz showed his sensitivity. For example, a childless widow came to him because she needed a religious service performed which would release her to marry again. In biblical times, it was the duty a a brother of the deceased to marry the widow in order to look after her. If the widow didn't want this, the brother had to renounce his responsibility at a service called Chalitza. For those who do not come from a very Orthodox background, it can be an awkward occasion. Rabbinowitz explained the procedure, but sent her to a rabbi who was more in tune with her religious standards to arrange the ceremony.

The rabbi was still expected and encouraged to lead the community in all matters concerning not just the services, but the exercise of the mitzvot. In 1927 the Beth Din in London wrote to the Honorary Officers, stating that they believed some of the meat being sold to the community in Sunderland wasn't kosher. The Honorary Officers replied that they had no knowledge of any such shortcoming and in future would the Beth Din kindly write to the Rabbi.

Sukkas is a very joyous occasion and for many years a popular part of it was a Reception held in the Rabbi's sukkah on Simchas Beit Hashoeva in the middle of the festival. Yiddish parodies of popular songs were a feature, composed and sung by Mendel Cohen, another son of Chatze Cohen.

The skills a number of members of the community brought to furniture manufacturing and sales went back a long way. In Krottingen the summers were a good time to gather timber from the abundant woods in the region. Then when the harsh winter set in, the wood could be fashioned into furniture for sale in the Spring. The Jews learned the skills of furniture manufacture in this way and brought their children to Sunderland, trained back in their Krottingen homes. Bernstein Bros, L.B.J, M. Davis and M. Linskill became well known firms and when hire purchase took off in the 1920s, the demand for the products of their factories went up steadily.

Life remained a struggle though with generally difficult economic times making for a great deal of industrial unrest, the worst of which were the General Strike. Lost wages during strikes inevitably reduced the disposable income of members of the Beth Hamedresh, at first or second hand, and many congregants failed to pay the bills for their seat rentals.

Rabbi Rabbinowitz's relationships with the successive ministers of the Englisher shul were cordial, but he remained in a different rabbinic league. While they worked hard to get their semichas, Moshe Rabbinowitz had been a rabbi since he was 20. He was old-school Eastern Europe. He lectured in yiddish. If you didn't understand the language, this was not his problem.

His opposite number in the 1930s was Rabbi Shlomo Toperoff who gave 17 year's service to the Englisher Shul. Clean shaven and wearing a vicar's collar, he did not look like a traditional rav. With a constant twinkle in his eye, Rabbi Toperoff presented a very different image from Rabbinowitz. He got more involved in the non-talmudic aspects of his ministry. It was Toperoff who persuaded Bishop Henson of Durham to join the anti-Nazis. During the war he would be a Chaplain to the Forces and wrote a monthly newsletter for servicemen with plenty of social gossip. There is a famous picture of Chief Rabbi Hertz at the time with a large selection of United Synagogue ministers at a conference. It is remarkable, by today's standards, for the fact that most of the ministers wore clerical collars and all but two are not wearing koppels. Salis Daiches, still In Edinburgh, has a particularly natty bow tie but no koppel.

Toperoff built up the Hebrew Congregation's cheder from seven to over 100. An emphasis on sound education remained paramount. Secular education counted as well, though. The Bede Collegiate Boys School was the best grammar school in the area and the ambition of many parents was to get their children admitted. The school offered 30 town scholarships and the competition for them was, naturally, very keen. The Bede governors were very tolerant towards their more Orthodox Jewish pupils and the time for lunch on Fridays was reduced to enable afternoon school to end earlier, so that all the Jewish children could get home in time for the sabbath. Non-Orthodox children would certainly become Orthodox for the afternoon.

The school had some very good Jewish teachers, including the senior maths master, Mr. Maccoby, who had been a senior wrangler at Cambridge. and had married David Rabbinowitz's daughter. Mr. Maccoby was the Kamminitzer Maggid's son and very devout; the same Zionist enthusiast who had come to preach the need to support Theodor Hertzl at the end of the previous century. As a Senior Wrangler, Maccoby could have obtained a good job anywhere, but he chose the Sunderland school because of the Beth Hamedresh. He was devoted to Jewish study. In class, after teaching, when he gave the pupils work to do, he would then don his mortar board, open his copy of the Gemara and happily settle down to studying it. Eventually Maccoby suffered a heart attack in class and died from it.

Bede Collegiate was a fine school and in one year four members of the sixth form went on to medical school and they were all Jewish. It often involved considerable sacrifice for the family though; one father paid out his entire salary for two years to enable his son to become a doctor.

Keeping the community together was a picnic (circa 1925)

Jewish Brigade of St John's Ambulance (1936)

Harry Black, Louis Mincovitch, Myer Gillis

Jackie Stern, Harry Isaacs, Maurice Woolf, Alan Foreman, Charles Goldman, Julius Gordon, Louis Berg, Issy Davis

Louis Oldberg, Vicki Gillis, Rev. Toperoff, Shalom Gillis, Syd Burnley, Ralph Grantham

Some of these will serve their country in the Second World War

Chapter 6
A pause for Gateshead

When in 1905 Rabbi Hurwitz had started the Sunderland Yeshiva, looking for local youngsters to provide the student body, Gershon Levy's foresight in starting a gemara class in the Talmud Torah was widely acknowledged. So it wasn't surprising that when Rabbi David Dryan, the shochet in Gateshead, decided in 1928 that he would try to start a Yeshiva in Gateshead, a small town 12 miles from Sunderland, that he went to Levy for support.

He didn't ask in vain and Levy set out to help Dryan to create what had always been a dream with the Gateshead rabbi. The importance of the Sunderland Beth Hamedresh members to the Gateshead Yeshiva in its early days is easily illustrated. Levy became the first President in October 1930 and was succeeded by two other stalwarts of the Beth Hamedresh, Solomon Cohen and Joseph Pearlman, who became Joint Presidents, in 1933. Another member of the family, Mark Pearlman, also served as President of the Yeshiva as well as of the Beth Hamedresh.

Gateshead, today, still seems an odd choice for a Yeshiva, but a quiet town, without too many secular attractions, is often a good choice for a college of higher learning. The Sephardim had one in Ramsgate for a number of years and even that remote Victorian watering place had an unacceptable level of night life which led students astray. Happily, Gateshead was even quieter than Ramsgate.

A Yeshiva, a Rabbinical college, is the oldest institution of Jewish learning, dating back to the biblical days of Hillel and Shamai. It was one of Hillel's disciples, Johanon ben Zakkai, who probably saved Judaism from extinction after the Romans expelled the Jews from the Holy Land in the first century. The rabbi was smuggled out of the Roman camp in a coffin to plead a case with Vespasian, the successful Roman general. He persuaded him to allow a school to be set up in Jabneh in order to continue to teach his pupils. That school led to other Yeshivot down the centuries and where the Roman Empire is no more, Judaism survived. Rabbi Johanon also made Jabneh the equivalent of the former Supreme Court in Jerusalem and it became traditional for the head of a Yeshiva to lay down the law in future centuries.

While the dispersed Jews had to survive in countries about which they knew little, at least in fields of commercial activity they had not entered into before, they had a universal body of law which would guide them in every aspect of their daily lives. To take just one area; Jews were able to trade with each other internationally, even in the Dark Ages, because the laws of trade were clearly and comprehensively set down in the Babylonian Talmud, which emerged from Rabbi Johanon's foundation. As the Talmud said (Yoma 286) "Our ancestors were never without a Yeshiva." Gateshead would be the latest in an unbroken line which stretched back 2,000 years. The similarities between biblical times and the emigration from Krottingen are obvious.

Why Gateshead, though? Well, ultra-Orthodox Jews didn't just come to London. In the 1870s Zachariah Bernstone, a Lithuanian glazier, emigrated to Newcastle. He decided, however, that the local community wasn't observant enough for him and so he crossed the river to Gateshead in 1881 to try to start his own community. Very slowly other Jews with a similar passion for the mitzvot gathered round him, most notably a young Austrian called Eliezer Adler who was only 19 years old. There was also a furniture manufacturer in a small way of business called Sol Wickes. His great grandson would, after his name had been anglicised, be Lyall Wilkes, who went to Balliol, became Secretary of the Oxford Union and MP for Newcastle Central from 1945 - 1951.

The small group managed to hire a room in which to pray during 1883, though they didn't even have a Sefer Torah. They called their community Chevrei Shomrei Shabbos and asked the Chief Rabbi, Hermann Adler, for help. He told them to rejoin the Newcastle community, pointing out that it would be unwise to fall out with a body which was providing them with both a mikvah and a cemetery. The community rejected the idea and a wealthy lace manufacturer in Nottingham came to their rescue and gave them a sefer torah. As the Chief Rabbi, himself, had suggested they should stop being independent, the sefer torah was kept in a drawer rather than in the Ark, as was normal. In that way, its existence could remain the congregation's secret and it did for many years.

This initial rebuff by the Chief Rabbi only strengthened the view of the founders of the community that it was important to retain their independence from what was, otherwise, universally accepted in the Jewish community in those days, as the paramount authority of the Chief Rabbi. From this time onwards, the Gateshead community and, later, those who founded the Yeshiva, would keep away from the authorities in London as much as possible. In time, they discovered that the Sunderland Beth Hamedresh had adopted the same view.

Their decision, however, involved, as it had with the Beth Hamedresh, a problem over the need for a marriage secretary. It was still the case that only the Board of Deputies could grant this and only then after the Chief Rabbi had issued a certificate that the congregation was made up of "a synagogue of persons professing the Jewish religion of Orthodox Jews." If a community was not thus recognized, then the only alternative which remained was to go to court to get acceptance of the congregation's validity.

For all of 50 years the Gateshead congregation was denied a Marriage Secretary because they would not accept the Chief Rabbi's authority. In not granting a certificate the Chief Rabbi could be accused of overextending his powers. While parliament had agreed that he was the only person to grant recognition, it was the status of the community that concerned the Commons; not whether it acknowledged his authority.

The first rabbi to be appointed by the Gateshead community in 1899, took the joint office of Minister to Gateshead and Newcastle. In 1905 Rabbi Mendel Berman became the Rav and he was from Krottingen. This should have strengthened the relationship between Gateshead and Sunderland. In 1911 the synagogue in Radheugh Bridge Road burnt down - Krottingen and fires seem to have had an unhealthy relationship - but by 1912 the congregation had managed to pay for a small synagogue which was known as the Blechena Shul - the tin shul. It cost £117 and if the final appearance was disappointing, at least the builder had kept to the clause in his contract that he should do no work on the site on Shabbot.

The result was really not much better than a hut and, as it was near a railway crossing, the noise of the trains passing interfered with hearing the congregant leading the prayers. If you were conducting the service it was also as well to avoid the pool of water on the floor when it rained, because the roof soon leaked and nobody could afford to have it mended. When the rain fell hard on the tin roof, you could hardly hear the prayers either. Many times people looking for the station would mistake the synagogue building for it and bang heavily on the door to try to get in. The community had its own Shechita, however, from an early stage and many of the very Orthodox throughout the North East would only eat meat authorised as kosher by Gateshead.

The tiny community then employed a new teacher, Rev. E. Gamzu. Gamzu was chosen by Rabbi Eliezer Adler, the same man who had come to Gateshead as a young man and was now the ultimate "figurehead and power house" in the community until after the Second World War. He was an inspiring educationalist and he set about organizing a really first class Talmud Torah. The school started with about 30-40 pupils, ranging in age from 5 - 15. For a small community this may seem quite a large school roll but the Charedim believed in large families to build up the ranks of the faithful.

When it was necessary to send the children to non-Jewish schools, a row broke out between the community and the educational authorities. The problem was that there was no way the Gateshead parents were going to send their children to school on Chol Hamoed, the days between the start and finish of the eight day festivals of Passover and Succot. Just as the Orthodox would not work on the festival days, so the very Orthodox would not have their children work on the intervening days in an eight day festival.

The Gateshead parents stood their ground and were taken to court by the Board of Education. The Magistrates examined this very unusual situation carefully and then decided that they weren't going to risk fighting an entire community and threw the case out. The city fathers learned to accept the complications of the Jewish holy days; it was agreed, for example, that the tickets for the toll bridge between Gateshead and Newcastle could be bought before the Saturday when they might be needed. A similar arrangement had been made for Jews wanting to attend the Great Exhibition in 1851 on the sabbath. What is obscure is that the sabbath regulations prevent you from carrying anything on the day - including a ticket - so how do you prove you've paid?

The children received a normal ultra-Orthodox education. Which meant three hours after school from Monday to Thursday, three hours on Saturday and six hours on Sunday devoted to Jewish studies. Twenty one hours a week on Chumash, (the Pentateuch), and Rashi, (The works of Rabbi Solomon ben Isaac, 1040-1105), Gemara, the prophets and Jewish law and ethics, outside normal school. It was very similar to the Beth Hamedresh curriculum in Sunderland. Where the children of United Synagogue members might go to classes on Sunday mornings, the Gateshead youngsters devoted their childhoods to learning, and most stayed with it as adults. If, as adults, they were going to give up Judaism, at least they would have a pretty good idea of exactly what it was they were sacrificing.

During the First World War the Gateshead congregation dropped by about half. This was due to those who joined up and to a number who were interned as potential enemies because of their German or Austrian origins. A lot of them never returned to Gateshead and it was fortunate for the sheer existence of the congregation that a number of Belgian refugees found their way to Gateshead. Rebuilding the community would take time in the post-war years and the condition of the synagogue between the wars remained deplorable.

Yet even if the community could not afford anywhere better to worship, they remained part of the very limited percentage of the Jewish population which strictly observed the Sabbath day. They were shomrei shabbot to a family, and if applicants to join the community were not prepared to make that commitment, they would not be accepted. The Gateshead community stuck to all of its guns. In 1923 Chief Rabbi Hertz visited Gateshead and saw the synagogue for himself. He was so upset by its condition that he offered the community a gift of £2,000 to build themselves a new one. This was the modern day equivalent of about £100,000.

The Gateshead congregation thought long and hard about this exceedingly generous offer - and then turned it down. They thought that if they took the money, it would be bound to draw them in more closely to the Chief Rabbi's authority and, above anything else, that was what they wanted to avoid. Their example must have met with the approval of the Beth Hamedresh in Sunderland, who provided them with an Aron Kodesh and some seats when asked to help in 1930.

The Sunderland Beth Hamedresh had promised to accept the Chief Rabbi's authority but had backtracked over the years. Seeing the sacrifice that the neighbouring Gateshead community was prepared to make in 1923 would have made their original decision to accept it appear more pusillanimous.

In 1927 Rabbi Gamzu went off to Liverpool and Rev. David Dryan, a shochet from Port Talbot, took his place. On the rock-solid foundation of the Talmud Torah, Dryan could see the opportunity to start a yeshiva. One who knew him well wrote:

> ....warm and smiling, noble of bearing, yet completely humble and self-effacing... above all he was possessed with a fierce and unquenchable love for Torah....you could have transported him anywhere in the world and he would have been just the same....

> completely impervious to such trivial considerations such as financial climate...and the indifference of the general population, he...only thought of building Torah and spreading Torah.

It is one thing, though, to decide to start a Yeshiva. It is quite another to attract the best Talmudic brains to teach in it. Here Rabbi Dryan was fortunate in his timing. Any famous rabbi in 1927 would probably have preferred to teach in a well established European Yeshiva rather than at a greenfield Yeshiva just begun in an undistinguished town in North East England, with no reputation, little money and very poor facilities. It wasn't even as if Britain was highly regarded from a strictly Orthodox viewpoint; it was alright, but no better than that. To choose Gateshead would have been like going from Cambridge to a College of Further Education.

By the early 1930s, however, the discussion on choice was not restricted to the subject of academic infrastructure in Central and Eastern Europe. It was far more to do with avoiding discriminatory laws, concentration camps, involuntary disappearance and state-supported anti-Semitism. The rabbis who saw the writing on the wall, read Juden Raus - and "Out" seemed a fine alternative to staying. Some of the greatest European rabbinic experts packed their bags for North East England.

As far as the students were concerned, it wasn't easy to get a visa to go to another country. The Slump had arrived and countries closed their doors and their hearts to the prospect of extra immigrant mouths to feed. The British Consul General in Frankfurt, however, soon became a staunch ally in Germany. Any student who said he wanted to go to Gateshead was immediately given a permit - and the Charedim never turned a student away, even though the education and the boarding were entirely free and the cost involved had to be found from donors. They all had to be housed as well and sometimes there would be as many as three boarders in one house. If, however, they could reach Gateshead they were safely in harbour, out of the way of the anti-Semitic storm.

Although Sunderland's Gershon Levy was Dryan's obvious first choice for financial backing for his dream college in 1927, the Rabbi worked hard to raise the necessary money from the North East communities as a whole . Elias Cohen from Sunderland opened the Yeshiva in 1927, the third in Britain, after London and Manchester. There was a dinner at the Cooperative Hall and a considerable number of speeches in Yiddish. The first two students came from Leeds, were enrolled in 1929, studied in a room at the Blechene shul and somehow, throughout the period -before the war, the money was found to keep all those who came after . More than 600 young men passed through the yeshiva between 1933 and 1939. Gershon Levy lived to see it well established before he died in 1935 at the age of 70. It was a blow to the infant Yeshiva to lose one of its most enthusiastic supporters, both financially and spiritually.

There grew up a kind of half-soup-kitchen, half-fund-raising action. It was called the Yeshiva tea and donations in kind were sold for the benefit of the Yeshiva to the highest bidder. Meanwhile, those who were hungry could tuck into a very substantial tea.

In the office of the Chief Rabbi in London, the idea of a new Yeshiva in Gateshead had gone down like a lead balloon. Joseph Hertz had his own Jews College in the capital, totally under his jurisdiction, and he recognized that a new institution could put competitive cats among many pigeons. For instance, there was the question of granting semicha, of enabling students to become qualified rabbis. This had invariably been frowned upon at Jews College. Semicha had been given in only a handful of cases over more than half a century. This had had the effect of raising the Chief Rabbi's status as the only United Synagogue minister who was allowed to use the title. Gateshead would expect to grant semicha to those pupils who deserved it.

Without qualified rabbinic competition, the authority of the Chief Rabbi in all spiritual matters was not difficult to maintain. A few of his ministers actually had semicha, but they were as likely to have obtained them overseas as in Britain. The first rabbi to be knighted, Sir Hermann Gollancz, and Simon Singer, the force behind the Daily Prayer Book, had both obtained their semichas on the continent. The Singer's Prayer Book was to be the authoritative prayer book for the United Synagogue communities for nearly 100 years, but the author on the front was always described as the Rev. Simon Singer, rather than Rabbi.

Now Hertz was faced with potential competition from what was formerly a tiny provincial community. What was more, it was well known that the standard of religious observance in the Gateshead community had, from its inception, always been much higher than in the Chief Rabbi's United Synagogue congregations. Chief Rabbi Hertz was seriously displeased - which was often a fearsome sight - but there was little that could be done except to discourage his supporters from going to Gateshead.

The competition between Jews' College and Gateshead would eventually result in an overwhelming victory for Gateshead, which left it in almost sole possession of the field when it came to producing rabbis in Britain. It really was down to who wanted to make the most sacrifices. Was it to be the United Synagogue, middle of the road and uncommitted even to shmirat shabbot, or the Gateshead rabbis prepared to do anything in their power to obey the mitzvot and the din. Jews' College foundered on a lack of financial support from the United Synagogue and the community. Gateshead succeeded because of the far greater commitment of the local community, its Charedi financial supporters and its sheer determination to succeed.

This became even more important to them after the war when the yeshivot in Europe were totally destroyed and they found themselves in the position of the sole survivor with the vital message of Orthodox Judaism still to deliver. Their attitude and example would inspire others across the world.

The religious authority to whom Dryan originally deferred was Rabbi Yisrael Meir Kagan of Radin in Poland. He was an eminent talmudist and was known as the Chofetz Chaim. In 1927, when Dryan first took control of the infant Yeshiva, Kagan was already 89 years old but he was still very active. Chief Rabbi Hertz was determined to oppose him in every way possible. Kagan wanted Rabbi Avrom Sacharov to come from Russia to head up the Yeshiva. He would, however, need an entry visa and a work permit from the Home Office. The Home Secretary was William Joynson Hicks, who was no friend to the Jewish community. Hertz consulted with this odd bedfellow and it was agreed that Rabbi Sacharov would not get his work permit.

Kagan was outflanked but not for long. In 1930 - and now 92 - he did get a work permit for another of his supporters, Rabbi Nachman Landynski, whose eminence, in itself, attracted scholars to join the fledgling institution. The Yeshiva was well and truly established but, in one way, on very different lines from the Continent. Where in Europe, the Yeshivot individually favoured one form of ultra-Orthodoxy or another, this did not apply in Gateshead. On the Continent there were Chassidic Yeshivot, Mitnagdim Yeshivot and Torah im Derech Eretz Yeshivot, to name but three. In Gateshead there was no distinction because their intake was from Galicianer, Litvak and Polak traditions; the teachers were free to follow their own definitions. Rabbi Kagan only concentrated on the need for everyone to study Torah. He died in 1933 at 95 but happily with yet another Talmudic study success story under his belt.

The Gateshead community got permission for its Wedding Secretary from Chief Rabbi Hertz in 1935. The Chief Rabbi had been persuaded to approve the application of a Liberal synagogue congregation in Leeds and would obviously have been in an impossible position if he had then turned down a very Orthodox community not that far away. His rationale was that, in the face of the threat from Nazism, the Jews had better sink their differences. He later regretted the Leeds licence and went back to his Orthodox last. The Gateshead synagogue hadn't compromised; they still agreed that they would officiate independently of the Chief Rabbi's office. They still do.

When the Gateshead students were awarded their semicha, they became eligible for pulpits all over the country, but they weren't always welcome in United Synagogue communities. The standards they set for themselves, most of them were inclined to expect from their congregations as well. If they didn't get the right level of commitment, they tended to castigate the worshippers from the pulpit or treat the worst backsliders with some disdain. The congregants affected often preferred to live in blissful ignorance of the size and number of their sins. With most United Synagogue ministers this was achievable, but with Gateshead graduates at the helm it was known it would be more difficult. The United had many problems in obtaining good ministers, but the London based and Gateshead communities tended to stay apart, even though both fully accepted that the other was legally Jewish.

There was a tendency in the Chief Rabbinate to refer to the Gateshead rabbunim as "foreign rabbis". It was true that the Chief Rabbi had been in office in Britain since 1913 but as he was born in Yugoslavia, brought up in New York and had served as minister for many years in South Africa, he could well have claimed membership of the same club. As many of these famous talmudic scholars fled to England, Gateshead was able to strengthen its teaching staff to a level that Dryan could only have considered possible in his wildest dreams. Rabbis Leib Lopian, Leib Gurwicz and Naftali Shakovitzky were just three newcomers with tremendous reputations as rabbinic scholars.

When they reported back their experiences of a tolerant Britain and a welcoming community, the word spread quickly. Rabbi Landynski also brought in a great talmudist, Rabbi Kahan, who had been a friend of his since student days, as the Menahel (Rector). As a young man Rabbi Kahan had founded the Yeshivas at Yostralenka and Polutsk, which would both perish in the Holocaust.

Of course the expanded community also included businessmen, and their new firms reduced unemployment in the North East quite considerably. The most famous demonstration against unemployment at the time was the Jarrow March from the North East to London and it seems unlikely that anyone connected with the demonstration would have considered part of the solution might lie with German Jewish refugees. The firms they created, however, did reduce the number of the unemployed.

By now another difficulty had arisen. To get a visa from the government for refugees, there needed to be a guarantee that the immigrant would not need to call on state financial support. They wouldn't apply for the dole. In 1933 practically every Gateshead family signed a guarantee for one refugee.

One family deeply involved was that of Moishe Kaufman and his textile business flourished. He was Polish but, ironically, his partner, Lesser, was German and had been awarded the Iron Cross in the First World War. Kaufman had four sons and eventually each took responsibility for supporting one of the Gateshead institutions.

The most pressing problem now was the synagogue. For years the condition of the Blechene shul had been a disgrace:

> It had rats. It had draughts. The roof was leaking, the stone steps were dangerous, the ventilation system was hopeless and the sanitary conditions were appalling. In fact it was a great wonder the town authorities had not stepped in and condemned it.

To add to its structural defects, there was now the problem that it couldn't house the enlarged congregation. Worse, there were now all the extra mouths to feed. Finding the money for a new synagogue seemed hopeless until one Gateshead stalwart, Dr. Chalk, suggested that the community build the synagogue itself. In December 1938 that was exactly what they set out to do and were triumphantly successful, laying bricks, plastering walls, installing plumbing and fixing roof tiles.

It didn't stop there. With so many brilliant talmudic scholars at Gateshead, after 15 years of building up the Yeshiva, Rabbi Dryan decided to go one further in the creation of academic centres. He gave thought to also setting up a Kollel, a postgraduate college for scholars who had left the yeshiva but wanted to continue their studies. At the time - and with hindsight - this has been well described as wild, impractical and heroic. After all it was 1941 and wartime. Sending a son to Yeshiva for two years was outlandish enough, but dedicating ones life to study, as the website history of the Kollel concludes "must have sounded like something from a different planet."

Nevertheless, Rabbi Dryan wrote to 22 distinguished rabbis to suggest they took on the task of becoming the Principal of such an establishment. Eighteen of them didn't bother to reply, probably thinking the idea too way-out to be worthy of a response. Three others stalled and said the time wasn't right. Only one said he'd be honoured to be considered: "My heart sees a great light in the matter which Your Honour suggested - your merit is very great." He was Rabbi Eliyahu Eliezer Dessler and his view of the world was very different from that of even the Orthodox bulk of the Sunderland Beth Hamedresh community, though they both came from the same Lithuanian background.

It wasn't that Rabbi Dessler rejected what most people considered were the honourable objectives in life of making your family financially secure and working hard enough to be publicly recognized, by appointment to an elevated role in some organization or another. As Rabbi Dessler wrote to his father:

> That level of emes (truth) could only be achieved after the complete separation from the non-Jewish nations - i.e. after a distillation process, like those in which Yishmael (Ishmael) and Esav (Esau) were filtered out of the Jewish people for good.

Rabbi Dessler was in favour of divorce from the culture of the country to which he had come, from Lithuania. He was not in favour of the torah im derech eretz approach. The danger of assimilation appeared far greater to him if there was an attempt to marry two ways of life. He went further, however, in his condemnation of the cultural norms he found in Britain. He found materialism *repugnant*; he found himself: "In a society in which the pursuit of money and honour was not even seen as a cause for embarrassment." For most people, to accept where Rabbi Dessler was coming from, would undermine their own philosophies of life.

As far as Rabbi Dessler was concerned - and the men in the Kollel would be likely to be more knowledgeable than the students in the Yeshiva - the right way of spending the vast majority of ones time was in study. The task was to absorb the knowledge in the Talmud and then pass it down to the next generation to propagate it and spread the word as widely as possible round the Jewish world. When Rabbi Dessler was a minister at a small synagogue in the East End when he first came to England 14 years before - he was paid 50p a week - he was often visited by congregants. As he wrote again to his father, those who came on social visits "steal my time for myself....(if they) knew how painful (their visits) were to me, they would surely desist."

The price Rabbi Dessler was prepared to pay to practice his beliefs was astronomically high. He had first come to Britain because his father had run up business debts in Lithuania which he couldn't pay. When he came to England, he had had to leave his wife and children behind in Lithuania for three years. It took the rabbi until 1937 to pay the last of his father's creditors.

In Gateshead, after Rabbi Dryan had been delighted to arrange his appointment to head the Kollel, a meeting in London of a wide range of rabbonim formulated a constitution for the Kollel. That was, perhaps, the easy bit. For Rabbi Dessler, from then on, the work schedule was monumental. To raise money for the Kollel - he was the only one doing so for most of the time - he would travel the country to call on possible donors.

He needed to raise about £5,000 a year just to keep going - and Rabbi Dessler wanted the Kollel to expand. He also went back to London for two nights a week to look after the education of the students who had gathered round him in the East End synagogue. Teaching was his only source of income because he refused to be paid for any of his work for the Kollel. In fact, he was only in Gateshead from Friday morning till Saturday night. Then he would be on his travels again. He would also have to prepare lectures - which was an absolutely meticulous task on which he spent many hours - and in addition he wanted as much time as possible for personal study.

The point was, of course, that Rabbi Dessler was setting new and higher standards. His students were being exposed to the finest kind of leadership, which is "Follow me" rather than "Go on". He would never try to exert his authority overtly in the Kollel. Even though he was 50 years old in 1941. He insisted on being treated as an equal and not even as a primus inter pares. He would refer to himself as the Assistant Shammas of the Kollel (the Assistant Caretaker).

On the one hand were his modesty, self-sacrifice and the academic standards he set himself. On the other hand there were his relative frailty - he worked on through his fifties and he drove himself unmercifully - his poverty, and his new separation from his family. His wife had been visiting their son at his European Yeshiva when war broke out and was stranded. The family miraculously escaped from Europe but Rabbi Dessler wasn't reunited with them for six years.

Who would want to settle for the rabbi's working life? Which was just the point. Rabbi Dessler, like his colleagues, inspired his students and played his full part in creating the Gateshead ethos. There hadn't been a Kollel in Britain before. When his students went on to other parts of the world, they took his example with them. Their standards in keeping the mitzvot and improving their talmudic knowledge even further, were higher than most of the communities they reached had ever seen before.

Rabbi Dessler was only one of the guiding lights in Gateshead. There were many others who had the same vision of the perfect life. All of the institutions, of course, continually needed financing and every avenue was explored. Even before the war, as the conflict seemed ever more likely, a conference was called of North East Rabbis in the summer of 1938 at the home of Moshe Rabbinowitz who presided. The objective was to stimulate interest in Gateshead and to raise a much needed £200.

The conference took the opportunity to bestow on Rabbi Rabbinowitz the title of Honorary Life President of the Yeshiva. He had been the first President of the institution, as the most Orthodox local rabbi, before the appointment of Rabbi Landynski, and he had been its Chief Examiner. The support from Sunderland in those early days was spiritual as well as financial. Now the Gateshead rabbonim were, more and more, able to take over. Where the Beth Hamedresh had previously set the highest standards, these were now being eclipsed by the regime up the road in Gateshead.

Over the coming years, those standards would influence Jewry throughout the world. Only a comparatively small percentage might try to emulate the Gateshead rabbis, but a far larger proportion of the younger generation would be affected and led to do more than their parents had managed. The Yeshivot and Kollelim in Israel, for example, would grow enormously in size and, very slowly, the great centres of talmudic knowledge which the Final Solution destroyed in Europe, would emerge again; in different locations but with the same ideals.

It was in 1938 that Ruth Kohn found refuge in Britain. She went to Gateshead in 1942 where her husband would be the head of the Cheder. Ruth and Avrohom Kohn's contribution to religious education would be the foundation of Sem - advanced education for girls, short for Seminary. Where their needs had been neglected in the past, Ruth Kohn created the framework in Gateshead by which hundreds of girls today are able to go to study and gain a deep understanding of all aspects of yiddishkeit. Thirty years later, there had been 247 graduates who had become Jewish teachers in Britain, 92 in Israel and 155 in the rest of the world. In 1944 the Gateshead Boarding School was started as well.

Ruth Kohn was only 26 when she began her work and she died, very highly respected, 50 years later in 1992. When it came to financing the creation of the Seminary, it was said that Rabbi Dryan converted his pension rights into cash and gave the money to her. He would have been abashed if the facts had emerged at the time, but it was in keeping with his determination to see that women could receive a proper Jewish education.

After the war the Rosh Yeshivas were Rabbi Leib Lopian (1947 - 1979), and Rabbi Leib Gurwicz (1947 - 1986). Today the Rosh Yeshiva is a past student, Rabbi Avrohom Gurwicz, the son of Leib Gurwicz.. From the synagogue came the Yeshiva and from the Yeshiva came the Kollel. And in 1945 there came to the Kollel, at the very early age of 18, the man who would spend all but a few years of his life, working for the Gateshead institutions; Rabbi Bezalel Rakow. Coming from a family which had produced rabbonim for 500 years, Rabbi Rakow received his semicha at the Kollel, married Miriam, the daughter of the Gateshead Rav, Rabbi Naftali Shakowitzky, in 1948 and spent a few years at the Montreux Yeshiva between 1959 and 1964. When Rabbi Shakovitzky died, it was the 36 year old Rabbi Rakow who was chosen to succeed him. At the dinner to welcome him to the post, every senior rabbi stood to acknowledge the seniority of the young man.

Rabbi Rakow led Gateshead until he died nearly 40 years later. He was a slight, unassuming, soft spoken, talmudic genius, who abhorred publicity and, according to one head of the Board of Deputies, had "an abundance of common sense and a tremendous sense of humour." It was said that he gave spiritual rulings which erred on the side of leniency and was endlessly charitable. Even so, it was under his leadership that Gateshead was widely perceived and roundly attacked by the less observant, as insisting on stricter and stricter adherence to the Mitzvot. Much fun was made, for example, of a rule laid down by Rabbi Rakow, that boys and girls should do their shopping on different days to avoid the mingling of the sexes.

The leaders of Gateshead didn't try to defend themselves and few pointed out that the increased strictness was in the nature of lashing movable objects to the ground when the winds of change grew to typhoon level. Rabbi Rakow took over in Gateshead at a time when the Lords Day Observance Society was still working hard to maintain the sanctity of their sabbath. They had much support throughout the country. A country which had previously looked down on premarital sex, had little problem with drugs and who had not known the pill. It was a country where, if you were divorced, you would not be allowed in the Royal Box at Ascot. The Lord Chamberlain censored plays, and pornography on television was unthinkable.

Over the years that Rabbi Rakow presided in Gateshead, these restrictions were abolished. Jewish communities suffered from out marriage which reached 50%, casual sex was acceptable, there were very large numbers of one-parent families. Drugs and alcoholism became major problems. Rabbi Rakow, unlike Rabbi Dessler, didn't just have to deal with opposing the generally perceived desirability of gaining wealth and position in society. He now also had to deal with a change in the nation's moral values, as his community saw it, for very much the worse.

It's a free country. If it isn't against the law - the pill never was, the Lord Chamberlain's censorship authority was abolished and Sunday opening became permissible - then there is nothing to stop people setting their own standards. Only the very Orthodox Jews didn't want to go along with the trend. They weren't going to go with the flow; they didn't care if they rocked the boat, were accused of being fuddy-duddies, of not keeping up with the times or living in cloud-cuckoo land. They believed in the biblical laws on the many subjects involved and they intended to bring up their children to practice these, rather than join the native culture.

If that meant trying to set up barriers to prevent their children even encountering these new moral standards, then that price would have to be paid. They had resisted the influence of other cultures over the centuries; from the Greeks and Romans to the Spanish and French. They felt they could resist the latest fads as well, but it started with divorcing themselves from the hedonistic world all around them. That was Rabbi Rakow's position and he held to it fearlessly. It was a fact that, from the very beginning of the Gateshead Yeshiva, some members of the local community found difficulty in maintaining the more stringent standards of observance the majority demanded. And if you're not doing the right thing in a small town, the word gets round pretty quickly. Many over the years would up sticks and go to other towns but, of course, without them, the majority of the Gateshead community would have less opposition to their desire to move to the Right.

Rabbi Rakow would also take on any authority within Judaism. In 2003, when the Chief Rabbi, now Lord Sacks, in the cause of improving relations between the religions in Britain, suggested that all might learn something from each other, Rabbi Rakow said publicly that this was heresy. The Chief Rabbi made minor changes to the book in which he had made his suggestion, but the word went round the community that the Chief Rabbi was no longer the ultimate religious authority in the country. That role it was said had now gone to Gateshead.

The anomaly is that so many of the families in Gateshead suffered most grievously from religious hatred in Eastern Europe. The Krottingen community was murdered by Lithuanians, many of the Polish survivors by Poles after the war had ended. Hatred between the members of various religions had been the cause of oceans of blood over the centuries. Yet Rabbi Rakow insisted that Judaism could not meet any other religion a hundredth of the way because Judaism was G-d given and perfect. Admittedly, this was at the core of everything Gateshead believed in, but it wasn't a good recipe for religious tolerance in the 21st century.

Apart from the transient Yeshiva community, the resident congregation remained very small. In 1954 there were 40 Jewish residents in Gateshead. Nevertheless, put it all together and the Gateshead Yeshiva today, 70 years after its foundation, is the greatest talmudic University in Europe. To great centres of learning like Heidelberg, Yeshiva University in New York, Cambridge, Bar Ilan, the Sorbonne, the Hebrew University in Jerusalem and Utrecht, you could now add Gateshead. The locals remain slightly bemused to this day, but a police chief once said that the only trouble the students gave him was that their lights were blazing at 2 o'clock in the morning as they went on working, and this could disturb the neighbours.

In 2002 a distinguished columnist in the Jewish Chronicle summed up the position Gateshead had attained in the Orthodox Jewish community in Britain. He said that

"Gateshead is the undisputed centre of Jewish religious Orthodoxy in the UK" and Rabbi Bezaliel Rakow "the undisputed final authority on Jewish orthodoxy". Which is impressive when it is remembered that the Chief Rabbinate in Britain is over 300 years old and Gateshead only 70. In fairness, there would be a lot of "if"s and "but"s about Gateshead's perceived hegemony vis a vis the Chief Rabbi's office but confrontation between the two organisations was always extremely unlikely.

Both Rabbi Dessler and Rabbi Dryan died within a short time of each other in 1953. The end came very suddenly to Rabbi Dryan, and Rabbi Babad came over from Sunderland to give a funeral oration; the link between the two communities remained very close and Gateshead powered on.

What qualifications do you need to be a distinguished university? Buildings like Kings College Chapel, or vistas like Trinity Great Court and the "wedding cake" bridge of St. Johns College in Cambridge are inspiring but not essential. Academic rigour, thorough research, and tremendous brains among the dons are far more important. Over the years Gateshead academics have produced a mass of scholarly work. Providing a first class education for the students is also essential and there Gateshead particularly scored from the beginning. The devotion of the teachers to their pupils was not to be matched in Oxbridge before the war, because the primary objective in Gateshead was that the students individually grow, rather than just turn up for a tutorial once a week, which could be the only contact between teacher and taught in the older universities.

For the Gateshead academics the aim is no less than to safeguard the continuation of a tiny minority religion by training up its future spiritual leaders. As far as the teacher/student relationship is concerned, the Gateshead Yeshiva rabbis recognize they are playing for far higher stakes than a university. The Sunderland Beth Hamedresh members who helped get Gateshead off the ground could take full credit for the achievement of the institution's noble ambitions.

Over the years the United Synagogue, even with the wholehearted support of successive Chief Rabbis, couldn't keep up with the Gateshead effort. Jews' College, which had produced excellent ministers, particularly after the Second world War, when its semicha class was led by the dynamic Rabbi Kopul Kahana, faded away as a powerhouse of Jewish academic effort. Today, Gateshead is the major force in Britain. There are approximately 300 residents, a considerable number of whom work in one or other of the educational institutions. There is also the continuously shifting student body. Rabbi Rakow has now passed away and his successor will find him a hard act to follow, for Rabbi Rokow was not only a fine scholar. He was also very popular with his non-Jewish neighbours.

Although, initially, Chief Rabbi Hertz had not welcomed the creation of Gateshead Yeshiva, the Jewish Orthodox community has come to depend more and more on their alumni to fill senior posts. Among those today are Dayans Ehrentreu, Abraham and Kaplin, educationalists like Rabbis Freilich, Posen and Segal, international university lecturers like Professor Franks of the University of Toronto, Professor Lev, founder of the Jerusalem College of Technology and Rabbi Schwalbe at Manchester University. There are heads of yeshivas, alumni running Kashrus Commissions, and, of course, many rabbonim of congregations. The student body in 2007 numbered 350, mostly from Britain, but also from every other continent.

The national Census in 2001 stated that Gateshead had 1,564 Jews living in the town, though this would have included the students. When Rabbi Rakow passed away in 2003 Gateshead had not only its Synagogue congregation, but a Kindergarten, Primary School, Boys' Grammar School, Girls High School, the Yeshiva Katanah, the Yeshiva and Girls Seminary, the Yeshivah Etzeirim, the Kollel HaRabbonim and the Beth Hatalmud Kollel. It even had the first scientific shatnass bureau to ensure that clothing was in accordance with the laws on the subject.

Financially, it still receives a great deal of support from well-wishers. Where the North East rabbis in 1939 tried to raise £200, Sir Maurice Bloch was only one benefactor to the building fund in 1959 and he donated £10,000. There have been even larger gifts since.

Today, Gateshead is the largest Orthodox Jewish education complex in post-war Europe. But what if it had failed to survive in its earliest years? Then there would have been no growth. So Gateshead will always be indebted to the Sunderland Beth Hamedresh for the help it received at the outset when it needed it most.

Chapter 7
The Difficult Thirties

In 1928 the Hebrew Congregation moved to its new shul in Ryhope Road. One of the main advantages for its members was that the new building was much closer to the suburban area of Sunderland to which so many of them had moved over the years. As their financial position improved they had been able to leave the run-down area of the East End of Sunderland for better homes.

The problem for the Honorary Officers of the Beth Hamedresh was that their members had moved out of the East End as well. In many cases, to walk to the Villiers Street synagogue now was to put a one and a half to two mile hike onto the journey, both ways, on the sabbath. Admittedly, there was nothing in the din to stop you walking a long distance to synagogue if you lived within the perimeter of a town. If you lived outside a town, though, 2,000 yards is the official maximum.

In cold, wet weather, however, - of which there is no shortage in Sunderland - it was an indisputable fact that the attractions of the shorter journey to the new synagogue were definitely impressive. Many families left the Beth Hamedresh, including one branch of the Chatze Cohen clan, who had recently produced Mordaunt Cohen, a name to be reckoned with in Sunderland in the future. Keeping up with the stringent religious standards of the congregation also proved too much for some of the less committed among the new generation. After all those who failed the test might find themselves among the most observant if they transferred their loyalties to Ryhope Road. Rabbi Rabbinowitz still set very high standards.

The new Hebrew Congregation synagogue didn't, in fact, have a minister, as Rev. Silverstone had accepted the call to Southport in 1927. His replacement would not be in the pulpit until 1933. The cost of a new synagogue is invariably greater than its progenitors plan, so the annual saving of the salary of a minister must have helped to bridge the financial gap. To make the books look even worse, the great slump started soon after the synagogue opened. Sunderland was in the wrong place at the wrong time. The effect of the Slump was that the North of England was harder hit than the South. There was usually work in the South and, as a consequence, in the Thirties a lot of Jewish youngsters left the town to make their fortunes in more economically hospitable surroundings.

Where a country's surplus work force is not prepared to act in that way it is known as an immobility of labour, but the long-term experience of the Jews often enabled them to avoid this pitfall. They had been accustomed for over 1,000 years to move on when the area in which they lived fell on hard times. For example, as trading ports like Falmouth and Penzance became less important, the synagogues shut. So this was not a new situation and many packed their tallith and tephillin bags and moved on.

Rabbi Rabbinowitz at the Beth Hamedresh had a serious objection to the layout of the Ryhope Road synagogue. The bimah, the area from which the service is conducted, is normally in the centre of the synagogue. The pulpit is normally by the ark. The snag is that there is a financial consideration for the Honorary Officers to take into account. If the bimah and the ark area are combined, there will be more space in the body of the building for seats. Furthermore, they will be the most prominent seats and will, therefore, command the highest rentals.

Before there is criticism that financial considerations should not be a factor in the House of G-d, it should be remembered that many charities depended on the support the synagogue was able to provide if it had the income. So Ryhope Road combined the two areas, even though the layout was not in accordance with the traditional form. After careful consideration, Rabbi Rabbinowitz decided that he couldn't worship or preach in the synagogue, and this did not go down well with the Hebrew Congregation. It would take 40 years for the congregation to change their view and build a bimah in the centre of the shul.

The unemployment brought by the Slump affected members of the whole community, profits dropped and many more Beth Hamedresh congregants fell into arrears with their seat rentals. Sunderland's heavy industry was badly hit. Spare cash to pay the tally men was more difficult for the workers to come by and the North East drifted into decline. Even so, in 1930 the Beth Hamedresh started a fund to buy a new house for the rabbi and a substantial sum was raised. Not everybody suffers in a slump, though, and one member of the Beth Hamedresh avoided the worst of it with some ease and moved to strengthen the community by finding the Talmud Torah a new home in 1933.

It was Elias Cohen, another of Chatze Cohen's sons, who bought Scotland House and its gardens from the estate of Sir William Allen on the corner of Mowbray Road for £3,875. He presented the handsome gift to the Beth Hamedresh as a memorial to his father and the Talmud Torah moved in. Henceforth, the house would be known as Beth

Yecheskel Hacohen after Chatze Cohen. Rabbi Rabbinowitz consecrated the building and Rabbi Hurwitz returned from Leeds to the town he always called his spiritual home, to join him in the ceremony.

The community also managed to raise enough money in 1930 to build a new Tahara house, a new chapel, at the Bishopwearmouth cemetery, at the substantial cost of £400. It was opened by Ben Joseph, the President of the Chevra Kedushah, the burial society, which still involved members of both congregations.

The Beth Hamedresh also agreed to provide the new Yeshiva in Gateshead with the Aron Kodesh and also managed to refinance the mortgage the community still had outstanding. The Sunderland Working Men Building Society lent them £1,600 for repayments of £11.20 a month for 20 years. By the time the loan would have been paid off in 1951, the total cost would have been £2,728, but rocketing inflation in the later years would still have meant that the community had done a good deal. Discussions also began in 1931 on the possibility of creating a Home for Aged Jews in the North East, but it would be a long time before that idea bore fruit.

As if all this was not enough to tax the financial resources of the community, members of the Beth Hamedresh responded to the approach of Rabbi Dryan from Gateshead to help him found a Yeshivah. Apart from Gershon Levy providing financial support, together with Joseph Pearlman and Solomon Cohen, Gershon Levy became the first President of the Yeshiva in 1930. A committee was formed to administer the college efficiently and after Gershon Levy's death, Joseph Pearlman and and Solomon Cohen acted as Joint Presidents for a number of years.

As the number of students swelled it became difficult to house them with the existing Gateshead community, and so the Yeshiva which had operated from a room in the synagogue, was moved to a large double fronted house which also served as a dormitory. The official opening took place in June 1931 and Elias Cohen of Sunderland did the honours. This would no doubt have been in recognition of his further generosity. As Lewis Olsover says in his book on the *Jews of North East England*:

> It is clear that the close proximity of the Sunderland Jewish community to Gateshead was a decisive factor in the founding of the institutions which were to make Gateshead a byword universally known throughout the Jewish world.

In the midst of all the economic problems, the Beth Hamedresh found another cause for concern, almost as potentially serious for its future. There was a well financed international movement which wanted to change the way the year was made up. Instead of having regular leap years, they wanted 51 seven day weeks and one 8 day week in the year. The effect of course, would have been to move all Saturdays after the eight day week to Sunday and on to Monday the year after. The Beth Hamedresh made representations to London, as did all the other communities in the country - and probably around the world. Today it may seem like a ludicrous notion but it still took a major effort by Chief Rabbi Joseph Hertz and other Orthodox Jewish leaders to get the idea quashed when it came up at the League of Nations. In Geneva it was referred to as the Battle of the Sabbath.

On a more parochial level, there was also an appeal from the Committee for the Mending of the Cemetery in Krottingen. It read:

> The Ancient cemetery of our town of Krottingen, dating back over 100 years (in which Great Sages and Geonim found their everlasting rest) is in dire need of repair.
>
> This place is not shielded from the ravages of time and is only protected by a weak wooden fence which is rotting away and now the cemetery is being vandalised by disgraceful neighbours. It is obviously clear that it is not honourable for the community and for the relatives of the deceased to allow this situation to continue and not to give protection to our beloved departed ones.
>
> We....have therefore decided to build a sound, beautiful wall, the cost of which will be borne by all Krottingen inhabitants, with an appeal for help to all who have left the town wherever they may be.
>
> We turn to you, dear brethren, from your old home town, whose relatives are buried in Krottingen, to help us in our worthy cause.

The Beth Hamedresh responded but the absence of help from the Krottingen Town Council was ominous. The problem of anti-Semitism was looming again in Lithuania. It is true that in Sunderland the Ayeres Quay Jewish cemetery was also falling into disrepair but it was indolence and a lack of money which prevented the Council from taking remedial action, not prejudice. It was also the case that the Sunderland community neglected its duty to arouse the Council to the deteriorating position. There was little sign of malice.

In 1932 the Sunderland Jewish community lost one of its most famous co-religionists with the death of its former MP, Marion Phillips at the early age of 50. She was the first Jewish woman MP and had been elected for Labour in 1929, though she lost the seat in 1931 due to the collapse of the Labour vote as the country moved towards a National Government. There were two Sunderland seats and they were both gained by the Conservatives, with majorities of over 20,000.

Marion Phillips was not from Krottingen. She came from a prominent Jewish family in Melbourne in Australia where one of the Jewish North East's most illustrious members in the future, Israel Brodie, was the rabbi. As a young woman she had come to London in 1904 on a research scholarship to the London School of Economics, which was a major achievement for a woman at that time. She worked on a committee investigating the poor laws and she was a major advocate of women playing a greater role in the young Labour party. She was never a suffragette but she did become Secretary of the Women's Labour League in 1912 and between 1917 and her death she was Secretary of the Standing Joint Committee on Industrial Women's Organizations.

Through her efforts Dr. Phillips persuaded hundreds of thousands of women to take up new responsibilities in areas where they are common today, but unknown then; school meals, clinics and play areas, and equality for women in the work place. She was particularly concerned about the safety of newly built Council homes and was appalled when they lacked bathrooms and toilets, as was the case with many in Sunderland. She once made a speech in which she said "If Labour councillors will not support us on the demand, we shall have to cry a halt to all municipal housing until we have replaced all Labour men by Labour women."

Marion Phillips became the Chief Woman Officer of the party and if she never married, she behaved with all the concern, tenacity and impact of a typical Jewish mother. In one respect, however, her views were definitely not those of the Beth Hamedresh congregation. It was Dr. Phillip's belief that the best solution to the problems Jewish communities faced was for them to become assimilated. If that was as likely as flying elephants, the Labour Party was very evangelical and fervently believed the world could and would be changed.

David Gillis, who had been the Secretary of the Beth Hamedresh for many years, as well as occupying other offices, died in 1933 at the age of 54. In the same year the Englisher shul appointed Rev. Shlomo Toperoff as their minister. Rabbi Toperoff in later life obtained semicha and was no mean scholar but it was still the case that only the Chief Rabbi used the title outside the minority Right and Left Wings. Born in Whitechapel, his father was an immigrant tailor and his mother a seamstress. His father couldn't get work because he insisted on keeping shabbos, which necessitated leaving work early on Friday. Shlomo was a star pupil at the Brick Lane Talmud Torah and left school to go to the Etz Chaim yeshiva. He also got a BA from London University.

Soon after he took up his position in Sunderland, when he was 28, he married the daughter of the renowned Rabbi Ferber of Soho. With Rabbi Moishe Rabbinowitz at the Beth Hamedresh, the collective rabbinic firepower in Sunderland was substantial throughout the dark days of the 1930s and during the war. A constant concern remained the effectiveness of the Talmud Torah when it came to educating the children. Those who ran it, however, began to balk at the subsidiary status it had always had within the Beth Hamedresh. It was agreed to reorganise it and to give it a separate constitution from the synagogue.

It was a good idea in another way as well. From the point of view of the senior members of the synagogue, there was always a problem of how to reward those who gave of their time and money for the benefit of the community. You couldn't pay them because the money wasn't available and they would have been offended at the idea of becoming paid officials. The key to the problem was to come up with ever more ideas to give them nachas; public honour for the work they did. Titles on committees, praise in speeches at dinners, the best tables at functions, lifelong awards. It was all in a good cause and the play-acting was harmless.

In future the Talmud Torah would be called the Sunderland Talmud Torah and it would have its own committee of management. The membership would consist of the President and Treasurer of the Beth Hamedresh and all the Trustees of the Talmud Torah building. The desired effect was to make it independent of the Beth Hamedresh Council as a whole.

The Beth Hamedresh members remained, automatically, members of the Talmud Torah and that applied also to the fathers of any boys attending the Talmud Torah who were members of the Englishe Shul. It was agreed - and this was 1932 - that in the primary classes, the teaching would continue to be carried out in Yiddish. It wasn't, of course, that the children couldn't speak English. If they did go on to Yeshivah, however, the teaching there would be in Yiddish and they would need a mastery of the language. The additional aim was to safeguard the continuation of Yiddish as a living language.

The defence of the Welsh language in the Principality today and the efforts to maintain the study of Gaelic in Scotland, are similar examples of the difficulties inherent in keeping alive a second language. It remains amazing that Hebrew, itself, survived for 2,000 years when it wasn't even the lingua franca of the Jews. That role belonged to Yiddish for the Ashkenazim and Ladino for the Sephardim, which is much like Classical Spanish. Yiddish has a rich and very extensive literature and culture, well worth retaining, but it is an ever more uphill struggle today to prevent it being dispatched to the basement store rooms of history. It is still because of the Right Wing that it is protected from this fate.

When Hitler gained power in 1933 the Beth Hamedresh knew very well what could be the outcome. They had ample experience from their own days - or those of their fathers - in Eastern Europe. They knew that many countries were already making life difficult for their Jewish communities and that anti-Semitism had a good deal of support in the general population. They took up the cudgels as best they could. Already that year a letter was sent to the Board of Deputies, noting their "disgust" at the half-hearted manner in which they considered the Board was dealing with the new persecution of German Jewry.

As early as that year the National Socialist victory in Germany saw the beginning of the flood of refugees out of the country. The reasons for their coming could have been the imprisonment of their parents or simply that the parents thought they would be better off away from Germany. Whatever the reasons for the families being broken up, the situation was tragic, though over the years the vast majority of the German Jewish community managed to find refuge abroad. It was, after all a problem which could be addressed for six years between 1933 and 1939 and the British Jewish community alone donated £3 million (nearly £150 million today) to help them. This level of aid was essential because agreement had been reached with the government that if they provided immigrant visas, the community would ensure that the refugees did not need state aid.

Krottingen and Germany were not the only trouble spots in Europe by any means. The Beth Hamedresh members also supported the appeal for Austrian Jewry which had been launched to help relieve poverty in the, primarily, Vienna community. The 8th list of subscribers in 1932 had, as usual many Sunderland names on it, and the amount raised had risen to £144,000. The peace of England contrasted starkly with the street attacks on Jews in Vienna, the "terrorism at Vienna University", and the published lists of Jewish shops which the Austrians were encouraged to boycott. Which they did to the point that suicides in the Jewish community reached 200 a year as early as 1935 and the *Daily Telegraph* reported that:

> something far nearer to the horrors of a Tsarist Russian pogrom than anything which has yet happened in Germany would probably be the first fruits of a collapse of Austrian independence.

Jewish doctors and teachers employed by the state were dismissed and the Austrian government had to station soldiers at bridges leading to Jewish quarters to prevent rioting. In Britain the situation was very different. The National Government under Stanley Baldwin, unknown to the public, had a quiet word with Lord Reith, the Director General of the BBC and agreed that Oswald Mosley's fascists should not be mentioned on the radio or have their spokesmen allowed to broadcast. Deprived of publicity, the fascists went into decline and the Public Order Act curtailed their activities even more.

In 1934 a minor domestic miracle occurred in Sunderland. The Beth Hamedresh and the Englisher Shul finally agreed on the creation of a Joint Board of Shechita. It had taken 30 years of on-off discussion, but finally there was agreement. Much of the credit was due to the two rabbis, Moishe Rabbinowitz and Shlomo Toperoff. The constitution of the Board of Shechita would have done credit to the drafter of the Articles of Association of Shell Petroleum, but the fact that every tiny detail had been thrashed out meant that no changes were, henceforth, necessary. There was also little likelihood that the slaughtering in the future would be ad hoc, as it was in 1931 when the shochet was discovered to be killing chickens at his home, as and when he found it convenient.

Sunderland Literary Circle

STANDING: *R Freedman, I Brewer, Lena Richenberg, Sol Cohen, Minnie Pearlman, Cyril Gillis, Ada Magrill, Rev. Burland, Rose Topaz, P. Cohen, Rita Olswang, Charles Gillis, Fay Cohen, Leslie Graham*

SEATED: *Sol Novinski, Rev. Toperoff, Israel Jacobs (President), Rev. Oler, S Light*

The social centre for the community

Some years later the inappropriate killing of a chicken cost the shochet his job. A farmer friend of a member of the Hebrew Congregation Council had lent one of his fields to the Jewish school children for a picnic. The farmer's prize cockerel decided to wander among the picnickers, at which point the shochet took out his chalif, the knife used for ritual slaughter, and dispatched the bird forthwith. This resulted in the extreme anger of the farmer, the dismay of the children and the dismissal of the slaughterer. The shochet still got six months notice, though; good shochetim were hard to recruit.

The social events of the Sunderland Jewish community were plentiful and very varied in the Thirties. Besides the barmitzvahs and weddings, there were Jewish Student Societies to attend all over the North East. At the annual conference in 1934, the Sunderland Jewish Dramatic Society won the Union's Shield for a play they performed which was written by one of their own members. In 1936 Sunderland won the sports trophy for the third time. In 1938 the Federation of Jewish Literary Societies held their Regional Conference in Sunderland and Sol Novinski continued to inspire the local members to greater cultural efforts.

The Sunderland community, if it could have known, had now reached the maximum size it would ever attain. There were no less than 2,000 Jews in the town, according to the *Jewish Year Book*. Certainly, the numbers warranted a new synagogue for the Beth Hamedresh. In 1934 a Building Committee was formed and it estimated that the cost of a new synagogue would be £3,000. An offer of £1,625 for the old building was accepted. There was a considerable gap to be filled. The "grave financial situation of the Beth Hamedresh and Talmud Torah took up much discussion" according to the 1934 minutes of the Council. They could have been content to just tick over - income in 1934 was £1,043 and expenditure only £1,066 - but in spite of the Slump they wanted to move forward. In 1938, in the grounds of the Talmud Torah, the last home of the community was built for £3,875. The complex also included the new mikvah and the Talmud Torah.

During the interregnum between leaving the old synagogue and opening the new, the Victoria Hall was hired for the festivals. On these Yomin Naroim the cost of sitting in one of the first three rows was set at 20p, in the middle three rows 15p and the rest went for 10p.

Beth Hamedresh, Mowbray Road
The old Sir William Allen Home

Opening of the Beth Hamedresh, February 1938.

Left to Right. Rev. S P Toperoff, Ald. J Cohen, A Yaffe, Elias Cohen, R D Pearlman, Lionel Gillis, J Pearlman, Rabbi M E Rabbinowitz, M L Pearlman, Rabbi H Hurwitz (Leeds), M A Cohen, Solomon Cohen P Cohen, Cyril Gillis (Hon. Architect), I W Brewer

It cost £3,875

The mikvah opened in 1936. It would cost 10p to use if you lived in Sunderland and 15p if you didn't. That included your towel and a bar of soap in a sealed wrapper. There was also an agreement to spend £10 to make sure the mikvah had a geyser in future which worked properly. As the mikvah is for naked immersion, the lady in charge of the bath would be kept at a discreet distance. The male caretaker was paid 50p a week. The Beth Hamedresh courteously asked Ryhope Road if they would like to be involved in the administration of the mikvah but the Englisher shul were happy for the Greeners to carry out that responsibility. It was unlikely that many members of the Hebrew Congregation would use the mikvah except for the ritual immersion of a forthcoming bride.

Naturally, the building of a new synagogue would involve the harmonisation of many different viewpoints and there would need to be compromise. Right at the beginning the Beth Hamedresh found that there were problems to resolve and the minutes of the 1937 Council Meetings recorded: "Much discussion took place on who should lay the foundation stone and who should open the new building!" The cost of the Mikvah had actually been donated by Philip Bergson but this was his gift to the community before going on aliyah to Palestine. Some more of the money for the new synagogue came from Israel Jacobs who wanted to mark his Diamond Wedding with a suitable gift to the community.

The architect was Beth Hamedresh member, Cyril Gillis, who was qualified. The front of the Talmud Torah house was given a handsome portico with the name of the Beth Hamedresh on it and the date in Hebrew. You would then walk through the old house to what had been the garden in which the new synagogue was erected. The design of the interior didn't present any difficulties except for the Ark. This is the focal point of the synagogue and everybody wanted an attractive design. It was said for years after that Cyril Gillis got his inspiration for the ark from the Eglise Madeleine church in Paris, a somewhat odd choice if true.

Beth Hamedresh
The Bimah in the middle

Tha Aron, Beth Hamedresh
Note the lowly position of the Omed

The Bimah, Beth Hamedresh
You got a lot in the 1930s for under £4,000

Beth Hamedresh
Not 'the lap of luxury' but everything they needed

Beth Hamedresh
The view from the Ladies Gallery

The Omed, Beth Hamedresh

Leining from the Bimah

The scrolls of the law, the Pentateuch

The new synagogue was opened in February 1938 by Sol Cohen, the current President and Joseph Pearlman, the Treasurer; the key moment being the placing of the sifrei torah in the ark. It was consecrated by Moishe Rabbinowitz and Hirsch Hurwitz, who both gave sermons in Yiddish. Rev. Warrantz conducted the service with a choir under Charles Gillis. As the Mayor and other visiting non-Jewish dignitaries would have made little of the addresses, it was as well that they were presented with copies of Chief Rabbi Hertz's *Book of Jewish Thoughts*. In fairness, it isn't a very imposing book, though the thoughts are profound. As the Beth Hamedresh had decided they were independent of the Chief Rabbi, it did suggest that if his contribution was likely to impress non-Jews, they might be prepared to make an exception.

The non-Jewish Mayor betrayed the same awkwardness as the Honorary Officers had when they decided on the appropriate gift of the Chief Rabbi's book. In his speech he paid tribute to the integrity of Sunderland Jewry. The proof he provided of that integrity was that "he had had very few Jewish cases before him" as a magistrate! With a religious body he would have used "integrity" in the sense of moral uprightness, which would seem to mean rather more than never having finished up as a defendant in a court case. It is highly unlikely that either faux pas would have occurred to anybody at the time.

At the inaugural dinner at the Victoria Hall there would only just have been time for the full grace after meals as there followed no less than 15 speeches; Rabbi Rabbinwitz, Joseph Pearlman, Rev. Toperoff, the Mayor, Rabbi Hurwitz, Sol Cohen, Alderman Jack Cohen, Alderman Ritson, E. M. Maccoby, Cyril Gillis, Dr. Joseph Gillis, I Gordon, M. Robinson, H. Levison and M. Jacoby all contributed.

The new Beth Hamedresh synagogue had the advantage, as would become apparent many years later, of having no architectural merit at all. It was just a large house with a simple frontage to make it clear that it was the Beth Hamedresh. The inside of the synagogue was traditional, although certain aspects of the synagogue were unusual. Perhaps the most remarkable was that there was no Ner Tomid. This, the everlasting light, burns constantly in almost all synagogues, to remind every congregation that the spirit of the Almighty was always with them. There wasn't one, however, in the new Beth Hamedresh.

Solomon Cohen
Sometime president of the Beth Hamedresh

The Menorah
Used at Chanukah to remember the miracle

Another unusual feature had always been the Omed. This was a reading desk which was built on the level of the synagogue floor in front of the raised Ark. The reading desk at the Ark was used for sermons. The one on the central raised bimah was used to read from the Torah when the sefer torah was brought from the Ark and the prayers associated with the reading were recited. Four times a year it was also used to read the Megillot. The fifth Megilla, Lamentations, is said on Tisha b'Av, which commemorates when the temple was destroyed and this was read from a low stool on the floor. The position of the bimah in the centre of the synagogue was in accordance with a centuries old tradition, but it was a little like having the stage in the middle of the orchestra stalls.

Most of the ordinary prayers at the Beth Hamedresh were, however, read from the Omed and the reason for this is very symbolic. No matter how desperate things may be, Jews always believe it remains possible to ask the Almighty for help. They were told so in Psalm 130: "out of the depths have I cried unto thee..." In leading the prayers from the Omed, the reader was physically below the Ark and the bimah. He was seen to be calling from the depths. The original omed had been given to the Beth Hamedresh in 1904 by Mr. Rafael, another member who had originally come from Krottingen with it. Unusually again, two prayers normally said in an Orthodox community in the Service on the Sabbath were not included. Yigdal and Adon Alom were omitted and only said at the beginning of the service on Yom Kippur.

Of course, the main synagogue was unnecessarily large for weekday services and these would be held in the annexe, the Shtiebl. Here the prayers were led from a shtender, a lectern which had been brought from Krottingen. There were two candelabra on the side of the shtender and wax dripped onto the surface as another reminder of olden days. Eventually, in the 1950s, it was decided to convert the candlesticks to electric light, but Rabbi Babad, the minister at the time, was most unhappy about the change, candles always having a perceived degree of holiness.

It so happened that the shtender was adorned with a brass plaque which read in Hebrew "Remember who you stand before." This was once innocently cleaned by a caretaker with the result that the reader would see his own face in front of him when he read the prayers. This was not who he was supposed to be standing before and the rabbi insisted that the surface be immediately dulled and gave instructions that it was never to be polished again.

Beth Hamedresh

The Shtiebl showing the Aron and the Shtender

Not all the forms of service met with universal approval. During the Passover Seder service at home, the joyous Hallel prayers form part of the proceedings. At the evening service in the synagogue which precedes the seder, Hallel is seldom said. It is, however, a Chassidic tradition to do so and the custom was introduced into the Beth Hamedresh by Rabbi Rabbinowitz to the chagrin of many members. It should be remembered that one segment of the Ultra-Orthodox is the Mitnagdim, and Mitnagdim means opposition. The Krottingens were not Chassids and as a consequence some of the members were so affronted that they walked out, but as it was still decided to continue the practice, it soon became a normal part of the ritual. In very Orthodox communities it is usually far more acceptable to add some additional prayers rather than try to cut any out.

After the morning service, every day, there was an exposition on part of the Mishnah, the Oral Law, and this was completed about every seven years At which point the congregation would go back to the beginning and start again.

Every effort was made to continue the Krottingen traditions. For example, before the reading of the law on the first day of Shevuot, there is a prayer called Akdamus. Possible uniquely in the entire Jewish world, the prayer was always said in the Beth Hamedresh by the Cohen who was the first to be called up to the bimah for the recital of the appropriate section of the law. There was also a continuing tradition that a collection of psalms, the Shir Hayichud, would be read in their entirety at the end of the Kol Nidre evening service. With a day long fast ahead of them, this was the straw that broke the camel's back for many members of the congregation, who hurried home instead.

One form of decoration to be found in most synagogues at the Festival of Shevuot is an abundance of flowers, for this is a harvest festival. There were, however, never any flowers decorating the Beth Hamedresh. The saintly and highly influential Vilna Gaon in Lithuania had decreed that the custom was inappropriate. The reason he gave was that it imitated the practice of other religions. Although this might seem a very minor point, it should be remembered that until comparatively recently, United Synagogue ministers were normally to be seen wearing those clerical collars. The fear in Right Wing circles was always that big and unacceptable trees could grow from little innovative acorns.

Beth Hamedresh

The Library

Another missing element was noticeable at the festival of Succot when most synagogues build a sukkah on the premises, to enable members to say the appropriate blessings in it. The sukkah does not have a solid roof, but rather a leafy trellis, to remind congregants that only the kindness of the Almighty enables them to shelter from the elements over their heads in the first place. No sukkah, however, was ever built at the Beth Hamedresh. It was expected that every member of the community would, instead, build their own, or would be welcomed by a fellow congregant who had completed the construction in his garden.

It is customary for synagogues to have a charity appeal on Yom Kippur but the Beth Hamedresh did not. It was felt that the appeal could be held on any other occasion and that to do so on Yom Kippur lowered the dignity of the great fast. Another link with the past was the magnificent silver Menorah, the eight branched candelabra which was used at the festival of Chanukah. This had been given by the members of the Chevra Tehillim and the Chevra Gemara when they joined together to form the Beth Hamedresh, now nearly 50 years old.

There are two major sermons each year, one before Passover and the other before Yom Kippur. These Shabbot Hagodol and Shabbot Shuva sermons were considered so important that references to the passages of the Gemorah which would be covered, were posted on the Beth Hamedresh notice board in advance. The congregation would then be able to study the background before they settled down to hear the Rabbi's exposition.

While the rabbi would preach, he would not be asked to lein, to read - without Hebrew punctuation - from the sefer torah, the portion for the week. It was a matter of pride that the lay members of the congregation would always be able to shoulder that responsibility. Most of the leining was done by Moshe Aron Cohen and Beril Pearlman.

Sol Cohen, the President, continued to be highly regarded in the new Yeshiva in Gateshead. When a siyyum was held there in 1935, it was Sol Cohen who was asked to preside. On that occasion the Yeshiva invited both Rabbis Rabbinowitz and Toperoff to speak. Gateshead took a lot of comfort from the support of Sunderland.

Sunderland Literary Circle
Silver Jubilee Dinner 28 Oct 1936
A long way from jeans and 'T' shirts

In 1938 Lionel Wolfe, a man well known to the wider Sunderland community, died at the age of 67 of a heart attack. He was a member of the Hebrew Congregation but typical of the Jews who created so much goodwill for both communities in the town. Lionel Wolfe was known locally as the "Poor Man's Solicitor". He did a great deal of work on a pro-bono or near-pro-bono basis for those who could not afford the legal help they needed. He was also a Director of Sunderland's famous football club, when the local team had some memorable players such as Raich Carter, who made his debut for the club - and his country - at the age of 18. It is an interesting sideline on the slump that one Wednesday afternoon in 1933 there was a Cup replay and still over 75,000 people turned up. The local employers obviously accepted this extraordinary level of absenteeism.

These were golden days for Sunderland FC and to be officially associated with it made you a local hero immediately. The team won the Football League in 1936 and the FA Cup in 1937, just a year before Wolfe died. When the final whistle sounded, it was Wolfe, rather than the Manager, who the team hoisted onto its shoulders in celebration. When he passed away it was reported that thousands attended his funeral from the worlds of politics, law, business and sport. There were a great many tributes paid to him, including a particularly warm one from the Chief Constable.

One charitable organization which had not previously been represented in Sunderland was the B'nai Brith. This omission was corrected at the end of 1938 by the inauguration of a new lodge (No: 1300) by the President of the District Grand Lodge, Professor Selig Brodetzky. The professor also served as President of the Board of Deputies, a key role in dealing with the government over immigrant visas. He was, however, very much an academic where the times demanded a great deal of thinking outside the box. Unlike, for example, the maverick Rabbi Dr. Solomon Schonfeld who used every trick in the book - and several which weren't - to save refugees from Europe, Professor Brodetzky would rely on the rules, which were often weighted against individual factions, notably the elderly and the very Orthodox. In the Bnai Brith, however, Professor Brodetzky was very much at home. The lodge was welcomed by a telegram of congratulations from the Mayor, the local MP, the town Clerk and the Chief Constable. It did a lot of charitable work for many years.

With the war clouds gathering, many of the Sunderland community prepared to join the colours. The first to be called up were the volunteers who were already serving in what were then called the Militia Men, and who we call today the Territorial Army. Still in civilian life, they had asked for training in their own time, to be ready when the call came. By 1938 over 100 of the 1,000 Jews in Sunderland had volunteered for National Service in the event of war.

Among them was Beth Hamedresh member, Joseph Landau, a grandson of Chatze Cohen. In his case, however, when he got his papers, he saw with alarm that he was ordered to report to his army camp on Saturday. Landau was not prepared to do this, so he decided to turned up on the Friday instead and was designated Militia Man No: 1. There was a great deal of publicity about his decision and by January 1940 he was the first militiaman to be commissioned from the ranks. He was only 21 at the time and, after a successful career, he finished up a Major. When he came back from the war he devoted much of his time to communal work within the whole community. He would also become Vice President of the local Conservative Friends of Israel and President of the Old Age Home. He died in 1994.

Philip Pearlman had joined the Territorials in March 1939 and the former boxing champion of the Bede was soon a sergeant. Another to join up with alacrity was Leopold Levine, the youngest member of the Beth Hamedresh Council and Chairman of the Jewish Literary Society and the Sunderland Young Zionist Association.

German propaganda was always going to try to pin the blame for the coming Second World War on the Jews. Josef Goebbels, the chief Public Relations minister, proclaimed it was an international Jewish conspiracy to achieve world power. In April 1939, the North East Jewish Ex-Servicemen's Association did its mite to prove the contrary and illustrate yet again the loyalty of British Jews to the crown. Their first reunion in the North East had been in 1936 when 300 had attended. Now 450 Jewish veterans from all over the area gathered under Lt. Col. Myers Wayman and they were inspected by the Mayor of Sunderland. They sang adon olom accompanied by the Band of the 47th Durham Light Infantry Antiaircraft Battalion. A definite improvement on the average synagogue choir.

The mayor set the tone when he said "We ex-servicemen have not forgotten that you fought with us, shoulder-to-shoulder, and today we have been proud to march with you in peace." The local MP also spoke and appealed to the government to offer a haven to refugee Jews somewhere in the British Empire. He justified his argument in terms which would be up for an award now, for the most politically incorrect statement of the year. He said:

> Surely it is not merely our duty but our course of greater wisdom to try to increase the white population of the British Empire at the present time.

Blatantly racist by the standards of today, it came from a member of parliament who considered himself a friend of the Jews and who would have weighed his remarks and decided that his views would find favour with his audience. many of whom would have been his voters. When we consider racism and anti-Semitism in the 21st century it is well to recognize just how far we have progressed towards a more tolerant world.

The events of the upcoming war would give at least the Western European world the kind of powerful shock it needed to change the system. As Bernard Levin, a great journalist, wrote of the 1930s in Britain, "Decent society in those days was filled with people who had forgotten what anti-Semitism *had* led to, and who could not guess what it *would* lead to."

Capt. Neville Laski, an illustrious figure in Anglo-Jewry, knew what it could lead to and spoke with biting scorn of the past and future enemy at the meeting. "To compare Nazi Germany with the barbarous Middle Ages is an insult to the Middle Ages." The bonds between the Jews and non-Jews remained firm, however, in the North East of England. When the King and Queen visited Durham that summer, Alderman Jack Cohen, Chatze Cohen's grandson, was presented to them.

In June 1939 a new Sunderland Hostel for Jewish Refugees was officially opened at 2, Kensington Esplanade by Julius Behrman. This was only for girls as mixing the sexes was now considered inappropriate. Thirty two children arrived between the ages of five and fourteen. Of these young refugees, relatives were located for eight of them, but the others stayed at the hostel. In the process of time it would normally be the case that boys would be put up by local families. The impending war unified the two communities and Rabbi Rabbinowitz officiated with Rabbi Toperoff. A free tea was offered, richly deserved, as it was estimated that 95% of the community had contributed to the fund to create the new hostel.

The first 14 girls for the new building had arrived in January, the results of Rabbi Schonfeld's Kindertransport efforts, to be greeted by Rabbis Rabbinowitz and Rev. Toperoff. The Jewish Chronicle, when listing Sunderland events, normally put Rabbinowitz first and this was no exception. When more hostel space was needed, it was found in Gateshead and in a large number of private homes in Sunderland, who looked after young male and female refugees throughout the war.

Attempts to rescue the Jewish communities in Austria, and Czechoslovakia were far less successful than with the German community. The war would break out with most of the European Jewish communities stranded, with horrific consequences.

One major problem to getting them out was the British government's White Paper restricting the number of Jewish immigrants to Palestine.

Although Rabbi Rabbinowitz was not a Zionist, like everybody else he strongly opposed the measure, but to no avail. The government knew very well it would need Arab oil if Britain was to have any hope of defeating a powerful Germany in the up-coming war and additional Jewish emigration would be a red rag to a bull for the Arabs.

There was strong non-Jewish support for the refugees, though, and Dr. Hensley Henson, the Bishop of Durham, was a notable voice of protest against the actions of the Nazis. When he retired in 1939 the community decided to present him with a Golden Book certificate and representatives gathered that January at Aukland Castle in Durham for the ceremony. Rev. Toperoff gave the Bishop the priestly blessing in Hebrew. "May the Lord bless you and keep you..." It was a moving moment and the Bishop was quite overcome. If age confers seniority, it was one of those occasions when Jews can pull rank on other denominations.

The world moved inexorably towards the Second World War and the Sunderland Jewish community got ready to cope and play its part.

Chapter 8
War and Peace

No less than 150 Sunderland Jews served in the armed forces during the Second World War. Five of them died. Among them was a Battle of Britain navigator, Israel Winburn, and Sergeant Harold Magrill, a descendent of the Maharil. His ship, taking him to a prisoner of war camp in Japan, was torpedoed by an American submarine and all on board were lost. David Davis of the 125th Anti-tank regiment died of cholera in the appalling conditions of a Japanese prisoner of war camp. Those who were in prisoner of war camps under Japanese control certainly had the toughest regime to survive, as it was a part of Japanese culture at the time that it was entirely retrograde to surrender to an enemy. It was felt that the honourable thing for the prisoners to have done would have been to die in battle. The Japanese, therefore, considered, that the Prisoners of War were traitors to their countries and treated them according to that yardstick. Bernard Jackson and Lionel Marks also lost their lives. There was relief at the fact that some of the soldiers finished up as prisoners of war rather than "missing".

Six of those who served received awards, including Maurice Minchom, who was Mentioned in Dispatches for his work with sick prisoners in his Japanese prisoner of war camp. It should always be remembered that out of companies of 300 British soldiers in the camps, often only a proportion would return after the war. There was much need for everybody to make a major effort just to help others stay alive.

The older members of the Beth Hamedresh would have liked to have helped more, but the Council could only make supportive gestures, like agreeing not to collect any arrears on payments due to the synagogue from members of the armed forces. As soon as the war started, though, the individual members of the community wanted to do their bit for the war effort. By March 1940 the local Women Zionists had started a Knitting Circle which was held at Mowbray Road every Tuesday afternoon. Appeals had to be made for the right colour wool to make the additional clothing to be sent to the serving men overseas.

Leo Levin, Lionel Gillis, Mordant Cohen, Issy Levine, Cyril Behrman
Phivie Pearlman, Israel Winburn, Rabbi Toperoff, Joey Landau, Maurice Minchom, Harold Magrill
Toby Book, Norman Cohen, Nat Goodman, Solly Gillis

Israel Winburn and Harold Magrill died in the war

Two members of the Beth Hamedresh had the distinction of serving at Bletchley Park, the ultra-secret centre for breaking the enemy codes. Joe Gillis and Hyam Maccoby were part of an elite group whose mathematical capabilities and general intelligence were outstanding and who were valued team members of an organization which did a great deal to defeat the enemy. One of the recruitment tests was to be able to solve the *Daily Telegraph* crossword in less than 12 minutes. Not a problem for the likes of Joe Gillis who had studied maths at Trinity, Cambridge and taught at Queens University, Belfast, before going on to Bletchley Park. After the war he taught at the Weizmann Institute in Israel. After the war Hyam Maccoby would become Professor of Jewish Studies at Leeds University and wrote prolifically on his subject.

The Beth Hamedresh provided 53 of those who served. They were Abe Bergson, Arnold Bloomberg, Toby and Wilf Book, Charles, Claude, Harold, Isaac and Sylvia Brewer, Pearl and Selwyn Caplin, Joey Charlton, Ernie and Solly Cohen, Austin and Hymie Davis, Nathan Ernstone, Archie, Charles, Ernie, Lionel, Max, Miriam, Solly and Zelda Gillis, Harry and Sam Isaacs, Harry Joseph, Charles Kersh, Charles and Edward Kolson, Arnold and Joey Landau, Leo Levin, Issy Levine, Dinah Levinson, Jack Linskill, Chaim, David and Lorna Maccoby, Rita Olswang, Beril, Miriam and Mottie Philip, R. David Reeva, Sheba, and Yankel Pearlman, David and Itsi Rosenthal and Jerry and Harold Shochet.

Sunderland was the sixth most heavily bombed city in Britain during the war. The shipbuilding yards were an important target for the Germans as the tonnage of torpedoed vessels rose and desperately needed supplies for the allied war effort finished up at the bottom of the sea. To stop the ships being replaced was a prime objective of the German Air Force. The Beth Hamedresh were taking no chances though that the synagogue might be a priority for the Luftwaffe as well. The sifrei torah at the beginning of the war were divided up between private houses to lessen the risk of losing them.

It was a difficult time for Rabbi Rabbinowitz, rallying the community, comforting the bereaved, hospital visiting and carrying out his religious studies. In 1942 the Council voted him £20 to take a holiday, as long as he arranged for someone suitable to continue the shiurim in his absence. Rabbi Rabbinowitz's custom was to visit his son in Manchester at regular intervals and he often returned to find that there had been new devastation in his absence. In the end he acquired an idée fixe that the bombing would increase in violence whenever he left the town, and so he told his relatives that they could no longer expect him until the air raids were over.

When the bombs started dropping during services, the Beth Hamedresh congregation would retire to the synagogue cellar and carry on praying from that point of relative safety. Some, however, decided to move to towns which were less attractive targets for enemy bombing and could be found, therefore, in places like Cheltenham and Buxton and in North Wales. When some of them didn't return after the war, the Beth Hamedresh membership was, naturally, reduced. There was also a shortage of teachers for the Talmud Torah and the Beth Hamedresh appealed to Gateshead to fill the gap.

One serious problem which prevented the use of the main synagogue was that it couldn't be blacked out. If you turned on a light, it could be seen from outside the building. This was because the synagogue had very large windows which couldn't be effectively covered. As it was totally forbidden to show any light after darkness fell, for fear of guiding enemy bombers to their targets, Air Raid Wardens would walk the streets. If they saw any illumination they would shout "Put that light out". When the older generation hears that phrase, their minds immediately revert to wartime.

So when it got dark, the synagogue couldn't be used and services were held in the upstairs hall where two rooms had been knocked together. This, however, was very difficult on one occasion during the year. On Yom Kippur, the Kol Nidre service on the evening, was always attended by almost the whole congregation. The numbers who could fit into the hall were far too small for the demand. So, throughout the war, the Kol Nidre service was started early so that the main shul could be used and the service could be concluded while it was still daylight.

Memories of wartime are only to be found in the minds of the very old today. It is hard, if you weren't there, to imagine leaving home to fight and possibly get badly wounded or killed. Or to have your children and relatives placed in extreme danger. To be on active service and never know whether tonight will bring an air raid at home which might kill or maim your family and friends. Most Jewish communities mentally shrugged and saw no way of keeping families together under those circumstances. Sunderland was different, thanks to the efforts of Rev. Toperoff who had the idea in July 1942 of producing a monthly magazine which would go to all the Sunderland Jewish members of the forces with news from home. It would also contain letters from them to their old friends in the community.

The last issue was in January 1946 and Toperoff gave an account of its origins:

> From the outset of the war when numbers of our lads joined up as Territorials, the idea of a Bulletin was conceived and we felt that it would be the means of uniting the serving members of our community whilst away from home....we realised that there would be the difficulty of finance. Other difficulties, too, appeared; should the Bulletin be restricted to members of the Ryhope Road synagogue only, or to all members of the Sunderland Jewish Community who found themselves in the services. Both these problems were soon solved by the initiative and generosity of Mr. I.E.Cohen, who originally undertook to defray the expenses incurred in the production of the Bulletin which was to be sent to <u>all</u> Jewish serving personnel of the town.

The Bulletin kept to its original format. It started with a page of comment on the Jewish events covered in the synagogue at that time. If you were disinclined to enjoy a drosha in peacetime, the commentaries on hallowed and age-old events in the Bible could be a comfort in battle; you were not alone. Toperoff didn't confine his remarks, however, to histories of the Festivals or wandering in the Wilderness. He linked the events of the month with the events of modern times.

The giant wave of sympathy which swept Britain when the ghastly results of the Final Solution were known, when the pictures of the liberated concentration camps were on the cinema screens, created a very different atmosphere from that which existed at the beginning of the war. At least 10 times as many Jews had died as had British citizens. In one of his earliest commentaries, Rev. Toperoff told of a Methodist minister asking why so many of the Jews "are guilty of sharp practices." Rev. Toperoff regretted that the vicar hadn't asked him why there was no juvenile delinquency among the Jewish kids and why there had never been a case of a Jewish parent in Sunderland being prosecuted by the National Society for the Prevention of Cruelty to Children.

He recommended those who had joined up to ask for a free copy of "The Jews - Some Plain Facts" which gave the information belying the accusations. He pointed out that while Egypt remained neutral even when invaded by the Nazis, there were 20,000 Jewish volunteers from Palestine to serve on the allied side, including 2,000 women. Of course, on occasions there was even a lack of sensitivity shown by the local authorities in the North East and there were obviously going to be some anti-Semites. The community was hurt when the Ottowa Jewish community raised enough money to send 12 mobile kitchens to Britain for the war effort. One went to Washington, Tyne and Wear, which is very near Sunderland but no representative of the local Jewish community was invited to attend the handing-over ceremony.

Rev. Toperoff dealt with ignorance about Jews in matters large and small. In one issue he dealt with the Jewish nose. He said "The Jewish nose is not Jewish. It is characteristic of the Armenoid peoples among whom were the ancient Hittites." On another occasion he lobbied for the numbers in all Jewish communities in Britain to be counted, so that they could be compared with the number of their members who were working for the war effort. This he felt would counter anti-Semitic criticism in some of the media. Nothing came of this and it would have really been a hammer to crack a nut, because the hatred of Hitler and the Nazis made anti-Semitism a non-starter in the responsible press. Sunderland Jews who were too old or unfit for active service, acted, like so many of the non-Jews, as Air Raid Wardens, Fire Watchers and as members of the Home Guard.

The rabbi also took the opportunity of lobbying for "a Jewish army as a distinct entity". One of the benefits would have been the ability of a Jewish general to liaise with the other commanders to obtain the release of Jews from concentration camps as Europe was liberated. Rev. Toperoff was right. After the war, Rabbi Solomon Schonfeld, Director of the Chief Rabbi's Religious Emergency Council, was able to do much good work in Poland by fitting himself out with an army officer's uniform and, as an official member of UNRRA, a United Nations organisation, giving instructions for the relief of Jews in the manner born. Few had Schonfeld's chutzpah, however. The Rabbi continued to wear his beard, the only one in an army uniform apart from the late King George V!

After the drosha on the front page, there was a quiz, information about the doings of various members of the community, light hearted social notes about who was going out with who, and who might be. The interest in sport was satisfied by the voluntary contribution of one of the Sunderland Echo's writers, who wasn't even Jewish; Captain Jack Anderson was the Military Welfare Officer in Durham with a very heavy work load, but he took pleasure in contributing regularly to the Jewish newsletter.

One of the stalwarts of the community, Sol Novinski, a well-known local tailor and the Literary Society engine room, had always been associated with the youth of the congregation. He regularly contributed memories of pre-war days. He had been a founder of the Union of North East Jewish Societies, the only president of the North East Drama Festival before the war and he had initiated the Sunderland Jewish Dramatic Society in the 1920s.

What was particularly striking was the tremendous sense of community which ran through the issues. It was one giant family. It becomes very clear that these were Sunderland citizens who knew each other from a very early age and knew they belonged within the community. Whatever happened in the future, they had once been closely linked. Charles Slater, the future head of the Labour Party in the town, was at the Bede school and won the speaking cup.

Harold Davis, who served as Secretary of the Beth Hamedresh for many years, was at the school at the same time. He won the 200, 400 and 800 yards races at the Sports Day and the long jump for good measure.

There were no reports of members dying at home, though if serving men were reported missing and later became prisoners of war, that was recorded. Also the experiences of coming across Jewish life in India, Africa, the Middle East and Europe. There was little in the Newsletter about rationing and hardship. It gave no information about the effects of bombing, even some damage to Mowbray Road synagogue in 1943, because such stories might have given useful information to the enemy about the effectiveness of their actions.

The synagogue damage was not substantial, but the repairs could not be carried out until after the war because of the greater importance of the war effort. Most foods were rationed, though it was possible for Jews to give up their allowances of foods like bacon and have rather more of something else instead. If you could get them, chickens were not rationed, so supplies of invaluable chicken soup were maintained. In March 1941, the Chief Rabbi appealed to all the British Jewish communities to give generously to the appeal for food to be sent to Jewish troops serving abroad which were suitable for Passover.

In 1941 there was an appeal for Fire Watchers and ARP (Air Raid Precautions) Wardens to which the community responded enthusiastically. They also decided to join the World Jewish Congress, which at least gave them some comfort that they were contributing to an international front against Fascism.

Sunderland, itself, could have been invaded from the sea and so the beaches were mined. Those with long memories might remember the outbreak of the First World War, when the German Navy sailed along the East Coast and shelled towns like Scarborough with considerable effect. The authorities were also concerned about the possibility of those born in Axis countries being spies. A number of refugees were made to leave Sunderland and live inland where there was no possibility of them helping an invading force.

There were also civilian casualties. A handsome gravestone in the cemetery records the death of David (48) and Miriam (38) Bergson, together with their children Arnold (6) and Millie (13) who were killed in the raid on Sunderland on May 24th 1943. David Bergson was the caretaker of the Beth Hamedresh.

Naturally, the Beth Hamedresh families were terribly concerned about the fate of their relatives and friends in Krottingen, in particular. The Jewish community there had had a chequered history since so many of their families had left for Sunderland 50 years before. Lithuania had become independent after the First World War and in 1939 64 of the 77 shops in Krottingen were owned by Jews. In the 1930s, however, the Lithuanian Organisation of Merchants had started a campaign to boycott Jewish owned shops and anti-Semitism grew in strength. A notice outside the local nunnery read "Entrance to strangers and particularly to Jews is forbidden." In 1940, when Lithuania was annexed by Russia, all the shops were nationalised.

The Jewish population of Krottingen in 1940 was about 1,000. After the German invasion in June 1941 the Nazis shot about 200 men at a farm outside the town on June 26th. The rabbi was burned alive. This was followed in July and August by subsequent massacres of the remaining men, women and children. Many had taken refuge in the synagogue which the Nazis set on fire, and the innocents were burned to death. The local fire brigade was told to protect the nearby houses but to let the synagogue burn.

Some non-Jews tried to help hide their Jewish friends. When this was discovered they, and their whole families, were killed. In 1958 there was a war crimes trial of the Colonel in charge at Krottingen at the time, Colonel Bernard Fischel-Schweder. Together with nine members of the Gestapo and members of the local Lithuanian police who had taken part in the massacres they were at last in court for their crimes. The trial lasted four months as 170 witnesses took the stand to tell of the horrors:

> Nauburas, a former Deputy Mayor of Polangen in Lithuania stated in court that Krottingen Jews had been forced before their execution to kiss the boots of the Nazi murderers. Children were torn from the arms of their mothers and beaten to death.

A mass grave was discovered in the Jewish cemetery with 356 bodies and another in the nearby forest with 700 bodies. All the defendants were found guilty but only received sentences of from three to fifteen years in prison. Words simply fail to convey the enormity of such crimes or the bestial behaviour of the murderers.

In Sunderland during the war there were protest meetings against religious and racial discrimination, supported by the good and great. In March 1943 there was a particularly large one where the guests of honour included the Jewish mayors of nearby West Hartlepool and Darlington, along with the Bishop of Durham and representatives of the Methodist and Roman Catholic churches. The Mayor of Sunderland had intended to be present but at the last moment was informed of the death of his son. By this time, although there were only 868 Jews in the Sunderland communities, there were over 120 in the forces.

That same year there were two other notable appeals; one was for 4,000 Danish refugees who had been spirited out of the country to Sweden but needed financial support. The other was a request by Rabbi. Dr. Solomon Schonfeld, on behalf of the Chief Rabbi's Religious Emergency Fund, for help in getting Jewish refugee children alternative foster homes with Jewish, as against non-Jewish families. Despite every effort, it was eventually estimated that only 35% of the Jewish children who came as refugees remained within the faith.

The social life of the youngsters of the community continued to centre around the Lit, the Literary Society, where they met, played billiards, borrowed books from the library, had dances, listened to guest speakers and often met their future husbands and wives. The dances were very popular and the young members of the Beth Hamedresh joined in the fun with the youngsters from the Englisher shul. Which, in strict Orthodox circles, remains a bone of contention today At Ultra-Orthodox social events there is no mixed dancing.

Before the full development of television, however, the 1930s was the heyday of the big dance bands and, for men on leave, the chance to dance with a girl was a way of meeting them which society considered harmless. Hollywood would make films on the lives of band leaders like Glenn Miller, the Dorsey Brothers and Benny Goodman to showcase their music. The big Lit dinner dance on December 3rd 1945 drew 200 guests.

On the other hand the Young Zionists were often members of a society called Habonim. This was normally secular in its outlook, as was the case with many of the Zionist founding fathers. Sunderland's Habonim was not only Orthodox - probably the only one in the country - but frum in its practices.

The war effort demanded that the women in the country play a major role, replacing the men who had gone to the front. Where before the war women had normally stayed home and brought up the family, now they worked in factories, served in the armed forces and did any job where there was a shortage of labour. This recognition of the equality of women had an effect in the Beth Hamedresh community as well and, in 1944, a girls cheder was founded to provide them with a better Jewish education.

With the end of the war came the end of the useful life of the Bulletin. Rev. Toperoff wrote in the last one:

> The Bulletin will live as a monument to the war effort of Sunderland Jewry that sent nearly 150 men and women out of a total Jewish population of 900 souls to the fighting fronts of the world.....though the Bulletin will cease to function, its contents and its message of hope, fortitude, courage and faith in G-d will live on. Our rabbis remark that when one parts from the dead we use the expression "Go in peace" but when we part from the living we say "Go unto peace". We cannot conclude without saluting the memory of those serving men who have passed on to the Beyond. To them the journey of life is over; to them we say "Go in peace". May their souls be bound up with the bond of eternal life, and rest in everlasting peace.
>
> Your friend,
> S.P.Toperoff.

It is very easy to see why Rev. Toperoff was not short of friends.

The Mayor said at the Reception to welcome home the Jewish troops after the war that he was "amazed at the Community's record of service". Many were distinguished, but perhaps the most able was Lieutenant Colonel Mordaunt Cohen, a grandson of Reb Cohen, who had been brought up in the Beth Hamedresh and would go on to distinguish himself as the leader of the town's Conservative party.

The history of most of the the founding families of the Beth Hamedresh had started with poverty, menial jobs and as immigrants in a new land. One of these at Moor Street was Barnett Smith who was a glazier. He would go round the villages with the glass on his back offering the service of mending windows. Jews are, however, justly famed for recognising niche markets before they become well known. Barnett Smith saw such an opportunity in the provision of glass for Miners' Safety Lamps and eventually supplied it for most of the local collieries. His son, however, decided to emigrate to the United States and, in 1944, rose to be Brigadier General Joseph Smith in the US army.

Even in wartime, domestic issues need to be addressed and one of the most pressing was the facilities which were badly needed to look after some of the older members of the community. After a number of discussions, in June 1945, Joseph Intract offered to make a gift to the community of a large property to be used as a home. It was agreed that the name would be The North East Joel Intract Memorial Home of Rest for Aged Jews and that it would be run on strictly Orthodox lines.

It would be for both elderly men and women and the refurbished building was officially opened in September 1946. By the end of its first year of operation it had 18 residents aged between 66 and 90. Joseph Intract explained his motivation in the first annual report of the home. He said he had remembered the verse: "Cut us not off in old age, forsake us not when our strength faileth." As a result: "here the old people can live quietly and peacefully, and receive every care, comfort and sympathy. Above all, they are able to spend the declining years of their lives in a truly Jewish atmosphere among friends of their own age, which is what they desire more than anything else."

The devastation of the Holocaust destroyed Yeshivot across the continent. Countless centres of talmudic learning for hundreds of years were wiped out, and all too often only those teachers and students who had managed to flee before the war, survived. The reaction of the surviving Jews to the Holocaust differed widely. Many lost all their faith in human nature, suspecting enemies on all sides and withdrawing from the world.

Others were simply crushed, giving up their faith, and were seen no more in the ranks of their former brethren. Still others never got over their appalling experiences and were mentally scarred for life. In addition to the 6 million dead in the Holocaust, there were a very large number who were severely injured, both mentally and physically.

The discovery of the concentration camps had a profound effect on the thinking of the Church of England. Where converting Jews was high on their agenda of desirable results for hundreds of years, the potential effects of the constant denigration of Judaism as a religion was finally brought terribly home as the death toll of the Final Solution rose higher and higher. It is from the Second World War that there emerged the Council of Christians and Jews, sponsored by the leaders of both faiths and dedicated to improving relations between the followers of the two religions.

During the war, two of the original leaders of the movement, the Rev. Bill Simpson and Rev. James Parkes came to Sunderland to talk of the importance of the new initiative. The atmosphere changed for good. When Rev. Toperoff was ill and couldn't edit one of the Bulletin issues, he called in the local vicar to do the job for him. The vicar was delighted to help.

Just before the end of the war Rabbi Salis Daiches died in Edinburgh at the age of 65. He had been a major positive influence in the Jewish community in Sunderland during his tenure and had remained a powerful Jewish spokesman when he accepted the call to Edinburgh. Like many other firm supporters of Zionism in its early years, including those in the Beth Hamedresh, Rabbi Daiches found himself not always in agreement with the way it developed. The future of the Holy Land after the war was on everybody's agenda but a year before he died, the rabbi - who served on the Executive Council of the Zionist Federation - warned against unthinking support:

> There were those who imagined that to be a true Zionist meant to endorse every move and every attitude of the official Zionist organisation and to approve all the methods adopted by certain Zionist spokesmen in furtherance of the success of Zionist effort. This was a mistaken view and might very easily lead to unfortunate results. The support of 'yes men' was of no real or lasting value to any cause which embraced such a lofty spiritual ideal as the regeneration of the Jewish people in its ancient homeland.

In 1945 Solomon Cohen died. aged 68. He had been instrumental in selling the Villiers Street synagogue at what was agreed was a very good price. In that year Chazan Warrantz finally retired after 40 years service to the Beth Hamedresh, when his health broke down. The Beth Hamedresh gave him a pension of £2.50 a week, the modern day equivalent of £255 - which just proves what inflation can do over the years.

In his place was appointed Rev. Jacob Kahn from Belfast. Kahn would be paid £7 a week but, in addition to acting as Chazan, he was also to be the shochet, the mohel and a teacher. It was agreed that if he was given a present by the parents of the baby he circumcised, that was acceptable, as it would be if he sung at a wedding and got a present from the family of the bride or groom.

With peace, life started to return to normal and the members of the Beth Hamedresh began to tighten up on any laxity which might have crept in under the pressures of the war. In a small town it is very difficult to hide yourself away. In a small community within a small town it is even harder. And if your father is one of the senior officers of the congregation, you know the eyes of many in the community will be peeled to pick on any shortcomings in the behaviour of family members.

So a conforming daughter would now be expected to attend Cheder every evening at the Beth Hamedresh, plus Saturday afternoons and on Sundays, now that the community had finally started to make provision for teaching girls. The teaching continued to be partly in Yiddish and there would now be explanations in English for those who needed them. One Pearlman daughter missed one Saturday afternoon and can still remember how furious her father was. Almost as outraged as on the occasion he found her carrying a book on the sabbath.

Where daughters went to synagogue every sabbath as well, the Beth Hamedresh wives usually didn't. Their responsibilities to their families took precedence according to the law. Wives would usually go to the Mikvah every month after they had their periods, and at different times the men used the Mikvah as well, particularly at Rosh Hashonah and Yom Kippur as a figurative cleansing of sins.

If all these observances seem to add up to a very demanding style of life, it must be remembered that the traditions had existed for centuries. The way of life left little room for loneliness and there was no reason for anyone to feel alone and isolated or without help at hand. Each member of the congregation 'belonged' and the need and desire to belong is one of the most fundamental aspects of a normal person's personality. One ex-member was asked how they regarded the intensity of observance demanded of them. "It was a way of life" she said "You don't question a way of life." The capacity to carry out so many of the mitzvot also created a pride in the membership. They continued to think of themselves as superior in that regard to the less observant.

While the comment on a way of life applied to the members of the Beth Hamedresh, there was always a new generation coming up and they would not always agree with the views of their parents. A considerable number of members over the years moved to the Englisher Shul although, in fairness, there was movement in the other direction as well. What was common to both communities was that they were becoming a lot more middle class than their parents and grandparents. Which was fine for their standard of living but led to smaller families than had been the case hitherto. Chatze Cohen was certainly exceptional in having 22 children but the norm for a middle class family after the baby boom at the end of the war, was more likely to be two and half. In these circumstances, the community would be likely to decline in numbers.

One communal activity found in many other Jewish communities was the communal seder on Passover. To make sure that everybody could attend the two seder services, the communal seder enabled the elderly or the less committed to avoid the cooking and preparation. No communal seder was ever held in the Beth Hamedresh community. Seder nights remained strictly family affairs and if there was an elderly widow or widower, without a family to invite them to the service, then there would be plenty of non-relatives who would readily welcome them to their homes.

There was a great deal of work to do at the end of the war to repair the ravages of the bombing of Sunderland and to get the town's economy back to its pre-war concentration on heavy industry, ship building and coal mining. According to the *Jewish Year Book*, the Jewish population in Sunderland had sunk from 2,000 in 1934 to only 950 in 1945, though it would grow again to 1,150 by 1955 and 1,350 by 1965.

Many young Jews continued to go into the established firms of tally men, where the more successful of the original traders had built substantial businesses, employing many agents. One newcomer was Gordon Abrahams who, when he was in his seventies, worked for a PhD at Sunderland University. It proved it wasn't always a lack of brainpower which led to the young men taking up comparatively menial jobs. It was often the lack of opportunity to do better for themselves. Even so, to their customers, the tally men were a significant part of their lives. Gordon Abrahams recalled:

> People would all have their favourite travellers, and often when a girl was getting married you would inherit her trade from her mother and so it carried on, and the daughter's house was added to your round. I remember one family particularly well; I used to have a real sense of pride when I went into that house because the lady and I had sat down together and we had chosen every stick of furniture in it. The husband wasn't interested....everything to do with the house was left to the wife to deal with.

The 1944 Education Act, however, would expand the number of student places available in higher education and the younger Jewish generation in Sunderland would take advantage of this like everybody else. The days of the tally men were beginning to come to a close. By contrast, in the 1950s there would be over 30 Jewish doctors in practice in the Sunderland area.

The Charedim who survived the war could have adopted many different ways of dealing with the tragedy of the Holocaust. The way they chose was to determine to replace all that had been lost, no matter how long it took. They would rebuild the destroyed communities and Yeshivas elsewhere. They would maintain every tradition, perform every mitzvah and prove by their devotion that Judaism remained indestructible.

Such a man in Sunderland was the red headed Rabbi Zushne Waltner, It is commonly thought among non-Jews that Jews are dark haired with prominent noses but, of course, Jews are an extremely mixed race. They have many blondes and redheads in their midst and there was no law that said that converts had to be brunettes. It was Rabbi Waltner who gathered support for starting a Yeshiva in 1946, though he was originally encouraged by Rabbi Dessler, the head of the Kollel in Gateshead. The Yeshiva of Rabbi Hurwitz had long disappeared but there were ways of starting again. First Rabbi Waltner asked a young Rabbi, Shammai Zahn, to help him and when Waltner moved on in 1950 and became the principal of the Toledano Foundation in Tangier, Rabbi Zahn took over. As he said, with some characteristic diffidence, 40 years later, "I was asked to help out and I've been helping out ever since."

Rabbi Zahn was a typical survivor of the Third Reich. He was born in Nuremberg in 1920 and because he came from a Polish family, there was an attempt to deport him to that country in 1938. As the border was closed, the deportees were sent back and Zahn decided to escape the country. Disguised as a farm boy he arrived in England in the spring of 1939 and two of his siblings managed to get out as well. His other two sisters and his parents died in the Holocaust.

In 1944 Zahn finished up in Gateshead under Rabbi Dessler and went to University at the same time. When he moved to Sunderland and joined Rabbi Waltner he travelled to the Displaced Person camps in Europe to find suitable students for the new Yeshiva. For the few he could take, it was the offer of a new life and the chance to recover from their ordeals. They were transferred from the squalor of the camps to a Yeshiva which was starting life in the now empty Sunderland hostel building. The one which had been used by Rabbi Dr. Solomon Schonfeld to house some of the refugees he had helped escape to Britain before the war.

It was now no longer needed and had been vacated. It would be adequate for a Yeshivah. Certainly, it would be shabby, with the carpets worn out, its furniture scanty and basic, and its heating non-existent in the dormitories. Nevertheless, serious study could begin again, albeit in just one large room. During the day group lessons would occupy about an hour and a half, but the rest of the time was spent in private study, with the teacher always present to discuss problems and provide any help that was needed. The Beth Hamedresh agreed to pay for 25% of the annual cost of maintaining it.

The visas were obtained for 35 students, mostly from Czechoslovakia, who were recruited to begin the first term. The lectures were to be in Yiddish and it was settled that seven to eight years study would be necessary in order to qualify as a rabbi. If the ambition was to become a shochet, it would take five years and for a teacher, four years.

When you study for semicha there is a great deal of Jewish law which you must master. That is the core of the knowledge you need, but Rabbi Waltner realised that his students would have seen levels of inhumanity which could destroy their belief in their primary responsibility, to live a good life.

They had been taught in the camps that the only thing that mattered was to survive another hour, another day, whatever it took. In the Yeshivah, to emphasise the overriding importance of morals and ethics, the curriculum for a good life is in a body of work called Musser. Waltner saw to it that this body of teaching was always prominent in the syllabus. In making sure there would be more well educated officials for communities in the years to come, Waltner wanted their hearts as well as their brains to be working well. It would take a steely determination.

Rabbi Zahn had the right personality and qualifications for the role of Rosh Yeshiva when Rabbi Waltner moved on. He had profound scholarship, even though he came from a non-rabbinic family, and over the years he wrote two major works on talmudic literature. He would serve the Sunderland community for the rest of his working life. Rabbi Zahn was also blessed with a very supportive wife.

Lottie Zahn was often to be found doing the *Daily Telegraph* crossword. Like her husband, though, she took her responsibilities to the communities very seriously - from her early days of marriage until she and Rabbi Zahn moved to Gateshead, she was the centre of Sunderland Jewish family life. She taught three generations of children at the Talmud Torah, she entertained widely and felt maternal responsibility for all the Yeshivah boys as well, particularly those from foreign countries. She was much loved by both communities and the Zahn simchas were occasions of universal celebration.

The rabbi's wife also involved herself with the Menorah School,, teaching at all levels until its final closing. She insisted that you learned Jewish history from studying the Tenach and, as such, she instigated a Tenach class, starting from Joshua, every Saturday afternoon. One day Shabbos Yomtov fell together and everybody was late coming home from shul. When asked whether there was still time for a Tenach class, she replied "Like the Windmill theatre, we never close." This was a reference to the slogan of a famous variety house in London at the time, which specialised in very risqué performances.

Nothing was too much trouble for Lottie Zahn; preparing brides for marriage, even preparing the Mikvah, which should have been outside the duties of the Rebbetzin - but she considered it a mitzvah. It was also an indication of the social cohesion of Rabbi Zahn and the North East's non-Jewish community, that the rabbi's son broke his leg playing rugby at his school, Newcastle Royal Grammar.

To his undoubted brainpower Zahn added a great deal of charm, kindness, humour and humility. The steel in his personality was carefully concealed, but it was there. He was a short, tubby man who combined extreme Orthodoxy with extreme tolerance. He did not press the case for a rigid performance of the mitzvot on the less committed. He knew that if he set the individual congregants impossible targets for observance, the result of him hectoring them would be to drive them away from the community. If, however, there was a seriously observant member present when he gave his generous ruling, he would wait till they were alone and then remind him "But that doesn't apply to you!"

In addition Zahn always looked the part. He was photogenic, another great after-dinner speaker, a keen supporter of Israel, and he had a wonderfully bushy beard. So he started with the advantage that he had all the credentials for a heimische rabbi. Rev. Toperoff may have looked like a typical vicar to the non-Jews in Sunderland. Nobody could mistake where Rabbi Zahn was coming from. By now the Englisher shul was less known for its scholarship. The Beth Hamedresh, the Yeshiva and the Kollel were admired for it internationally.

For the less committed, there is a temptation to dismiss a rabbi like Shammai Zahn as peripheral to the serious business of daily life. The sacrifices he makes and the problems he overcomes seem outlandish and unnecessary. With Zahn's talent and brainpower, he could certainly have been successful in any number of other professions.

Instead he set out to sustain a yeshiva. So let's remember what a yeshiva is. It is a centre for the academic study of Jewish legal literature, which is immense in scope. Unlike a typical university, the students are not an inevitable distraction preventing the teachers from doing research, as is the case when a government make the amount of useful research done by the faculty the yardstick for its success. Again, unlike a university, the students see their teachers continuously. At the Sunderland yeshiva the teachers always sat with the students as they studied, and Rabbi Zahn would sit in their midst rather than take up a position of importance at the top of the room.

The students were cherished by the rabbonim as the next crop of religious leaders without whom the religion would become rudderless. All the emphasis was on bringing out the best in the students, inspiring and teaching them. The cost of all this was often provided free to the students. Certainly, in the early days, the youngsters from the camps on the continent would have been quite incapable of paying. The yeshiva teachers, the maggids, were paid, but the Rosh Yeshiva - in time, Rabbi Zahn - would have to give up lecturing in order to devote himself to raising money to keep the yeshiva in being.

When the students leave the yeshiva and get married, some want to continue to devote themselves to study. That where the Kollel comes in. Their daily work then becomes the study of the ancient texts and commentaries. If there is any money coming into the home, it is either going to come from charity, from the support of their family, or from the efforts of their wives. A bride who marries a husband who wants to be a member of a Kollel knows what she is letting herself into. She will be the breadwinner and without her wholehearted support her husband and family couldn't survive.

The charitable contributions came regularly from supporters like Mac Goldsmith of Leicester, the Reichman Brothers in Toronto, the Hubert Trust, Sebag Cohen of Jersey and members of the local community. To such eminent and successful businessmen the importance of the work of the Kollel had a priority they would succour as they did their companies, even if the institution started with only 10 students.

Inspiring and teaching the students, building up their confidence and preparing them for a life of service to others, was the task of men like Shammai Zahn. It would appear that those who adopted a more hedonistic view of life, who had the power and the status in the wider community, who dismissed the rabbi as old fashioned, misguided and out-of-touch with the modern world, had all the weapons. The truth was they hadn't any hope whatsoever of undermining the efforts of men like Zahn. If the Nazis hadn't been able to achieve it, nobody else would.

If the successful businessman is the one who goes the extra mile, rabbis like Zahn would understand Chairman Mao in China - "a journey of a thousand miles starts with a single step." They had all chosen to start the journey and would stay with the task for the rest of their lives. The yeshivas in Europe had been wiped out in the Holocaust. Men like Rabbi Zahn would build them anew.

When the Displaced Persons Camps closed, the supply of Yeshiva students dried up. This could have been the end of the institution but Rabbonim Waltner and Zahn were nothing if not innovative. A serious problem was identified for young men in Morocco. After the 1948 war of Israeli Independence no Jewish community in the Arab World could be considered safe. There were a large number of desperately poor youngsters in North Africa. So a considerable number of young Moroccan Jews were encouraged to enrol in the Yeshiva. and from 1950 to 1957 Rabbi Zahn made annual visits to find new students.

There were problems; they didn't speak Yiddish. The men from Morocco were, of course, Sephardim, where the Displaced Person camps had mostly housed Ashkenazi Jews. So adjustments had to be made. Moving from a hot Morocco to an unheated Sunderland was spartan. The teaching was conducted in Yiddish before the Moroccans arrived but the Sephardim spoke French and Arabic rather than Yiddish, so compromise was needed there as well. With good will on both sides in the actual Yeshiva, the problems were overcome. There was a belief among the Sephardi, however, that the Ashkenazi, also very short of qualified synagogue officials after the Holocaust, did their best to persuade the Sephardi students to change sides, with some success.

It was decided to teach in Ivrit (Modern Hebrew). This produced the strange situation of a German Headmaster teaching Moroccan students in modern Hebrew. Somehow, everybody coped. For many years the ranks of Jewish community officials were swelled by the Sunderland graduates. Both the Ashkenazi and the Sephardi communities filled many gaps around the world with well-trained men. Future graduates would include those who went on to become Chief Rabbis of Venezuela and Argentina.

Chapter 9

The peak years

In May 1946 Rabbi Zvi Hirsch Hurwitz died at the age of 83. He had been a practising rabbi for 62 years, starting in Lithuania - he was born in Vilna - when he was just 21. After his eight years in Sunderland, he had gone on to Leeds and become the Ab Beth Din in the city, its senior officer. His Chevra Tehillim synagogue maintained all the traditions of the Sunderland Beth Hamedresh and so the apple hadn't fallen far from the bough. "the clergy officiating there do not wear robes or any insignia of office."

Rabbi Hurwitz was also appointed to the Chief Rabbi's Rabbinical Commission. The Sunderland Beth Hamedresh had not consulted the Office of the Chief Rabbi before appointing Hurwitz, but obviously that slight had been long forgotten.

Hurwitz was a pioneer in the teaching of Modern Hebrew and, as a lifelong supporter of Zionism, when he died, he must have been one of the last survivors of the delegates to Theodore Hertzl's final Zionist Congress. He was also considered an expert on Kashrut and Taharat Mishpocha, the laws of family purity. A husband's conjugal rights were restricted by law in Judaism, where as in many other religions it would have been considered eccentric to have done so.

The rabbi had remained in office until just a few weeks before his death. Among his last work was the sending of instructions to local institutions on standards of Kashrut and paying tribute to the retiring headmaster of a Jewish school. Although very widely respected and admired, Hurwitz never sought popularity. His legacy to the the rabbis who came after him was summed up when he was given an 80th birthday party by his community and spoke of a rabbi's duty. "A rabbi should not receive too much honour or praise: that would be an indication that he had not spoken forthrightly always or condemned wrongdoing when he saw it". With Rabbi Hurwitz there was no danger of that. In an appreciation to mark his 70th birthday it was remarked that he had "endured much criticism from many quarters."

Within a year of his death, however, there came into being the Rabbi Hurwitz Memorial Hall at the Leeds Mizrachi Youth Centre. He would have been pleased with that. Five thousand trees were also planted in Israel in his name; the Hurwitz Memorial Forest.

Rabbi A Babad
A national and international figure

In the same year the Beth Hamedresh suffered a further loss when Moshe Rabbinowitz died, ending a family connection with the congregation which had been maintained for over 40 years. Rabbi Rabbinowitz was 68 and his wife, Chaya, would outlive him by more than 20 years. As for the Beth Hamedresh, the problem was now to find a successor to Rabbi Rabbinowitz. As was reported in the Council Minutes for that year, "the funeral of Rabbi Hurwitz at Leeds allowed some discussion on the suitability of the three candidates" (to replace Rabbi Rabbinowitz.) It must have been a variation on "Le roi c'est mort. Vive le roi."

In 1947 it was Rabbi Abraham Babad who was installed to replace a spiritual leader who had done sterling work, guiding the Beth Hamedresh community for over 20 years. It was significant that the old rabbi's son, Rabbi Gedaliah Rabbinowitz, was not invited to succeed his father. This, in no way, reflected on the son, but did create the precedent that the Beth Hamedresh did not feel itself bound by an old Chassidic tradition that the office might go down the family line if a son was properly qualified. This would become important in the future. Rabbi Babad was inducted by Dayan Grunfeld, a German lawyer who had fled his country in the 1930s and taken Semicha in London. Grunfeld became one of Chief Rabbi Hertz's right hand men when he was appointed a Dayan of the London Beth Din but illness shortened his career. He was very much a power in the land in 1947 though.

Babad was the 5th rav of the Beth Hamedresh. Like Hurwitz and the two Rabbinowitzs, he was a tremendous talmudist. He was a tall man, very scholarly and a very heavy smoker, which suggested he was normally under some stress to cope with the many demands made upon him. If he had the appearance of an East European sage, he had a command of English - a qualification demanded of all candidates now - which he could use with elegance, irony and wit. At least one very eminent candidate, Rabbi Gurwicz, who would go on to be the Rosh Yeshivah at Gateshead, disqualified himself because of his poor command of English.

Ewen Montagu, the lay head of the United Synagogue and no mean performer himself, said he was amazed at Babad's skill as an after-dinner speaker. Rabbi Babad was fond of colloquial English and would criticise an action as "not cricket" or excuse the behaviour of a youngster by insisting that he was just "sowing his wild oats." The rabbi read *The Times* every day, taking a particular interest in the Law Reports. It would have interested him to contrast the decisions reached by the higher courts with those applicable in Jewish law.

There was one major difference between Rabbi Babad and his predecessors in the Beth Hamedresh fold; Rabbi Babad was a national figure. For a number of years, on behalf of the British Agudas Yisroel, he was Chairman of the Central Council of the World Organisation. He took over the Chair of the European Executive from a famous figure in Anglo-Jewry, Harry Goodman, after the latter's death in 1961. He was the founding Editor of the Jewish Tribune, which he started after Harry Goodman's own paper stopped with his demise. Rabbi Babad wrote all the Leaders in the paper. When he spoke in his official capacity, he was faithfully recorded in the Jewish press. The Beth Hamedresh rabbonim had served the community most effectively, but Rabbi Babad gave it additional nachas because he was a very senior representative of the world Right Wing.

The Agudas Yisroel organisation was founded in 1912 and set out to co-ordinate an Orthodox response to problems affecting Jewish communities around the world. Today it has consultancy status with the United Nations. Rabbi Babad came to it by a traditional route. He was born in Poland in 1909. and became the seventh generation of rabbis in his family. He gained his semicha at 24 from the Tarnopol Yeshiva and married into a renowned Chassidic family when he wed the daughter of the Przemyslaner Rebbe, Chaje Margulies.

With such impeccable Right Wing credentials, he came to London when he was 28 to be the Principal of the Or Yisroel Yeshiva. This was a creation of Rabbi Dr. Solomon Schonfeld when he was making heroic efforts to get Jews out of Germany. It was his idea that exit visas might be obtained if the youngsters said they were coming to London to study at a Yeshiva. So he created the Or Yisroel Yeshiva, brought in Rabbi Babad, and visas became that much easier to obtain. The Yeshiva started with 20 pupils and the local community agreed rotas by which a family would provide a student with free meals for one week in eight.

During the war Rabbi Babad went on to ministering to a North London community before he moved to Sunderland. If he had been a United Synagogue minister, there would have been no public career, as the synagogue laymen normally hogged the limelight. In the Beth Hamedresh, however, Babad expected to be, and was the leader.

Rabbi Babad had been brought up to be a Chassid which meant that his traditional stance had been to advocate withdrawal from the secular world. As the Sunderland Beth Hamedresh rabbi, however, he realised when he applied for the office that he couldn't carry his community with him if he maintained the same attitude. For example, when he started, mixed dancing continued to be the norm at Beth Hamedresh weddings. This had always been the custom although, officially, the sexes do not dance together. Babad knew this perfectly well, but as everybody carefully refrained from asking his opinion, he did not feel it necessary to take the initiative and condemn the practice. At so many functions he just left the room before the dancing started. It was only after 13 years, at a meeting in Leeds of the Shomrei Torah in 1960, well away from his home base, that he attacked the practice. At this point Rabbi Babad said that the rabbis had talked too little on the subject.

When it came to Jewish shops opening on the Sabbath, both Rabbi Babad and Rabbi Zahn looked the other way, rather than criticise. After his death, Chaim Bermant, a noted columnist in the *Jewish Chronicle*, described him as "Hospitable, tolerant and devout without being fanatical." Which, of course, depended on your definition of fanatical.

Rabbi Babad was also Vice President and then Chairman of the Agudist Keren Hatorah, Vice President in 1949 of the Agudas Israel World Organisation and still found time to be President of the Sunderland Yeshiva. He often went fund raising in London on its behalf, but was always back in Sunderland by Friday. When asked by one rabbinic colleague why this was so often the case, he said "Friday's pay-day!" The rabbi's duties would often take him abroad, though. Seventeen rabbis from the UK went to the Agudas World Conference in Jerusalem in 1954. The leader of the delegation, which numbered 47 in all, was Rabbi Babad.

The Agudas Yisroel position was summed up by Harry Goodman when he said that it "looked at the world from the viewpoint of Torah. Others looked at Torah from the viewpoint of the world." This was an organisation which was founded to fight for the greater observance of the mitzvot against, as often happened, the Zionist approach. When Israel was founded, a whole string of decisions had to be made about what was going to be legal in the new state. When the decisions went against Orthodox practice, Agudas protested.

In 1958, for example, there were demonstration in Jerusalem against the legality of mixed bathing. In London the Agudas protested that Zionism was aiming at destroying Judaism: "The Zionists are enemies of the people of Israel and have now for 60 years been pursuing the aim of destroying the Jewish religion."

There was another major row a few years later when the very Orthodox inhabitants of the Mea Shearim section of Jerusalem, protested against cars being driven in the holy city on the sabbath. Kibbutzniks invaded the district and Rabbi Babad complained that "the police allowed the organised riots against the inhabitants of Mea Shearim which brings nothing but disgrace to the State and people of Israel." When you remember that the Beth Hamedresh had a congregation of about 150 families in the North East of England, it was remarkable that influential international protest emerged from such a small community.

When Harry Goodman died in 1961, 1,000 came to the funeral service in North London including both the Chief Rabbi and the Haham. There was a half mile procession of cars to the cemetery and it was Rabbi Babad who gave the address at the internment.

One area which was of major importance and the cause of much conflict between the Zionists and the Agudas was education. When the State of Israel was founded, there was a desperate need for more immigrants. The Zionists realised that one source of newcomers could come from the pupils at Jewish schools around the world and it was, therefore, decided to support such schools financially. It was hoped that the curriculum would include Ivrit, modern Hebrew, and that Israeli flags and the Israeli national anthem would become a normal part of school life.

Seeing the secular development of the state, the Agudas was much against this involvement by the Zionist Federation. In 1956 Rabbi Babad presided at a meeting of rabbis in London which passed a strongly critical resolution:

> The conference views with the gravest concern and disquiet the intention of the Zionist Federation of Great Britain to establish day schools under its aegis. The Zionist organization being a purely secular and political movement, the conference feels that it is not qualified to be entrusted with the establishment and supervision of Jewish schools which, in the first instance, must necessarily be of a strictly Jewish traditional character. It calls upon Anglo-Jewry to disassociate themselves from that effort.

The proceedings were all in Yiddish and it was an early example of British Right Wing rabbis taking the lead, rather than abiding meekly by the opinions of their lay leaders. There was no compunction about attacking the Chief Rabbi, who was accused of approving the establishment of one or two of the Zionist Federation schools. What was also significant was that Rabbi Babad presided even though other delegates includes such luminaries as Rabbi Eli Munk of what is now known as Munks synagogue in Golders Green in London, Rabbi Shakovitzky and Rabbi Gurwicz of Gateshead and Rabbi Halpern, the President of the Union of Orthodox Hebrew Congregations.

A further bone of contention for the rabbonim was that to occupy a United Synagogue pulpit, a rabbi had to have semicha from Jews' College or a board approved by the Chief Rabbi. This was condemned as being against procedures which went back hundreds of years and here the rabbis were absolutely right.

In the long run the Zionists had little success in influencing Jewish schools in Britain.

In spite of carrying out so much international work, Rabbi Babad always found ample time to serve the community in Sunderland. He undertook a prodigious workload. What was always needed of the Beth Hamedresh rabbis in Sunderland was the ability to maintain harmonious relationships with the Englisher shul and to continue to merit the warm and friendly regard the non-Jewish community had for the Jews in its midst. So Rabbi Babad was always quite sociable. He also saw to it that the lessons in the Talmud Torah would in future be given in English and not Yiddish. It was Babad who ensured that the daily shiur on the Gemorah was conducted in English.

Rabbi Babad was once asked what it was like to be a Chassid in a non-Chassidic congregation. He answered wryly that it was much better than being a non-Chassidic rabbi in a Chassidic community! It was generally recognized that the Chassidim were likely to be less tolerant than the Beth Hamedresh congregation. Indeed, there were some Ultra-Orthodox families who wondered whether the children of Rabbi Babad could be considered suitable brides and grooms for their offspring, considering how far they felt the rabbi had strayed from the straight and narrow. After he died one eulogy remarked on his "brilliant mediating qualities (which) enabled harmony to be maintained." Which it was - on most occasions. The community did, however, start to move to the right and what was acceptable in 1947 when Rabbi Babad took office, was not always equally approved when he came to the end of his tenure.

There were, of course, many Jewish communities around the world even more strict than the Sunderland Charedim. On the other hand Rabbi Babad had only received his appointment by agreeing to one condition insisted upon by the Beth Hamedresh Council; if he wanted to wear his Streimel on shabbot, he could only wear the fur hat indoors. He was not to wear it in shul or in the street. For his part, while Rabbi Babad agreed to be responsible for the shechita of the meat sold by the kosher butcher. What he wouldn't do was eat it himself, even if he had authorised its consumption by others ! Both Rabbi Babad and Rabbi Zahn only ate fish at community functions.

Nevertheless, Rabbi Babad was pretty pleased with the situation he inherited at the Beth Hamedresh. As he wrote:

> The proportion of Sunderland laymen with a good knowledge of Torah is higher than in any other place in the country (the neighbouring Gateshead excepted). The Hebrew classes, or Talmudei Torah - there are two of them in town - are amongst the best in the country. Almost all Jewish children are attending Cheder. Attendance on weekdays is higher than anywhere else in the country. In the Beth Hamedresh it is 100%. No child misses Cheder without a justifiable excuse. Synagogue attendance on Shabbos is no less encouraging. Here also, in the Beth Hamedresh, it is almost 100% of the membership. It is pointed out, with justifiable pride, that attendance on High Festivals does not exceed an ordinary Shabbos by more than a handful of worshippers, a feature rather uncommon in Anglo-Jewry.

He would also have wholeheartedly approved of the Council's decision in 1948 not to build a communal sukkah during the festival of Succot. It was still the case that there were plenty of individual family sukkahs in the town to enable anybody to use them who wanted to do so.

In the wider world the death of Chief Rabbi Hertz in 1946 led to the election of his successor after a suitable time had elapsed. In 1948 the Beth Hamedresh Council now represented a community of 149 members. According to the report at the AGM, 89 of them were "fully paid". The Council now considered its position as far as its commitment to the Office of the Chief Rabbi was concerned. There was no definite conclusion, but as the successful candidate, Rabbi Israel Brodie, was a Newcastle man, there would have appeared to be a case for a degree of support, as long as the Beth Hamedresh could maintain its traditions under his auspices.

In 1949 this argument did not carry sufficient weight. Soon after he took office, Rabbi Babad had to deal with this difficult question of relations with the new Chief Rabbi. In January the Council decided "to write to London to ask if we (the Beth Hamedresh) could be contributing members to the Office of the Chief Rabbi, without accepting his authority should it differ from that of the Beth Hamedresh." Before asking, however, it was decided to consult Rabbi Babad.

The Rabbi responded that such an affiliation would cost the Beth Hamedresh its independence. Furthermore, as they weren't being asked to join the United Synagogue, why open a discussion with them on the subject anyway? Finally, if there was a falling-out in the future with London, it would be far harder to withdraw their affiliation than it would be to agree it now. The Council decided to leave well alone. The agreement with Hermann Adler which had enabled the community to have its shochets licensed and a Marriage Secretary appointed, was conveniently forgotten. The new Chief Rabbi chose to ignore the slight and, when he visited Sunderland, he went to the Beth Hamedresh for the afternoon service on the Shabbot.

Rabbi Babad was a good diplomat and in any congregation this is a useful attribute for a rabbi. This did not mean that he never disagreed with a member of the congregation but he always saw to it that the argument was patched up. Indeed it is customary on Yom Kippur for the rabbi to give an example to the rest of the congregation by asking forgiveness for any offence he might have given during the year. Jewish law does not approve of long feuds between members of a congregation.

The Rabbi settled in and 1949 was a truly significant year for the whole community. For it was then that the first Jewish Mayor of Sunderland was elected. Jack Cohen, another grandson of Chatze Cohen, donned the robes of office as the representative of the ruling Labour party. His wife, Kitty, was also elected an Alderman, the first time that this had happened to a husband and wife in the town. It was a very proud moment for the generation who had followed their refugee parents and grandparents out of Krottingen. Jack Cohen was knighted and in 1967 his wife, now Lady Kitty Cohen, was elected Mayor as well. For the Beth Hamedresh in 1949 the icing on the cake was that collections and offerings were at an all-time high and the silver ornaments were now so extensive that it was decided to insure them.

The Beth Hamedresh was always keen to help the Yeshiva. When they needed another sefer torah, the Beth Hamedresh lent them one. The only condition was that it had to be returned to the synagogue before the Festival of Succot every year. During the festival all the synagogue's sifrei torah are paraded before the congregation. Thus it was ensured that the Sefer Torah would continue to be recognized as Beth Hamedresh property.

In 1950 the Yeshiva moved to a better address at 3, The Cedars. This was a middle class area, formerly known for its Quaker, industrialist and trade residents. There was some objection from the locals that a Yeshiva on their doorstep might bring down the property prices in the neighbourhood. Simply because it was a Yeshiva and it would bring with it additional noise. It was, in fact, true that when you got outside the building you could hear "the distinctive chant of voices, each chanter in the same manner a different portion of Gemara". If that was a negative, the residents were at least spared the potentially rowdy behaviour of students; Yeshiva students are not known for wild living.

It was obviously the introduction of a number of Orthodox Jews into the area which concerned the residents, but their fears were groundless. A distinguished body of senior rabbis came for the opening of the new campus, including Chief Rabbi Brodie, Haham Gaon and Dayanim Abramsky and Dayan Grossnass.

Even as the Beth Hamedresh flourished in its many-faceted activities, the effects of emigration to Israel, smaller families than their forebears and intermarriage slowly began to take their toll. In 1950 the Greeners numbers had dropped to 92. A lot of members had decided to emigrate to Israel where the new state was now able to welcome them. For many years Jewish immigration to Palestine had, of course, been severely restricted and the pent up demand to go to live in the Holy Land led to a larger migration than would normally have been the case in future years.

Where Right Wing families remained very large, the Beth Hamedresh didn't fit the pattern. Indeed, there were a number of ways in which the Beth Hamedresh customs and traditions were difficult to adjust to other very Orthodox communities. For example, very few of the wives wore sheitels, the wigs with which married women traditionally cover their hair in public. Few of the men wore beards, the families went to the theatre, had television sets (considered distracting and a bad influence by many Right Wing communities) and they seldom had more than four children.

As was to be expected, the first danger signals for the Beth Hamedresh were to be seen in the financial stability of the community. In 1948 the Treasurer was able to report a surplus of £80 and in 1949, £70. The redecoration of the Beth Hamedresh had been completed at a cost of £316 and the War Damages Commission had contributed £288 towards this. By 1953, however, there was a deficit of £156 and this deterioration continued until, by 1963, the shortfall had risen in that one year alone to £2,540. This was in spite of the fact that, over the period, over £2,000 was raised for redecoration and special projects.

The congregation continued to nudge the 100 family mark. There were 92 full paid-up members in 1950 and 104 in 1951. the Talmud Torah had about 30 children. With such a small community, it could well have been expected that the Beth Hamedresh would be just one more minor provincial community. In fact this was not the case. A group of rabbis were talking in Israel in 1953 and were asked about their views on Sunderland by a visiting member. "Sunderland is Wunderland" said Rabbi Sorotzkin, head of Vaad Hayeshivoth, and everybody around the table agreed.

What made the Beth Hamedresh so special was a combination of many factors. You can have a synagogue with a couple of thousand members but with only seating for half that number in the synagogue. This creates no problem except at the time of the New Year and Yom Kippur, when halls are hired for overflow services, as a much larger proportion of the faithful gather for these festivals. It wasn't true of the Beth Hamedresh. The size of the congregation on Yom Kippur was hardly larger than the norm for any sabbath. Almost everybody came for every service.

There was also the normal reception given to those representatives of charitable foundations who visited the communities to raise money for Yeshivas, Kollels and other worthy causes around the world. They often found doors shut in their faces when they called. They were often treated with discourtesy. In Sunderland, however, they called first on the Beth Hamedresh and the congregation provided them with a member to go with them to call at the houses where they hoped for a donation. They were genuinely welcomed and, indeed, they were allowed to make an appeal from the pulpit on the Sabbath. This generous behaviour on the part of the Beth Hamedresh was very unusual among the country's Jewish communities.

The attitude of the Kehilla led to visits from many very eminent talmudists. One of the most prominent was the Ponevezha Rav, Rabbi Kahaneman, who had been a member of the Lithuanian parliament in the Thirties. He had been out of the country when it was invaded and lost his family. After the war he went to Israel and started a yeshiva in Bnai Brak. This is a particularly famous location because the discussions of rabbis in biblical times in the town is recorded in the Haggadah service at the Seder table at Passover. The Kollel building at Bnai Brak is dedicated to the memory of Joseph Pearlman.

Like other communities, Sunderland helped any number of good causes. In 1958 they collected no less than 25 sackfuls of surplus clothing for the Federation of Jewish Relief Organisations and three hampers of baby clothes for the Crippled Childrens Home in Jerusalem.

It was also necessary to recognize the steadfastness of the families in keeping to the faith. By this time the children of the founders of the Moor Street Shul were seldom to be found in the ranks of its members. They had left the community which their grandparents had fought so hard to create. In both the Beth Hamedresh, and the Hebrew Congregation, however, the grandsons of Chatze Cohen presided over the two congregations.

As with any other Jewish community, the continuity of the congregation depended partly on new members coming to live in Sunderland and partly on maintaining the adherence of the children to the tenets of the congregation. The latter task has proved a major obstacle for communities all over the world and over the centuries. The gravestones of vanished communities stand as mute reminders of failure, though the closing of synagogues was also often due to extraneous reasons, from massacre to expulsion, and from economic decline to emigration.

At the Beth Hamedresh the children were taken to the synagogue from an early age and it became part of their life. There are a number of elements to particular services in the synagogue which appeal to children; for example, on the mention of Haman's name at Purim, the powerful politician who wanted to destroy the Jews in the book of Esther, the children are encouraged to shake rattles and bang the shelves in front of their seats. Or after the barmitzvah boy has completed his reading, sweets can shower down from the Ladies Gallery. There is room for fun in Judaism. And at Passover in the Beth Hamedresh there were games played with hazelnuts.

The games included guessing how many nuts your opponent had in his clenched fist. It was called How Many Men In the Boat. If you were right, you got his hazelnuts; if you were wrong you had to hand over the number he was holding. Kupskas was another game with four nuts forming a pyramid and you had to throw a nut at them like a cocoanut shy. At the end of the festival the nuts were put away until the following year.

The core of the children's involvement with Judaism was the Talmud Torah, where they studied for some 15 hours a week. Attendance was more important than almost anything else. Inspectors would say that the teaching methods were archaic, but the results were certainly outstanding.

The Hebrew Congregation appointed Rabbi Turetsky to replace Rabbi Toperoff in 1951. When Rabbi Turetsky got engaged, his fiancee came to stay in Sunderland and it was the Beth Hamedresh Pearlman family who were the preferred hosts. There would be no question of their standards of kashrut being defective, and obviously the Englisher shul members were not considered equally safe in this regard.

Hackles were raised in the ranks of the Hebrew Congregation, but Turetsky walked the tightrope of many Orthodox rabbis. If their congregation wasn't prepared to observe all the mitzvot, should he meet them halfway and have his fiancee staying in what he considered a less than sufficiently Orthodox home? Turetsky wasn't about to give way on anything affecting his personal life and the community had to accept that he was within his rights.

On communal issues he kept his head down on occasions, but when he accepted a new post years later, he used the pulpit for the last time to criticise the synagogue's management and the ban they had imposed on him on talking about a new Jewish primary school in the town. The need for Jewish schools was a contentious matter in those days. Rabbi Turetsky said that the rabbi should be free to speak about anything at any time. With its emphasis on rabbinic, rather than lay, leadership that would always have applied within the Beth Hamedresh. From Norman Richardson to Mordaunt Cohen, religious leadership did not always outweigh the views of the Honorary Officers of the Hebrew Congregation. Rabbi Turetzky went on to serve the Western Synagogue in London for the next 14 years and then taught rabbinics at Jews' College.

It was generally accepted that Rabbi Babad was, talmudically, in charge of the whole Sunderland community. Even Rabbi Zahn was prepared to ask his advice. On one occasion Rabbi Zahn was returning from Scandinavia and his boat was due to dock on Friday. It did, but it had been delayed and it would arrive after the sabbath had begun. Rabbi Zahn used the ship-to-shore radio to contact Rabbi Babad and check what he could and could not do. They agreed that he could get off the boat but couldn't carry his luggage. Who was going to help him get it to a hotel? Who could understand the importance of keeping the sabbath? Rabbi Zahn approached a Catholic priest on the ship and explained his dilemma. The priest agreed to carry his luggage for him!

Where there were knotty religious problems to solve, it was quite possible for the Sunderland rabbonim to set up their own Beth Din. Babad actually means son of the head of the Beth Din, so the Rabbi was carrying on the family tradition. With Rabbi Gelley available and a number of other talmud chochomim, it was more likely that the Beth Din in London would consult with Sunderland than vice versa. Indeed, when the problems came from the North East, the London Beth Din would be prepared to refer them to Rabbi Babad.

For the Rabbi it was always a necessity to tread a fine line between maintaining acceptable standards of Orthodoxy and not imposing his own more rigid Chassidic rules on the Beth Hamedresh members. He was indeed a martinet in upholding the din in the Beth Hamedresh but, as Chaim Bermant, a great observer of the British community once wrote: "The men of Sunderland would thus nod approvingly to his remonstrances, bow their heads to his admonitions, and do as they had always done." He was almost revered by his flock, even though, to an outsider, he might have appeared pretty stern. On the other hand the Rabbi lived very much in the modern world and recognized the need to marry the innovations of modern times to the ancient laws of the Talmud.

In Victorian times it was advisable to know a fair amount about how to look after horses as so many farm implements, public transport and private carriages were pulled by them. Today it is not necessary for the general public. The same applied, as far as Rabbi Babad was concerned, to the invention of the frozen kosher chicken and he wasn't happy about it. What could possibly be the problem here?

Well, before you could get them frozen, you got them from the butcher's shop and they had to be koshered at home. Just cutting the animal's throat was only the start of the process. The carcass had then to be put in water, then covered in salt, then in the water again, until all the blood and impurities had been removed. Jewish women knew that when they got married, they would have to know the rules for this if they were to be able to put the food on the table properly koshered. Rabbi Babad recognized that if the butcher did all this for them when producing the frozen chicken, the skill would disappear from the Jewish housewife's expertise. And he was right; far fewer women now know how to carry out the mitzvah of kashering meat and chickens.

The financial rewards offered to Rabbi Babad were relatively meagre. Why Jewish communities so often take advantage of a rabbi's dedication, to pay him far less than he merits, is not a situation peculiar to any one synagogue. It is also true, though, that gifts to the rabbi, when he comforted the mourners, officiated at a circumcision or married a happy couple, could be a considerable supplement to his official salary. In Babad's particular situation, his brother-in-law was the property magnate, Ephraim Margulies, so, in extremis, there would have been plenty of support to fall back on.

At the time, the real financial muscle in Sunderland remained Elias Cohen, another of Chatze Cohen's sons, who owned a great deal of slum property. He supported many charities and while slum property has not the same commercial status as, say, leasing flats in Mayfair, it is still perfectly respectable. Another very wealthy family in the Beth Hamedresh were money lenders, which also attracts a social stigma. If you called money lenders Banks instead, or Credit Card companies, the status would rise for no reason other than the alternative etymology.

Babad's status in the entire Jewish community in Sunderland was soon very high. There is a tradition that, before Passover, a pious Jew would give anything which was not kosher for Passover (chametz) to the rabbi for sale and collect it back after the festival was over from the titular new owner. It was a point of pride for the Beth Hamedresh that both the Beth Hamedresh members and a considerable number of the Englisher Shul congregation would bring their hametz to Rabbi Babad.

In 1952 there occurred yet again that event which epitomised the difference between the Beth Hamedresh and the average Anglo-Jewish community. Normally, Jewish study would be restricted to the occasional shiur, a visiting rabbi invited to speak from the pulpit and some lectures given by the rabbi, sometimes as often as once a week.

In July 1952 the complete study of the Babylonian Talmud was completed by Beth Hamedresh members for the third time. It had taken no less than 28 years on this occasion. Every weekday for over a quarter of a century, for half an hour between the afternoon and evening services, the rabbi led the study which was taken that little bit further on. It was Moshe Rabbinowitz who had been the rabbi when the vast enterprise began in the 1920s.

It says in the Bible that it is not your duty to finish the work, neither are you permitted to desist from it. Rabbi Babad completed the last part of the study, some years after Rabbi Rabbinowitz died. He was supported by members of the congregation, some of whom were present at the start, some who weren't born when it began, and in the absence of some who had died in the meantime. At the Reception to celebrate this historic achievement in its history, the Beth Hamedresh faithful were addressed by no less than nine rabbonim.

The Tyne & Wear communities still socialised and the girls and boys would join in the Maccabi meetings in Newcastle. An exception was that any daughter of the rabbi would not attend a mixed party after the age of 12. The fact that the communities enjoyed themselves together did not, however, mean that they were now religiously as one. With the appointment of Rabbi Turetsky at Ryhope Road, it was not long before there was a difference of opinion which, through general misunderstanding, did not reflect well on either congregation.

It was quite simple; the two rabbis set different times for the beginning and end of the sabbath and the festivals. The timings are based on the setting of the sun and this differs according to how far North or South you are. Sunderland wouldn't have the same time as London and Rabbi Turetsky and Rabbi Babad took it upon themselves to set the minutes and hours. As a consequence, there was the extremely odd situation on July 23rd 1954 that the sabbath started for the congregation of Ryhope Road at 8.30 on Friday evening and ended at 10.23 on Saturday evening. At Mowbray Road, 500 yards away, Rabbi Babad decreed that it started at 9 o'clock and ended at 10.30.

Charles Slater, the nephew of Jack and Kitty Cohen, who would become the long-time leader of the Sunderland Labour party, took up the cudgels in the *Jewish Chronicle* and poured scorn on the inability to agree. He posed the problem of congregants who belonged to both communities and at what time the kindling of lights at the end of the Sabbath should be observed. The fundamental problem seemed to be that both communities were still struggling for the religious high ground after more than 50 years. Charles Slater appealed for "the starting point of a change of outlook on the part of many who would do well to forget their animosity and cleanse themselves of deep-rooted prejudices."

What Charles Slater failed to realise was that there were different authorities who had made the case for when Shabbot and the Festivals should start and finish centuries before. Working out the time is a complicated study and Rabbi Nathan Bushwick explains the full background in his book *Understanding the Jewish calendar* (Moznaim Publishing, New York, 1989.) It seems unlikely that most of the critics had studied the subject which involves Molads and Chalokim and even the effects of the Molad Zoken. While we can rely on others, better versed in the subject, to decide on the rights and wrongs of the arguments of Rabbis Babad and Turetsky, they are different theological arguments rather than just trying to be more Orthodox than the other side. In fairness, it is not surprising that this went right over the heads of the majority of the lay members.

In 1956 Sol Novinski died in London and a memorial light was dedicated to his memory in the Intract Home. While the spotlight falls on Honorary Officers, it is the Sol Novinskis who make the committees work by many hours of unpaid labour. Another loss to the community was the death of the Krottingen born Arnold Levy, who died at 69 just before his book on the Sunderland Jewish congregations was published. Arnold Levy was Gershon Levy's son and, like his father, he worked untiringly for the Gateshead Yeshiva. He also served on the Board of Deputies for 35 years and, in national terms, he was a very important member of the Rubber industry and was the pioneer of their 45 hour, 5 day week.

A new kindergarten was started in 1958 by Rabbi Babad, Charles Gillis, Maurice Mincham and Chaim Pearlman, called the Menorah School. It was for children between the ages of 4 and 11 and it began life in one room for eight children, As it grew it continued to use the Beth Hamedresh in term time but it soon became popular enough to need its own building. Jackie Leach raised a lot of money by running a highly successful football pool and in 1961 it moved to Thornhill Park with four primary classes and 60 - 70 pupils.

The Head Mistress was the highly effective Jennie Shochet and Mrs. Zahn took responsibility for the Jewish Studies lessons. In the school curriculum Jewish Studies had a distinct role and were taught when the youngsters were fresh. It was in marked contrast to the necessary demands of a Talmud Torah which, perforce, had to hold its classes after school, and on Sundays when the children would very probably have preferred to be at play. In 1969 the Ministry of Education would recognize the Menorah as efficient, a grade of distinction almost unique for schools of its size.

The Chief Rabbi, Israel Brodie, came to open and dedicate the building. He went to Ryhope Road on Shabbot morning but attended the Beth Hamedresh for mincha on Shabbot afternoon and was the guest of honour at a Shalos Suedos, (the third meal of the sabbath). As Rabbi Babad was delighted to announce, every Jewish child now had a proper Jewish education. This applied even though the pupils were from an eclectic mix of non-observant and very observant families and as there were, perforce, mixed classes from a lack of numbers to make it a single sex school, Menorah required religious compromise from everybody. Rabbi Babad was happy for the children to get a sound Jewish education at an early stage in their lives, but he was not against them eventually finishing up at University. Today, in Chassidic circles, the authorities are not so sure. The challenges and temptations the students face are more challenging.

Financially, the school was supported by the Yavneh Foundation, part of the Jewish Agency, but the Menorah school governors allowed the Zionist Federation no say in the school curriculum. They even made sure that the Hatikvah, the Israeli National Anthem, wasn't sung at the school, but a considerable number of young Jews in Sunderland went on aliyah anyway. In all, more than 100 of the Beth Hamedresh community emigrated over the years.

1958 was also the Barmitzvah year of the Sunderland Talmudical College - the Yeshiva. It had 60 pupils; seven came from Britain, there was one Hungarian and everybody else was still from French or Spanish Morocco. It was also expected, though, that soon there would be a considerable influx from Iran. If you added to this that the teaching methods were still deeply rooted in the Lithuanian tradition, the international scope of talmudic training was amply illustrated. It was said that the only things more worn out than the carpets were the library books from constant use.

The thrust of the Talmudic teaching in the Yeshiva concentrated on learning in depth rather than the sheer amount of ground covered. The philosophy of the Yeshiva was not that all work and no play makes Jacob a dull boy, but it had no facilities for physical training or recreation. Football was played against the local Jewish team, but the Yeshiva players were at a considerable disadvantage, as they had to stop if their yarmulke fell off in order to retrieve it!

1948 Sunderland Jewish Football Team

Charlie Kolson, Bernard Morris, Phivie Pearlman, Hymie Brechner, Norman Pollack, Wilf Book, Charlie Marks, Tom Book
Leonard Book (Boy), Syd Leslie, Addy Van de Velde, Alan Foreman, Harry Black, David Rosenthal

Only Yeshivah footballers wore Yarmalkes

There was, however, an annual camp in the summer. A friendly member of the Durham Agricultural Executive Committee had a farm and provided free tents, paliasses, ground sheets, blankets, table and beds for the students. In return they worked for the local farmers, helping to bring in the harvest. It was definitely a win-win situation; everybody benefited.

In those 13 years more than 200 graduates had left the Yeshiva to bolster the religious knowledge of communities all over the world. Of the 30 graduates in the last few years, six had become rabbis and 17 had gone home to North Africa as teachers. From Chief Rabbis in South America to school teachers back in Morocco, to shochtim and mohelim in Europe and the United States, the Yeshiva had a record of which to be proud.

At the dinner Rabbi Babad produced a felicitous analogy when comparing the Yeshiva with Sunderland, talking of the symbolic connection between coal and the Yeshiva as a power house of yiddishkeit. What he couldn't foresee was that the coalfields would become economically non-violable while the Yeshiva would continue to provide light to the world-wide Jewish community. Rabbi Toperoff, speaking for the Englisher Shul, pointed out an extra advantage obtained from the Yeshiva. He said it instilled in the whole community a reverence for learning and a stricter adherence to Jewish observance, which, of course, was absolutely right.

To mark the 20th anniversary of Mowbray Road, the whole building was redecorated in 1958, thanks to the donation of £1,000 by the members. Even then, the expenditure for the year exceeded the income. The main structural alteration was the levelling of the sloping floor in the Ladies Gallery. A rail with metal scrollwork was fixed to the front of the gallery, which was a discreet improvement. It was later changed to a higher wood parapet. One newcomer to the community that year was the Rev. Beril Lewin, who took on the roles of Chazan, Shochet, Teacher and Mohel. Another event was the revival of the Bnai Brith Lodge which had remained dormant since 1938.

The additional question, however, was now the kosher status of the kitchen equipment the community had used and which was still in their homes. This is also covered, however, in the din. The rule is that if there is more kosher meat than non-kosher sold in the shop, then all the kitchen equipment can be considered kosher. Except that used for liver which was all deemed non-kosher. If the Beth Hamedresh community were highly embarrassed, they had at least done their best with a prompt damage limitation exercise, while feeling sore at some members of the local Kollel, who had had their suspicions many months earlier, without informing the community.

As the 1960s dawned, the influence of the Yeshiva, to which Rev. Toperoff had referred, began to affect the community's viewpoint on a number of topics. Lax practices which had been acceptable, now began to be questioned. Rabbi Babad felt it was now possible, for example, to condemn mixed dancing at weddings, though he did so diplomatically from the distant platform of the meeting in Leeds in December 1960. He said: "According to Jewish law it was quote immoral for married men and women to dance with anyone but their respective partners." It had, however, taken him more than 10 years to criticise Sunderland weddings on these grounds.

When Rev. Toperoff moved on, his successor, Rabbi Ephraim Gastwirth, assured the *Jewish Chronicle* in 1960 that relations with the Beth Hamedresh were excellent and "the matter referred to in your report was no more than a friendly exchange of opinions." The matter in question was whether Rabbi Gastwirth should sell chometz at Passover. While this mitzva can be performed by any rabbi, a number of members of the Hebrew Congregation had preferred to sell their chometz to Rabbi Babad. It was a practice carried out normally by only the more Orthodox and they were more akin to Rabbi Babad. Also he had been for some years the recognized head of the Board of Shechita.

Rabbi Gastwirth asked Rabbi Babad out of courtesy whether he would have any objections to Rabbi Gastwirth fulfilling the same function. Rabbi Babad made it very clear that he would, insisting that it was, by custom, the prerogative of the Beth Hamedresh. There is a thin line between local custom - minhag - and the din, but Rabbi Babad certainly had no authority in Jewish law to stop any member of either community selling the chometz to whichever rabbi he chose.

Rabbi Babad's dependence on minhag would lead to more serious consequences within a few years.

The Ryhope Road Synagogue built 1928
"the Englishe Shul"

Chapter 10
The Babad succession

Meanwhile, in 1960 there arrived in Sunderland Rabbi Chanoch Ehrentreu to be the head of the Kollel. As a Kollel is for married men who want to continue to study the Talmud after they have finished at Yeshiva, it requires an exceptionally able talmudic head because, in university terms, its students are all studying for Ph.Ds.

In Rabbi Ehrentreu the Sunderland Kollel found the right candidate. Ehrentreu came from a rabbinic family. His father, Rabbi Yisroel Ehrentreu had served the Manchester community - and his son, Chanoch, had been rescued at the last minute from Nazi Germany when he arrived in England on Rabbi Solomon Schonfeld's Kindertransport in 1939. He was only six when war broke out and was evacuated with the other pupils at the Jewish Secondary School in North London to Shefford in Buckinghamshire. He well remembers the hospitality of the foster family who took him and his brother in, but even at such an early age, he warned his sibling that he couldn't eat the fried eggs which had been cooked for them because they weren't kosher.

Rabbi Ehrentreu went on to the Gateshead Yeshiva and graduated at the Institute for Higher Rabbinic Studies. He had been brought up in the Lithuanian Yeshiva tradition, which meant that his studies were very deep and analytical. It was considered that the Chassidic approach was not as thoughtful, and it was in the Lithuanian way that he ran the Kollel.

Even as a young man Ehrentreu was a very impressive figure. He did not go in for the absent minded professor, heimische, rumpled appearance. A crease in his immaculate dress would only have been there to be removed. Even today, when he is nearly 80, it is necessary to put your brain into overdrive if you want to keep up with his lightning thought processes. His wife, too, was very popular, teaching at the Cheder and always ready to help the community in any way she could.

In 1968 there were only 12 men studying at the Kollel but then higher talmudic study was never a mass movement. Producing sufficient experts of a high quality was considered more important than educating a large number of less qualified students. The sheer existence of the Kollel gave an example to the Yeshiva students of what they could attain, just as a graduate student can see the possibility of obtaining a doctorate.

The Kollel students were initially very much self-contained and hardly communicated with the outside world while they studied. At a meeting of the Chevra Kedushah there was once an appeal for them to set out to interface more with the other members of the Jewish community which they took to heart. At the time the President of the Beth Hamedresh, Dr. Ernie Gillis, promised that the suggestion would receive 'serious consideration' from his Council, but its influence on the running of the Kollel would have been very limited.

By the early 1960s, the original world of the Beth Hamedresh tally men had changed greatly, though there were still similarities. A lot of the community was engaged in the furniture industry, both in its manufacturing and retail side. Since the introduction of Hire Purchase, it had become possible for poorer people to furnish their homes by paying for the goods over a year or two. This was really the tally man system extended to products of greater value. The small Jewish furniture companies in Sunderland were, however, now coming under pressure from the chain stores and would shortly have to face the introduction of supermarkets and shopping centres. People would look back nostalgically to the days when "the business was frequently in court for obstructing the pavement, but it was obviously worth paying the fines, for goods were soon outside the shop again to attract customers."

With the younger generation wanting something better from their lives than running a small shop, increasingly there was nobody to carry on the business when the older generation had had enough. The small furniture manufacturers also started to fail although at one time they constituted the second biggest industry in Sunderland. In time Winburn & Sons, M. Davis & Sons, Linskills, B. Bernstein & Co., Isaac Brewer and Stan Goldberg were just some of the Jewish companies which closed their doors.

In addition, however, to the members who remained businessmen, there were also a growing number of Jewish professionals in Sunderland; Doctors and Specialists, Lawyers and Dentists, Accountants, and Pharmacists. Rabbi Ehrentreu decided to start giving a weekly shiur designed for Doctors and Lawyers. Jewish law is not identical to any other system and Jewish medical ethics have significant differences from British law as well. While the rule is always to follow the practice in the country in which you live, there are many instances when Jewish law can be applied where British law is not involved.

Jewish law on transplants is another area where study is necessary to understand the din. Contraception is acceptable in Jewish law but only in certain circumstances and in certain ways. Rashi's grandson had said that a woman could wear a contraceptive device many hundreds of years before; time became meaningless; it's like referring to the continuing authority of Magna Carta, only over a much longer period. Much of Jewish medical and legal law was, of course, massively ahead of the ruling civilizations of biblical times and it still provides valuable insights into the correct approach to many moral and ethical dilemmas.

Relations between the Hebrew Congregation and the Beth Hamedresh continued to be correct and in 1964, when the Hebrew Congregation minister accepted the appointment of Director of Jewish Studies at Carmel College, a prestigious Jewish boarding school, Chaim Pearlman presented him with a pair of silver candlesticks on behalf of the Beth Hamedresh.

It wasn't easy to finance a Kollel either and in his last years Rabbi Babad and the young head would travel widely to find benefactors. Sir Isaac Wolfson of Great Universal Stores, a tallyman writ large, donated an entire library to the Kollel in memory of his parents. The Sunderland community were generous as well but both the students' application to study and the money to keep the Kollel going made heavy demands. Unusually for Sunderland the members of the Kollel suffered from abuse from hooligans in the area, but dislike of strangers is not confined to any particular group, as the experiences of Catholics and Protestants in Northern Ireland would starkly illustrate in the years to come and in a much more virulent form.

It was remarkable that a small provincial community could boast the talmudically eminent Rabbi Babad, the Sunderland Talmudical College under Rabbonim Zahn, Gelley and Lopian, and the Kollel under Rabbi Ehrentreu. No wonder that in Orthodox circles around the world, the name of Sunderland was well known and admired. Rabbi Babad once reflected on the community:

> Secession may not always appear commendable, yet the history of the flourishing Jewish community in Sunderland has shown that the act of secession 'perpetrated' by a few stubborn Jews from abroad some 60 years ago, who established the Beth Hamedrresh, was an act that proved beneficial to the community. It has proved that consistency, perseverance and sometimes even obstinacy and fighting spirit, on behalf of traditional Judaism can only result in healthy survival.

Behind the scenes, though, a lot of hard work was done, as ever, by the shul Ladies Committee, particularly in raising money for charity. The Rebbitzin was the President, Doreen Gillis was the Chair and Lottie Zahn's acted as Vice Chair. The Yeshiva Ladies Committee was run by Leah Cohen and Phyllis Pearlman.

Rabbi Babad's good humour didn't desert him as the years passed. There was once a discussion on the difficulty of getting a minyan in the winter for morning services at 7 o'clock in the morning. The suggestion was made that a later start would encourage more people to get out of bed and brave the weather. Rabbi Babad commented "If you start at 9 o'clock there will still be 10 Jews in Sunderland who haven't dovened!"

In the Beth Hamedresh the old customs continued to be strictly maintained. For example, fasting, as part of the plea to the Almighty for the forgiveness of sins, is at the heart of Yom Kippur. There are other occasions, however, when fasts exist for the same purpose, though they are not as universally observed. Two are for three days on Mondays and Thursdays in the Hebrew months of Iyar and Cheshvan. They are to atone for sins committed during Passover and Succot. A special prayer was said in the Beth Hamedresh on the sabbath before the fasts began, and whoever answered "Amen" would be taken to have agreed to fast.

In later years the fast days in Iyar would sometimes cover Israel Independence Day and it became the custom to sing the joyful prayers of Hallel to celebrate the state coming into existence. In the Beth Hamedresh about a third of the congregation said the prayers for fasting (selichot), another third the Hallel prayers and another third clapped loudly. When asked why they were clapping, the reply from the Rabbi was that this was the traditional split on such occasions; three different approaches to cover all possibilities.

There remained family traditions of service to the Beth Hamedresh. For many years, for example, the Black family provided the wine for Kiddush and Havdolah on Shabbot. It was Harry Black's generosity at the time and he was following in the footsteps of his father and grandfather.

Beth Hamedresh

The Abraham and Dulcie Merskey Hall

No mixed dancing at any time

When the massive Adelphi Hotel in Liverpool was opened, its Chairman said what a great help it would be to the development of tourism in the city's economy. Unfortunately, it opened in March 1914 and in August 1914 the First World War broke out, which ended Liverpool tourism for the foreseeable future. There were overtones of this kind of unforeseen disaster in the building of the Abraham and Dulcie Merskey Hall at the Beth Hamedresh in 1964. It was financed by Abraham Merskey at a cost of £6,500 as a memorial to his wife and it made a very good setting for the community's functions. It would now be expected that men would cover their heads when using the hall at functions and there would only be kosher milk and drinks served. Mr. Merskey was presented with a silver cake dish, Cyril Gillis, the architect was given a table lighter and Rabbi Babad now gave clear instructions at the outset that there was to be no mixed dancing in the hall.

In the past, while the food was always kosher, wines were allowed from any country because it isn't easy to make wine that isn't kosher. The change to kosher wines was a boon, of course, for the Israeli wine industry, which, in fairness, was improving its products. One non-Jewish wine importer had produced a book some years earlier describing and commenting on the world's wines. There were pages and pages for the French varieties but when it came to Israeli products, there was but one line: "Israeli wines are drunk for sentimental rather than oenological reasons."!

Many other members contributed to the upkeep of the synagogue. In that same 1964 there was new carpeting laid down in the shul and the President recorded in the Annual Report that: "We're grateful to Mr. Charles Gillis for securing the carpet on very favourable terms and to Mr. I. J. Charlton for defraying the cost of preparation and laying." Even with such help, the overdraft continued to rise, though a collection in 1963 had improved matters.

As had the decision not to replace the Chazan. Unfortunately, what was looming on the horizon, though it couldn't be predicted, were events which might make all the investments superfluous to requirements.

Relations with the general non-Jewish Sunderland community remained excellent, though there were occasional difficulties. In 1967, for example, the increased emphasis on Health and Safety led to the Council considering forbidding the use of kerbstones in cemeteries. It was considered a possible danger for pedestrians as they might trip over them. From the Jewish community's point of view, such an ordinance would be highly undesirable as there would be less protection for the graves and, therefore, there would be a greater likelihood of "walking over desecration" which the kerbstones helped to prevent. Jews feel awkward walking over the gravestones you can find in the aisles of many cathedrals. On a less contentious occasion the Sunderland Library system was presented with 32 books for its Anglo-Judaica section.

Rabbi Babad continued with his Agudas Yisroel responsibilities. In January 1965 when the European Executive met in London, the subject of reparations from Germany came up again. The Agudas wanted representation on the Memorial Foundation for Jewish Culture which was funded with German money.

The Rabbi's work load continued to cover the Beth Hamedresh affairs and the national scene. It was hard work but it was coming to an end. In 1965, Rabbi Babad fell desperately ill and was diagnosed with inoperable lung cancer. He was only middle aged and his thoughts went particularly to the future financial position of his wife after his inevitable death. It was true that his wife's brother was a very rich man, but Babad felt that it was up to the community to look after his widow, rather than to rely on her relations. He also had a 17 year old son who he believed should be able to succeed him and he wanted to try to make that acceptable to the community before he passed away. On March 1st 1966 he wrote a letter to the congregation.

> To my Friends the President and Honorary Officers, Member of the Council and to all the Members of the Sunderland Beth Hamedresh.
>
> Friends,
>
> You will appreciate that I am writing this letter in the most fervent hope that the occasion with which it deals will never arise.
>
> In my own humble opinion for close on 19 years (March 47 - December 65) I served your community to the best of my ability. I take pleasure in the thought that in the course of my stay in your midst a mutual friendship has developed which I hope will be of a lasting nature. I am ill at the moment but hope and pray to return to you in sufficiently good health to continue to enjoy my duties and privileges in your midst. The ways of Providence however are not known to us and our fate is in the hands of [G-d.]

I am writing to you now to tell you how much it means to me to feel confident that you will, in case of need, take care of my wife.

I have no doubt that the people of [the community] will follow Jewish Tradition according to which a son is the natural successor to public office held by his father, provided of course that he is reasonably capable to fill such a post. My Son is only 17 now (at the time of writing) and I am confident that within a few years he will be able to obtain [semicha] from authoritative traditional [rabbis] who will testify to his ability to be a Rav.

In my own humble opinion he is a promising young scholar.

In the interregnum, my Son-in-law who is an outstanding [rabbi] and a man of very high qualities generally, as you all know, is fully prepared to bridge the gap and I have no doubt he will fill the post admirably, with the help of God, until such time as my Son will be able to take up the post. This is to the best of my knowledge in accordance with Jewish Tradition and custom.

My friends, I am highly appreciative of all your kindness to me and I thank you one and all for everything you have done for me. I do hope that you will fulfil this my last and most fervent wish.

I raise my hands in prayer to [God] who has guided us all these years that He will continue to guide you in the preservation of Jewish Tradition as handed over to you by your forebears. May He continue to help you to upkeep the [commandments] as a Tower of light and strength for the preservation of Yiddishkeit.

May [God] grant you all long and happy lives, much naches and joy in your private lives and may the [Beth Hamedresh] go from strength to strength.

Yours most sincerely,
A Babad.

It was a humble and gentle plea from such an eminent rabbi but what Rabbi Babad asked for was dynamite.

Knowing that he was dying, Rabbi Babad asked Rabbi Zahn to accompany him as he went one last time to the synagogue to say good-bye. He kissed all the sifrei toroh and remembered all the good times that he had enjoyed over the years he had served the community. He died on March 31st at the age of 57 but the effects of his letter lived on for the next 15 years. At the memorial service there were eulogies by his son-in-law Rabbi Ben-Zion Rabinovitch, Rabbi Rakow from Gateshead, Rabbi Zahn and Rabbi Gurwicz. Summing up his life's work, it was said that "He was one of the last remaining bridges between the sages of Israel of pre-war Europe and the present generation."

It is not unknown for a son to succeed his father and do just as good a job. A Prince of Wales after a King and the Younger Pitt after the Elder Pitt are two examples. The difference was that Rabbi Babad's son was only 17. There was no guarantee that he'd even get semicha though, in the event, he became a most learned rabbi. The second problem was that the community had basked in Rabbi Babad's national fame for many years, and to go back to obscurity with a youngster was not an attractive alternative.

Rabbi Babad was going to be a very hard act to follow. If you only take into account the funeral orations, though, it is possible to get a hagiographic and very biased opinion of the deceased. It is as well to balance such praise with the views of someone who didn't like his views. Ben Azai, a columnist in the *Jewish Chronicle* gave a balanced judgement after the rabbi died

> He was an uncompromising Agudist and I was often appalled by the extremeness of his views, but I knew them to be accompanied by infinite compassion and a sense of humour reflected both in the glint in his eyes and the wit of his utterances. For an unworldly man he had a worldly way of expressing himself and he was a master of the English phrase, pithy, balancing and biting....what was a rav with such rigid views doing in a Lithuanian shtetl transplanted to an English shore with its easy going Lithuanian ways and irreverent attitudes. Although few presumed to live up to his standards, he was regarded with an awe not far short of worship.'Rabbi Babad is the apology for our shortcomings" I was told. The fine name which Sunderland enjoys is partly a reflection of his name.

The journalist was from Latvia originally and his reference to "easy going" and "irreverent attitude" would have been severely questioned in the Beth Hamedresh community. Still, This was the man, Rabbi Babad, who wanted his 17 year old son to succeed him. His position as Chief of the European Agudist World Executive needed to go to someone as eminent as Rabbi Leib Gurwicz of Gateshead. Yet here was Rabbi Babad asking from the grave for his Beth Hamedresh position to be kept open for some years for someone at present without qualifications.

After the rabbi's funeral the Council called a special meeting for April 10th. The easy bit was to tell the treasurer to pay Mrs. Babad sufficient money for her needs, up to the salary of her late husband. What was to happen in the way of a pension, capital sum or annuity was far more difficult "in face of complicated tax contingencies." The minutes are not more explicit.

When the question of the succession came up, the Council didn't know whether the wishes of Rabbi Babad were binding on them as being din, or whether they were a minhag, only reflecting a Chassidic tradition. This was obviously a very important point. When Rabbi Babad had first been appointed, it was well known that he came from a Chassidic background. The ethos of the Beth Hamedresh was not, of course, Chassidic but very strongly linked to the non-Chassidic Lithuanian tradition.

Rabbi Babad had understood this and ensured that it did not create a problem in the way he conducted his ministry. Now, however, the Chassidic background came right to the fore and the council rejected it, under the Chairmanship of Chaim Pearlman. The next rabbi "it was generally felt, in the absence of a Halachic ruling to the contrary, should not be subject to an automatic family succession, irrespective of who the finally decided candidate should be." That, after all, had been the decision when Rabbi Rabbinowitz died.

That was all very well but the late rabbi had taken that decision out of the hands of the leaders of the Beth Hamedresh. By distributing the letter so widely, there was no chance of a knowledge of its contents being confined to a small circle like the Council. Everybody would know of the wishes of the rabbi and that meant that every candidate for the post would be told as well. In such circumstances, every rabbi would withdraw his candidature when he knew the facts. In Orthodox circles you didn't ignore the clearly stated wishes of your predecessor and a candidate of the necessary ability would not seek to put his head into a hornet's nest, because the congregation couldn't reach anything like a consensus on the subject.

It is the opinion of Rabbi Ehrentreu, the former head of the Kollel and later the head of the London Beth Din, that Rabbi Babad's wishes were, halachically, not binding on the Beth Hamedresh. Dayan Ehrentreu was, however, a young man at the time and not involved in the arguments. A temporary executive had taken it upon themselves to break a long and highly regarded tradition of the community. They asked for the views of the London Beth Din. The council members felt this action was beyond the executives authority. Criticism poured on to the heads of this unfortunate group and they resigned as one body. The Council decided to reconvene on April 24th. Things had become a little clearer. First, £700 was paid to the family to settle the late Rabbi's bills for medical expenses during his last illness. That is the equivalent in today's money of £20,000. Then it was agreed that Mrs. Babad could remain in the house with which the congregation had provided the family, until the end of September, with the Beth Hamedresh paying all the expenses except the telephone bill. After that Mrs. Babad was offered either a pension of £10 a week (about £285 today) or a lump sum of £5,000 (over £140,000 today). Of course the problem with either offer was that their value would be depreciated by inflation and, though it couldn't be foreseen, there would be massive inflation in a few years time.

After much further discussion it was decided "that the Beth Hamedresh be free to select any candidate for the office of Rav as it may so desire." The voting in favour of that resolution was 9-4 and that meant the community was seriously split on the subject. It was, of course, open to Rabbi Babad's son-in-law, Rabbi Benzion Rabbinowitz to question the decision at a Din Torah, that Jewish court where highly qualified talmudists could hand down an official decision. It had happened before David Rabbinowitz (no relation) was appointed in 1913, but until the problem was thrashed out, as would become clear to the Council, no rabbi would accept the job.

The question was what to do in the meantime and the congregation was fortunate that they had within their midst a rabbi who was prepared to undertake all the duties of their religious head without asking for the title. This, of course, was Rabbi Zahn, the head of the Yeshiva. There was really nothing that Rabbi Zahn wasn't fully qualified to do. He presided at marriages, funerals, brissim etc, but there was one ceremonial act he completely rejected. He wouldn't sit in the rabbi's chair in the synagogue.

Some of the burdens he was able to transfer to Rev. M. Berdugo who was appointed in 1966 to be Chazan, Shochet and a teacher in the Talmud Torah. Rabbi Ehrentreu agreed to take over the Blatt, helped by Rabbonim Kahn, Lopian and Kauffman. There were also members of the community who were quite capable of giving shiurim and were asked to do so; David Pearlman, Ruby Rabbinowitz and young Benjamin Cohen, to name but a few. The Pearlmans and the Cohens were now the 4th generation to have worshipped in the synagogue.

Rabbi Zahn's influence was always exercised towards maintaining harmony between the two Sunderland congregations. In 1970 he was instrumental in the setting up of a Joint Co-ordinating Council for the Promotion of Communal Unity. The Jewish world in Britain was changing, though, and the effects could be seen particularly clearly in Sunderland. The chief change was a steady growth in the polarization within the community.

Until the refugees arrived from Eastern Europe between the 1880s and 1914, the British community was very middle of the road; it was Orthodox but its standards of observance were not very high. The arrival of the refugees did not change the approach of the community, for while there was an increase in the number of more observant communities - like the Beth Hamedresh - the leadership remained with the Chief Rabbi and the United Synagogue. The arrival of the refugees from Nazi Germany in the 1930s strengthened both the very Orthodox communities - like Gateshead - and also the Reform section, as many of the refugees were well educated German Reform leaders.

Now, from the 1960s onwards, the polarization grew apace. The *Jewish Chronicle* columnist was reflecting what was probably the majority view. The position now was more and more that either the Orthodox became more Orthodox or they drifted to the Reform and Liberal communities or drifted right out of the faith. Intermarriage increased to a great extent, so that the total community has sunk from around 400,000 at its post-war peak to less than 300,000 in recent years.

The growth of Gateshead and the work of Rabbi Ehrentreu and Rabbi Zahn with the Sunderland Yeshiva, make Sunderland a microcosm for the change in the Orthodox communities. The Beth Hamedresh became more observant than ever. They were keeping up with the standards of the Yeshiva and the Yeshiva was careful to keep up with the standards being set in Gateshead. Its critics would dismiss this as a competition for who could be "holier than thou" but this is to demean a genuine attempt by most of the congregation to live more in accordance with the dictates of the mitzvot. Many of the next generation, influenced by the even more extensive Jewish education they received, persuaded their parents in the same direction.

The effect on the relationship between the Beth Hamedresh and the Hebrew Congregation was not always beneficial. There were members of the Beth Hamedresh who were not slow to criticise the less stringent approach of the Ryhope Road congregation. They, for their part, did not want to apply the same degree of religious discipline to the way they lived their lives. They might dismiss the practices of the Beth Hamedresh as extreme, old fashioned, fanatical or out-of-date. The atmosphere became strained at the senior level in the synagogues. Obviously, the family members might belong to one or both. They would normally remain on good terms with each other socially, but there were more snide remarks than had been the case in the past.

Take as an example the relative position of men and women at a wedding. In all Orthodox congregations the men and women sit separately in the synagogue. But what about at the Reception afterwards? The first answer would be to sit together with your husband. That was the United Synagogue approach. The next arrangement in a more Orthodox community would be to sit with your husband on one side, but another lady on your other side. So the seating would be man, man, woman, woman, man, man etc. Then it moved on to all the men sitting together on one side of the table with the ladies sitting opposite them. The final separation of the sexes in the most Orthodox receptions would be to have the ladies sitting on different tables from the men. As the Orthodox moved to new levels of Orthodoxy, the gap between them and the United Synagogue members became greater and greater.

In many other areas of everyday life, the distinctions grew as well. The middle-of-the-road Jews had been in the ascendancy for so long, that many of them resented their likely future as a minority within the overall community. The Orthodox families had large numbers of children where the United Synagogue families were not reproducing their own numbers. Admittedly, the future of the community as a whole was being safeguarded by the very Orthodox - their children didn't marry out to anything like the same extent and there were more of them - but laisser faire Judaism was representing a far smaller percentage of the Jewish population than it had for centuries.

The religious standards of Sunderland Jewry appeared to have an effect on the Jewish students at the Sunderland Polytechnic. Their membership was very low and efforts were made to find out the problem. One student, when asked, why he didn't join, referred to 'the community's terrifying Orthodoxy which keeps many away." The *Jewish Chronicle* sprang to the defence of the Rosh Yeshiva, Rabbi Zahn.

> Certainly 'terrifying' would be a most inappropriate description for Sunderland's venerable and benign Rosh Yeshiva. Rabbi Shammai Zahn, through whose resourceful hands thousands of young men have graduated in England to become teachers, ministers, shochetim and communal leaders in Britain and overseas.

Naturally, Rabbi Babad's death was also a loss for the *Jewish Tribune* which had been founded as a triumvirate by Rabbi Babad, Elchanon Liff and Simcha Unsdorfer. With hindsight it seemed a most unlucky publication, as the rabbi died in 1965, Elchanon Liff in 1966 and Simcha Unsdorfer in 1967, when he was only 43 years old. They must have been an exceptional trio because the same *Jewish Chronicle* writer said of Simcha Unsdorfer:

> He settled here at a mature age, yet acquired an extraordinary grasp of English and there were times when he could make even the Agudist creed seem not unreasonable.

Within the wider Sunderland community there was a well deserved knighthood for Jack Cohen. In 1967 Abraham Merskey died, the donator of the Merskey Hall and a former Chairman of the Yeshiva Building Committee.

Another of Chatze Cohen's sons finally passed away at the ripe old age of 91. Isaac Cohen had come from Krottingen with his father and had grown up to be a stalwart of the Sunderland community all his life. He wrote 300 typed pages about his experiences in both towns, which remains a fine example of Yesterday's Witness.

Like Florence Nightingale, Isaac Cohen was always ailing and sure that the end of his days was nigh. His book is full of dire prognostications of the results of his failing health but he still made it into his nineties and had the pleasure of seeing that his lifelong work for Zionism came to fruition.

Rabbis Zahn, Dayan C Ehrentreu, Isaac Brewer and Jack Mendoza

Consecration of the Sifrei Torah from West Hartlepool at the Old Age Home

Congregations may die but the Sifrei Toarah lasts for centuries

The 1967 war in the Middle East turned out to be a quick and brilliant victory for the Israelis, but that can be seen with hindsight. As war appeared ever more likely, the Beth Hamedresh members instituted a programme of prayer and fasting. There was, of course, a collection for Israel and three members went there during the fighting to replace Kibbutz members who had gone to join their units.

One local casualty of these years was the Literary Society. The ever-growing popularity of television made the Lit's events less attractive and, with attendances ever dropping, it was decided that the Lit had come to the end of its useful life. On the other hand, the post-war Menorah School was continuing to receive excellent reports from the Schools Inspectorate and the new Chief Rabbi, Immanuel Jakobovits was happy to come up to Sunderland to be the guest of honour at the school's 10th anniversary dinner. The visit of the Chief Rabbi was marked by a civic reception where he was welcomed by the mayor and he came to the Beth Hamedresh for the evening service.

It would have pleased Rabbi Moshe Rabbinowitz that the Chief Rabbi also consecrated the new central bimah at Ryhope Road. After 30 years, the new bimah had been built in its traditional place in the shul. Now any Orthodox rabbi would be happy to worship there.

Financially, the congregation were not doing too badly. Ironically, it helped not to have to pay a rabbi. It continued to guard its independence, even after it received a plea from the Chief Rabbi to join the other Orthodox synagogues under his aegis. The Chief Rabbi explained that he felt that the very Orthodox Beth Hamedresh would be a good example to the other synagogues acknowledging his leadership.

The Beth Hamedresh Council had a lot of time for the Chief Rabbi, who was an eminent talmudist and came very much from their background. Indeed, one of his daughters had married a boy from the Beth Hamedresh. They argued the case for a long time but, eventually, they decided that the threat to their independence which could come from such an association was too much of a risk. If, however, the Beth Hamedresh continued their policy of seceding from their original agreement to accept the authority of the Chief Rabbinate of Hermann Adler, they were about to suffer from a defection of their own.

The problem was the membership of the Kollel. These men who devoted their lives to study were role models for the Yeshiva students. They were the men who were prepared to go the extra mile. In the 1960s and '70s however, when they looked at recent developments in the national culture, alarm bells started ringing very loudly. The nation's morals and moral outlook were changing - and they believed for the worse. What the majority of the population considered the liberalisation of old-fashioned laws, the members of the Kollel, like the community in Gateshead, saw as a decline into serious sin.

There were many examples; the Wolfenden report which led to the decriminalisation of homosexual acts between consenting adults. The invention of the pill, which removed the danger of an unwelcome birth from premarital sex. What Rabbi Rakow was recognising as a serious threat to accepted Orthodox philosophy, was equally concerning the Kollel down the road.

The Kollel members started to pull down the shutters and put up the barricades. How could they protect their children from the new influences which they believed could corrupt them? Starting near home, they recognized that the children at the Menorah school, where their own small children were educated, might not have parents taking the same views they did. If they made friends, would their children be encouraged to adopt different standards? The Kollel members recognized that the new cultural norms were attractive, in that they relaxed prohibitions and reduced any feelings of guilt. Indulgence was not criticised as it had been.

There was another problem, as they saw it. The new school might be acceptable for the children of Rabbi Zahn and the other rabbonim, but its high standards of Orthodox teaching were still the cause of criticism within the Kollel, who wanted them higher still. So the Kollel members tried to start a new school for their own children, only there weren't enough of them and the effort was doomed to failure. At the same time, while their school existed, it weakened the Menorah by reducing its school roll. When they gave up the idea of a separate school, Kollel members didn't admit they had made a mistake in giving up a good local Jewish school by returning to it. Instead they started to bus their children to the schools in Gateshead.

The inconvenience of this led to the question of whether it was better to live in Sunderland near the Kollel and bus the children, or live in Gateshead and bus the men to the Kollel. Many decided on the latter route. The Yeshiva students then started to wonder whether they might be happier living in Gateshead as well. Where they were a tiny minority in Sunderland, there would be far more similarly minded in Gateshead. The question was whether they would be allowed to move. Because the result of moving would be, of course, that they would not be in Sunderland for the sabbath or yomtovim.

Furthermore, the members of the Kollel and the Yeshiva did a lot of good work for all kinds of Jewish endeavours. They could lein the torah, read the weekly portion of the law in synagogue, if a regular was unwell. They were often part of the Chevra Kadisha, helping with burials. They could teach barmitzvahs and help with youth activities. If they were to live in Gateshead, they would start to become divorced from the Sunderland community.

They approached Rabbi Zahn and Rabbi Ehrentreu. Could they go and still stay at the Yeshiva and the Kollel. The two rabbis recognized that, for the Sunderland community, it would be a retrograde step, but there was both a Yeshiva and a Kollel in Gateshead. If they stopped their students living in Gateshead, all they had to do was switch their academic alma mater.

It was agreed that those who wanted to live in Gateshead and study in Sunderland could do so. It was the thin end of the wedge. It was almost bound to lead to the closure of both the Kollel and the Yeshiva in Sunderland. Within a few years, Rabbi Ehrentreu moved on to the Manchester Beth Din and later to head the London Beth Din. In the 1980s the Sunderland Kollel was no longer in Sunderland and the Yeshiva had moved itself to Gateshead where it is still known as the Sunderland Yeshivah. The Kollel members had large families. Those children had they continued to provide for the Menorah, would have been important in maintaining the viability of the school. Without them, the school was doomed to eventually close.

Synagogue communities don't disappear overnight in a democracy. It takes years for them to wind down and there is always the hope that, as with Dickens' Mr. Macawber, something will turn up. There are a number of Jewish communities in Britain today who are in the same position, although, in fairness, other long-dead communities, like Exeter, have taken on a new lease of life as new jobs and opportunities appear. Unfortunately, the position is Sunderland as the Sixties drew to a close was that this was very unlikely to happen.

Chapter 11
The end of the story

It would always be a great mistake to underestimate Rabbi Zahn. Behind the modesty, the charm and the flexibility there was a very shrewd brain indeed. One example of this occurred on the 25th anniversary of the creation of the Yeshiva, which came in 1971. One of the most generous supporters of all the very Orthodox charities in the North East was the Hubert family. So it was not surprising that Arthur Hubert was invited to be Guest of Honour at the Yeshiva's Silver Jubilee celebration. In due course the benefactor offered to make a handsome donation to the organization - and Rabbi Zahn turned it down. He managed to negotiate and double the original offer but not before he had given his supporters some very worrying moments. Only then did Rabbi Zahn accept it. As he said to his staff "Don't tell me how to collect money!" It was well known that when Rabbi Zahn made the appeal for charitable support for Israel, the response was usually better than on those occasions when the community was approached by the official JIA (The Joint Israel Appeal.)

Rabbi Zahn's general appeal was also founded on his generous and positive attitude to the problems that crossed his path. When his father-in-law died, his mother-in-law came to live with his family until she, too, passed away. Although the very Orthodox no longer had television sets in their homes for fear of their youth being corrupted by some of the programmes, his mother-in-law enjoyed hers and nobody raised a fuss about setting the children a bad example. When she died, Rabbi Zahn's youngest son was most upset and Lottie Zahn, with a twinkle in her eye, said that maybe the tears for grandma were a little mixed with regret that the television was departing with the cortege.

By nature Rabbi Zahn was not judgmental but on one subject he was very clear. There are 613 mitzvot in Judaism and the question was posed to him of who would go to heaven; would it be the Jew who had kept 612 out of the 613 or the Jew who had kept one. Rabbi Zahn chose the Jew who had only kept one! His rationale was that the Jew who kept 612 tried to argue that the last was not important. The Jew who only kept one was at least making an effort and didn't deny that the others mattered.

Perhaps the most contentious problem within Jewry as a whole remains the question of conversion. If someone decides that they believe in the Almighty and in Judaism, there is no major obstacle to them being converted. On the other hand, if the application is in order to get married to a Jew, with the consequent concomitant religious observances as something of an afterthought, that is not acceptable in any way to the Orthodox. One of the most serious arguments between the Progressive and Orthodox sections of the community today is over the question of how rigourous should be the conversion procedures. While there is no ban to conversion to a Charedi community, the demands are more stringent than with the Progressives.

In Rabbi Zahn's case, there was a lady who applied for conversion and the Gateshead Rav praised her as a modern day Ruth; a book in the Bible about a genuine convert. Now, to learn the performance of the mitzvot a potential convert to the Beth Hamedresh had to live with an Orthodox family for a considerable period of time. This particular lady was welcomed into Rabbi Zahn's home, was converted in due course and joined the Beth Hamedresh.

On another occasion a prostitute was murdered and it was suggested that she might have been Jewish. It was only hearsay but Rabbi Zahn agreed to the burial being within the Jewish part of the cemetery. If he could find a way out of a difficult situation, he would.

Rabbi Zahn was also very conscious of the importance of public relations with the non-Jewish community. He was a great friend of the Bishop of Durham. There was also an occasion when the Queen came to Newcastle to distribute Maundy Money and about 60 members of the North East Jewish community were invited to attend the lunch which followed. The problem was that the event was going to take place in the middle of Passover. Now it is difficult enough to serve Jewish guests with properly kosher food in a non-Jewish setting, but doing so during Passover, when so many additional regulations have to be strictly observed, is almost impossible.

Rabbi Zahn told the only kosher caterer in the North East, Shirley Davis, that she had to accept the challenge; if the Melech, the Queen, was involved, the Jews must pay their respects. Shirley Davis is a fine cook and had actually come into kosher catering when the Gateshead kosher caterer had lost the licence. She set a high standard for many years and was even allowed to prepare food for functions in her own kitchen with Lottie Zahn as the nominal rabbinic supervisor. This showed a very high regard for her kashrut by Rabbi Zahn.

On this royal occasion, the first necessity was to buy entirely new crockery and cutlery. The utensils and china in use at other times of the year cannot be used during Passover. After the new purchases were packed up, a cold menu was prepared in Sunderland and transported to Newcastle. So far, so good. When Shirley Davis arrived, however, it was to find that the Jewish guests were seated among all the other invitees and not in a group.

So each Jew had to be pointed out to the waiting staff as the future recipients of the special food. Which solved all the problems until a waitress, designated to put bread rolls on the side plates of the guests as part of the setting up of the room, also put them on the plates of the Jewish guests. Disaster! The whole point about Passover is that no bread is eaten during the festival and no plates can be used on which bread has been placed before. So all the side plates for the Jewish guests had to be removed and new ones put down in their place. At the end of the day, proper Pesachdik food was served to all the Jewish guests and due respect had been paid to the sovereign.

As the 1970s dawned, the Beth Hamedresh faced very serious problems. Not only was it without a rabbi but membership was diminishing at an alarming rate. The problem was that the eldest members were dying off and many of the children of the community were choosing to leave Sunderland. More than 130 Sunderland Jews went to Israel on aliyah over the years, and this applied to many of the older members as well as they followed their children. There were also the attractions of the larger British cities for the youngsters where, like the slump in the 1930s, economic prospects looked better than those in their home town. In 1975 the last paid official of the Beth Hamedresh, Rev. Berdego decided to leave to set up as the town's Kosher Butcher.

The Sunderland economy had depended to a considerable extent on shipbuilding, and a combination of inadequate management and short sighted union leadership had led to a collapse of this important manufacturing industry. There was also the work that came through the Durham coal fields but these were equally undermined by constant union-management disputes. It looked as if the prospects for Sunderland were bleak and many of the Jewish youngsters gave up the ghost and went off to seek their fortunes instead in London or Manchester. When they settled down in those cities, their parents might well join them when they retired, in order to be near their children and grandchildren.

It was ironic that, as the membership diminished, the eminence of members of the community continued to grow in the corridors of Sunderland power. Sir Jack Cohen and Charles Slater, grandson and great grandson of Chatze Cohen, led the Labour party councillors; indeed, Charles Slater was the City Council leader for nearly 20 years, from the early 1970s till the early 1990s. Mordaunt Cohen, another grandson, served as an Alderman from 1967 - 1974 and led the Conservatives.

Mordaunt Cohen had married a particularly able barrister who became Myrella Cohen. She took silk and became one of the first women judges in the country in 1972. It was significant that over a 13 year period presiding on the bench in Newcastle, she did not try one Jewish defendant. It fell to Myrella Cohen to draw up the first Prenuptial Agreement to help engaged couples to decide on the distribution of the family assets in the event of a future divorce; possibly the least romantic piece of legislation ever. For his part, Mordaunt Cohen became the Chair of the Northern Regional Industrial Tribunals, dealing with cases of alleged unfair dismissal.

The Sunderland Directory Year Book in 1953 had listed one Jewish accountant, four dentists, 12 doctors and three solicitors. Over the years, from the ranks of the tally men and furniture makers came a crop of offspring who became professionals. If it is remembered that the community never exceeded 2,000 souls, it was remarkable that the number of consultants included physician, Bernard Chazan, psychiatrist, Ernest Gillis, pathologist, Harvey Wax, gynaecologists, Sydney Cohen and Harry Doberman, ophthalmologist, Jack Frankenthal, and dermatologist, Benny Gordon.

No less than 24 Jewish doctors had ministered to the sick in Sunderland over the years, including Harold Benson, Sonny Bindman, Geoff Caplin, Charles, Grant, Sam and Sheila Cohen, Alex and Ralph Blakey, Leon and Ralph Collins, Vikky Gillis, Bernard Gusack, Harold Halson, Babette Hertz, David Keidan, Joseph Priceman, Brian and Simon Posner, Monty Raphael and David Rowlands.

In the local courts, apart from Myrella Cohen, Aubrey Gordon was the Recorder of the Crown Court. Gerald Cohen was the Magistrates Clerk in South Tyneside and Isidore Isaacs was the Clerk of the Justices in Castle Eden. Six Jews were appointed Justices of the Peace in Sunderland, two in South Tyneside and one in Durham. Four of the nine were women.

Two of the Jewish community were appointed Deputy Lieutenants of the County - Charles Slater and Mordaunt Cohen. Another prominent Sunderland-born politician was Lt. Col. Marcus Lipton, MP for Lambeth from 1965 - 1978 and, of course, there had been Marion Phillips serving as the MP for the town in 1929. Three members served as Mayor of Sunderland; Jack and Kitty Cohen and Charles Slater. Three were Alderman, including Mr. Levy who served in 1832. It was a record any community could be proud of, and the fact that the vast majority of those elected and appointed came from refugee families shows the benefit that Britain has always enjoyed from opening its doors to the less fortunate and persecuted from overseas.

The problem with replacing Rabbi Babad did not lack for willing helpers to try to solve the problem. After a couple of years there was a suggestion that the Babad family might be prepared to give its blessing to the appointment of a new rabbi from outside the family, but this fizzled out. The eminent Rabbi Padwa from London also offered to help but there was no settlement. Rabbi Seruya was employed as Maggid Shiur and many of the congregation, the baalebatim, could still conduct services, lein the Torah and give shiurim as well. Rabbi Ehrentreu would help to conduct the morning Mishnah studies and yet another Rabbinowitz - Ruby - worked with the Pearlman brothers to maintain the daily shiur, while Michele Rabbinowitz conducted the Sunday classes. So the normal activities of the community continued unabated but the divisions within the congregation were unconstructive.

There were soon only fifteen girl pupils and nine boys in the classes. The standards were still high; the smaller the class, the more personal attention. Mrs. Zahn taught the children their "O" level Classical Hebrew and they all took the exam successfully. With the boys at school in Newcastle, it was more difficult for them to attend classes after school as punctually as their forefathers had done before them. Most of them had lessons from members of the Kollel, starting at 10 o'clock in the evening. Four of the potential boy pupils had, however, gone to the Gateshead Boarding school.

Rabbi Zahn's views on education were in line with his torah im derech eretz upbringing. He accepted that some of his yeshiva students go on to university where this course was becoming increasingly frowned upon in Chassidic circles. They simply didn't want to expose their children to a world where such distractions as casual sex and drugs were becoming increasingly prevalent Rabbi Zahn had sent his own children to the Royal Grammar School in Newcastle and still believed that youngsters could benefit from both the talmudic and national cultures.

Rabbi Zahn
Not to be underestimated

If there was one blot on the community's post-war copybook it arose in a very unlikely way, but the handling of the problem was typical of the Beth Hamedresh. One day the owner of the kosher butcher shop, Yehuda Berdugo, a brother of the Chazan, was seen coming out of the butchery department of a local cash-and-carry food store. An immediate investigation was undertaken and non-kosher meat and liver was found in the butcher's shop. Now, to keep kosher, any Orthodox community has to rely on the integrity of its suppliers and they had now been very badly let down by the butcher buying treifa, non-kosher meat. The ecclesiastical authorities were Rabbis Zahn and Rabbi Gelley and they immediately withdrew the butcher's licence, Yehuda went back to Marseilles and the shop had to close down. It was, however, reopened as a communal venture soon after.

The Beth Hamedresh community was now definitely declining in almost every aspect of its normal way of religious life. The 1979 Annual Report talked of difficulties in even mustering a minyan (10 male Jews over 13 years old make a quorum) for the morning service. The President, however, spoke of this resulting in a new spirit of determination among the hard core who remained and was able to announce that there would now always be a minyan for all the services. Unfortunately, this was in the nature of a last hurrah and the task of gathering the necessary numbers would become more difficult with every year that passed. As the community reduced in number, the synagogue building seemed to deteriorate in sympathy and in 1979 serious dry rot was identified.

At the beginning of the 1980s the problem of the succession to Rabbi Babad continued to plague the Beth Hamedresh, still trying to find a suitable candidate. The settlement with the family was only one part of the problem. In 1981 Rabbi Zachariah Gelley had become Vice-Principal of the Sunderland Talmudical College. Rabbi Gelley had been one of the original students at the Yeshiva and now he tried again to find a solution. He was reported in the council minutes as having told its members that an appointed rabbinic authority was really essential. He agreed that, although the Sunderland rabbunim were usually members of the Beth Hamedresh, they very seldom interfered in its running, but he had taken the initiative in discussing the position with the Hebrew Congregation. Nobody objected to this but there was no real progress.

In March 1981 the Beth Hamedresh Council were able to agree that only Rabbi Zahn would be acceptable to them, but if Sunderland, as a whole, was to have a communal rabbi, they were concerned that Ryhope Road might take offence if Rabbi Zahn had already been appointed at Mowbray Road. They compromised by announcing "that Rabbi Zahn be invited to occupy the Rav seat in the Beth Hamedresh whenever he attends." Rabbi Zahn was flattered but too much of a diplomat to actually take the seat. Eventually, Rabbi Gelley wrote to Rabbi Babad's son and reported the subsequent negotiations. He told Rabbi Babad:

> "that in view of the fact that his own appointment as Rav of the Sunderland Beth Hamedresh is not a practical proposition, he (Babad) should enable the congregation to appoint a Rav of their choice, should they wish to do so." In answer Rabbi Babad states clearly that he has no objection for the Congregation to make an appointment of their choice and and he wishes the (candidate) well and success for the future.
>
> I have shown the letter to the leading (rabbis) of the North East, namely Rabbi Zahn, Rabbi Rakow and Rabbi Gurwicz and we are all agreed that this frees the (congregation) of any further commitment and are free according to the (law) to do as they wish.
>
> I would like to add that in all my dealings with Rabbi Babad, I found him gentlemanly and well disposed to the future of the (congregation) a true son of his illustrious father.

Rabbi Babad had written to him in Hebrew, in that flowery prose which has been used in rabbinic circles for centuries:

> Peace and all goodness, SELAH! To the honourable friend who is trustworthy, Rabbi and Gaon, man of many talents, crowned with good character traits and good behavioural traits, he who spreads Torah to young flocks and busies himself in the needs of congregation with trustworthiness, our teacher, Rabbi Z. Gelley SHLITA, head of the academy Netzach Israel of Sunderland, may G-d strengthen and protect him!
>
> After addressing him with the appropriate honour; his letter I have received, and reply to, in the holy tongue, for in it I am more able to express myself - please forgive me.
>
> As I have understood from the letter of our rabbi SHLITA, the situation of the Beis Hamidrash is such that - my being appointed as their rabbi to lead the congregation is not practical at this time; such that, for the sake of peace and truth, I have come with these words for the betterment of the congregation, to state that as far as I am concerned, there is no impediment to fulfil the position/ office of becoming Rabbi: and to bless our friend, the elevated, Harav Hagaon, our rabbi and teacher SHAMAI ZAHN SHLITA, to merit the effect successfully the elevation of the

> HORN of TORAH and ISRAEL, in a situation conducive to happiness and personal satisfaction, of complete health, up until (and including) the arrival of the righteous saviour speedily in our days Amen!
>
> So do I bless all the members of the Kehilla to merit that they continue in the prayers and torah lectures/learning constantly, in self satisfaction and tranquillity and complete health, long days and years in goodness until and inclusive of the reinstatement of the Priest wearing the TUMIM URIM quickly and Amen.
>
> So are the words of the one who seeks your peace (and fulfilment) with all my heart and desire of my soul, and who hopes for the salvation of the Lord quickly.

It was a great pity that it had taken so long to arrive at this point. At last agreement was reached with Rabbi Babad's widow and son. For £9,000 the Babads gave up any claim to a pension for Mrs. Babad or for the money which might come from selling the house in Belle Vue Park where they had lived. In addition they agreed to pay any tax which was claimed by the Revenue on the £9,000.

When eventually the family agreed to settle all their disagreements with the Beth Hamedresh, the figure arrived at in 1981 was the equivalent of £38,000 today. With that payment the Babad family indemnified all the members of the Beth Hamedresh, "jointly and severally in respect of all claims and demands in connection therewith."

It had been a very long 15 years and both sides had tried to justify their position, making for a lot of argument and dissension. By 1981, however, it was becoming likely that there wouldn't be a Beth Hamedresh congregation for much longer. The two congregations in Sunderland had declined in numbers to the point where there was a move to appoint a communal rabbi, rather than to have one in post for each community. The Hebrew Congregation had been approached on the subject but had not replied. The Beth Hamedresh Council agreed that the only candidate they would now accept would be Rabbi Zahn, who had served the community so well in the interregnum.

Rabbi Zahn was the likely - and the only distinguished - nominee for the post of communal rabbi and the question was still whether the Hebrew Congregation would be offended if he was appointed Rabbi of the Beth Hamedresh before they had decided on the question of having only one rabbi for both the Sunderland synagogues. In March 1981 the Beth Hamedresh lost patience and decided to go ahead and invite Rabbi Zahn to be their rav anyway.

More of the members of the Sunderland Kollel had now decided to live in Gateshead but continue to study in Sunderland. Now they set up their own small school for their children in Gateshead and took advantage of the various religious foundations in the town. They eventually abandoned the Sunderland kollel building. Without them, Rabbi Zahn faced the problem of the difficulty of keeping up the numbers of students studying at the Yeshiva. Compared to Gateshead, it was a disadvantage for them not to have the opportunity of going on to the Kollel if they wanted to, when they finished at the institution. There were also the economic problems associated with the continuing decline in the number of Jews in Sunderland to consider. The fewer the Jews, the higher the financial contribution that would be required of them individually to support the Yeshiva.

Eventually, Rabbi Zahn decided that the only way to keep the Sunderland Yeshiva going was to move it, lock, stock and barrel, to Gateshead. Arrangements were made with the religious authorities in Gateshead to absorb it and today the Sunderland Yeshiva continues as an entity, but 12 miles from its original foundation. The move finally took place in June 1988 with 40 students still enrolled.

Although it was only 12 miles up the road from Sunderland, it was a vast step in the wrong direction, if there was to be any hope of the Sunderland community surviving. For some it was a Dunkirk evacuation to the safe shores of Gateshead, and to others a final capitulation. For the students were the lifeblood of the future. A lot of money was spent on renovating the premises they were to occupy in Gateshead and soon the first sefer torah, specifically for the Yeshiva in its new location, was paraded under a chuppah through the Gateshead streets. But while the future of the Yeshiva was secured, the defection of so many supporters was a heavy, if necessary, blow to the Sunderland community. In 2007 the Sunderland Yeshiva in Gateshead had 100 students and most of them were British.

At the end of the 1983 summer term, the Menorah School closed because there were no longer enough young Jewish children in the town to educate. It was in its 25th year. In the book on Jewish Education published in 1982, the Head Mistress, Jean Winter, had written:

> It has, over the years, attained a high standard of education for children up to 11 years old, with a high rate of entries to the local independent and public schools. Our pupils have gone from there to professional and rabbinical careers. Great stress is paid in the school to Jewish observances and to Mishnah and Gemara studies.

Mishnah and Gemara at eleven! And, in fact, earlier. Pretty impressive by normal British Orthodox standards. The school only had one full-time teacher by this time and the help of nine part-timers. Jewish Studies took up 25% of the curriculum.

There was still a small group of dedicated Honorary Officers of the Beth Hamedresh, one of whom was the Treasurer, Motte Pearlman. Now by this time most members paid their subscriptions by cheque, but a few of the poorer families still paid in cash weekly. Mottie Pearlman one time Chairman of a public company quoted on the London Stock Exchange, still went to visit those who wanted to pay in this way. He talked of one family who always had four piles of coins waiting for him; 10p for the Beth Hamedrresh, 10p for the Yeshiva, 10p for the Old Age Home and 10p for the Joint Israel Appeal.

It was a considerable percentage of the income of the family and Mottie Pearlman admired their generosity greatly. As a gesture of thanks, he would arrive with eggs and cakes and other foods for them, so that, at the end of the day, he probably paid out more than he took in subscriptions.

Over those last years the organisation of the synagogue services was carried out by Max Guttentag. He would leyn from the sefer torah and the megillot, and lead the services, particularly on the Yomim Naorim and the Festivals. He was the convener of the Blatt, reorganized the library and dealt with the repairs. He even supervised the revitalisation of the mikveh.

Which left Mottie Pearlman as the elder statesman. He had been an active member of the Beth Hamedresh all his life and though he modestly refused the title of President, he did agree to be the Chair of the Council. He was tactful, talented and highly intelligent and he guided the shul through the difficult years of the interregnum and amalgamation.

By 1984 the membership of the Beth Hamedresh had fallen to a level where it seemed only sensible to amalgamate the community with the Hebrew Congregation altogether. Receipts had dropped from £6,500 in 1983 to £5,300 in 1984 and although the congregation was solvent because of its ownership of the synagogue building, the future prospects were bleak. The Hebrew Congregation had about three times the membership of the Beth Hamedresh and by June 1984 efforts were being made to sell Mowbray Road.

Mottie Pearlman
The last treasurer and elder statesman

Next door to the synagogue was a church high school and the governors enquired whether it was permissible for a Jewish synagogue to be sold to a church foundation. Having been assured that, as long as they didn't want to turn it into a church, there was no problem, they made an acceptable offer. When they bought the shul, it was to knock it down to provide more classroom space but, with great sensitivity, they wanted a reminder of the synagogue to be there for future generations. The Mikvah was physically intact but, in addition, in the foundations of their Science block in the new building the High School buried a time capsule with details of the synagogue's history, written in Hebrew, together with photographs, floor plans and other memorabilia. All that was now needed was planning approval and the agreement of the Charities Commission, which were forthcoming.

Rabbi Zahn had undertaken to discuss with the Hebrew Congregation an agreement for amalgamation and was able to report that he had resolved the matters most important to the Beth Hamedresh. These included the continuation of the daily Mishnah and Gemorah Blatt, which was agreed, and minor changes to the form of the services. The Beth Hamedresh library would be housed in a room allocated for the purpose in Ryhope Road and membership of the Hebrew congregation would be offered to all those in the Beth Hamedresh who wished to join.

One of the by-laws of the Beth Hamedresh had always been that any member who married out of the faith would lose all the privileges inherent in being a member of the community. These included the right to be buried in the Jewish section of the cemetery. This would have been a bone of contention with the Hebrew Congregation and Rabbi Zahn overcame the problem by creating a special row for use in such cases. This is somewhat comparable to the royal graveyard at Frogmore near Windsor Castle. All the graves in the little cemetery are on one side of the grounds except those of King Edward VIII and the Duchess of Windsor, Mrs. Simpson, who are buried on the opposite side.

The disposal of the accoutrements of Mowbray Road was a depressing necessity after so many years of keeping them cleaned and polished. It was agreed that two of the sifrei torahs would be given to Ryhope Road and a third would go to the Sunderland Yeshivah. The fourth would be presented to the Sunderland Kollel and the bimah would be sent to the London synagogue of Woodside Park. These included the Ark and the Almemar, whose meticulously crafted woodwork would have been difficult to reproduce in modern times. The Shtender in the shtiebl and the Oren Hakodesh went to Ryhope Road, and eventually the Shtender finished up in Newcastle and the Oren in Gateshead.

When the building was sold, it was agreed that the most important concern for the Trustees would be the maintenance of the Mikvah on which £6,000 had only recently been spent for it to be completely renovated. It was also agreed to make the payment of the salary of the Maggid Shiur a priority. The Beth Hamedresh chuppah would be given to the Kahal Chassidim in Salford.

By February 1985 the Shabbot service and the Daily Blatt had been transferred to Ryhope Road, although the sale of the synagogue had not yet been completed. During that winter, however, the heating system had collapsed and there was now little alternative to the move. It was agreed to close the synagogue in April. Rabbi Zahn was still going through the traditional motions of the Sunderland community, proposing the toast to the Chevra Kedushah, marrying and burying and giving advice on any number of problems, but the numbers were continuing to dwindle and the end was in sight.

The Hebrew Congregation had dealt with the amalgamation insensitively on two points. The first was that the new community would be called the *Sunderland Hebrew Congregation incorporating the Beth Hamedresh.* It would have been just as easy to call it the *Sunderland Hebrew Congregation and Beth Hamedresh* but this idea was rejected. It was also insisted that members of the Beth Hamedresh would have to be members of the new congregation for two years before they could stand for office. As both congregations were declining at an alarming rate, this was akin to rearranging the deck chairs on the Titanic after it had struck the iceberg. Mottie Pearlman was not the only one though who realised that the amalgamation would only last for a limited period before the community vanished altogether.

There could have been additional difficulties in sorting out the differences between the services of the two congregations. Here, however, Rabbi Zahn put his foot down. He announced categorically that services were his province and he'd decide what was put in and what was left out. Both communities settled for that.

At the last service in Mowbray Road, Rabbi Zahn summed up the legacy of the Beth Hamedresh:

> Although the Aron of the Mishkon was entirely overlaid with gold it is always referred to as having been made of wood. Likewise, the Jewish community of Sunderland came to England from *der litte,* imbued with *Ahavas Torah* and *Yiras Shomayim*, and in the course of time grew prosperous. But the wealth they earned lay on the surface-

> like the gold of the Aron - whereas the profound Torah values (the wood) of the congregants remained at the heart of the community and on these its reputation was built.

The congregation numbered some 250 "mostly ex-Sunderland people who now live in Antwerp, the USA and various parts of Britain" and after the mincha service, the Emeritus Minister from Middlesborough, an ex Beth Hamedresh boy, sang Keil Molei Rachamim which is said over a grave. Max Guttentag was in the chair and he congratulated David Pearlman on having attended the Blatt for 57 years and completing the shas three times; a remarkable record.

A kiddush was arranged to welcome the new members to Ryhope Road and one result of the amalgamation was that there were now enough attendees to guarantee a minyan again for morning and evening services. A newly constructed Daily Prayer Room doubled as a Bet Midrash, thanks to the hard work of the Treasurer, David Berg. It was significant, however, that having completed the work, he emigrated to Israel.

What happened in Israel also affected the Jewish students at the Sunderland Polytechnic. In 1985 the Student Union banned the formation of a Jewish society because it was committed to defending Zionism and Israel. The students might have benefited from recalling the words attributed, if incorrectly, to Voltaire "I disapprove of what you say, but I will defend to the death your right to say it."

As the community declined, it was ironic that October 1988 marked the 150th anniversary of the first time a Sunderland representative had been elected to the Board of Deputies. To mark the anniversary the Board of Deputies held a meeting in Sunderland but it was as if it was gathering round a death bed. Life went on as usual, though. If the membership was growing ever smaller, it was still possible for a coffee morning in March 1989 to raise £1,865 for the Sunderland Yeshiva. That year, though, saw the end of the WIZO branch which had been started in the 1930s, but now lacked the membership to continue.

The cost of membership of the combined Ryhope Road synagogue was not set at a high level. Class A seats were available for £130 a couple, £100 for a single man or £70 for a single woman. Class B were £80, £70 and £45 and Class C £70, £55 and £40.

The search for a good home for the Sunderland treasures continued. In 1991 a sefer torah, which had been specially written for the Sunderland Yeshiva, was transfered to Gateshead for the Yeshiva's new home. It is not the continuity of synagogue buildings which has the prime emphasis in Judaism, but the survival of each sefer torah is definitely of major importance. The little synagogue in Dubrovnik in Croatia has seen far better days and the community is only 25 strong. In its tiny museum, however, after all the depredations of pogroms, the Nazis and Civil Wars over the centuries, its 14th century sefer torah is still as clear as if it had been written yesterday. The Sunderland Yeshivah sefer torah was written in Israel and donated by Israel Goldlust of Toronto in memory of his parents who were killed in the Holocaust. Why then give it to Sunderland? Because his son-in-law was a former student of the college.

Inevitably, in 1999 the combined community ceased to be viable as well. Although the synagogue had 130 nominal members, as many as 80 of them no longer lived in the town. Effectively the history of Sunderland Jewry had come to an end. It is not unusual in the slightest for Jewish communities to form and dissolve over the centuries. If, however, the dissolution is voluntary, as against being the result of pogroms or banishment by the state, the congregation does have one major asset; the actual synagogue building can be sold. The land value has usually increased enormously over the years if it is sited in a good district and that should have been the case with Ryhope Road as well. There was an offer of £165,000 but there arose an enormous snag. In September 2000, on an application by Sunderland Council, the building was listed Grade II. This meant that an official body, English Heritage, had decided that the building was of sufficient architectural and historical significance to merit its preservation for the nation.

The original architect, Marcus Kenneth Glass, had done too good a job, though there was much in the appearance of the front of the synagogue that, to a layman, resembled an Odeon cinema. It had a barrel ceiling, painted with the stars and sky and there was light from semicircular glass windows on either side. It had been designed, according to Marcus Glass, "in a free Byzantine style". Jewish Heritage call it art deco and say that Marcus Glass is under-appreciated. "The colourful facade features corner towers, red and yellow *ablaq* striped brickwork, arcaded porch with Byzantine basket capitals, mosaic and abstract stained glass." Nikolas Pevsner, who described every building of importance in Britain said that it was "vigourous and decorative."

So whatever its financial value, no part of it could now be knocked down or even materially altered. It was a financial disaster for the community from which there was no appeal. There was no comparable state fund which would pay for the building's maintenance either. That task remained with the owners, though if it was allowed to fall into rack and ruin, there was not a great deal anybody could do about it.

While it is understandable that the Sunderland Council wanted a memento of the Jewish presence in their midst over so many years, there are many other synagogues throughout the country which might be considered of more architectural merit. What can be said for certain is that there is no Jewish architecture anywhere, to even remotely compare in beauty with buildings like York Minster, Kings College Chapel in Cambridge or St. Pauls Cathedral. The case for Preservation Orders on synagogues in England, like Bevis Marks in London or Princes Park Road in Liverpool are undeniable, but Ryhope Road does seem to be stretching a point.

The problem with Jewish synagogue interior architecture is not just because no reproduction of the human face is permitted in a synagogue decor; it would be a graven image and, therefore, against the commandment. It isn't just that the Jews haven't produced any Michaelangelos. It is, primarily, because they didn't want to risk their buildings being considered superior to those of the majority religion, so they constructed them modestly. They also often didn't have the finance or the number of congregants to justify any kind of superb edifice.

That didn't stop them being involved in paying for parts of cathedrals. It is a fact that, in early Mediaeval times in England, Aaron of Lincoln, the richest Jew in the country, had financed the building of Lincoln and Peterborough Cathedrals, and Henry III had later extorted nearly half a million pounds from the Jewish community in special taxes to pay for the rebuilding of Westminster Abbey.

So while it is a great compliment that the Sunderland Council wishes to pay to its Jewish citizens, past and present, the synagogue isn't quite as important as it may appear. The building in Ryhope Road was eventually purchased by an American Jewish charity, the Shlomo Memorial Fund, for £65,000 and they agreed that the remnants of the Sunderland community could carry on using it for services. They would have liked to make it the core of a new Yeshiva but there was really no call for such an organization with Gateshead cheek by jowl with Sunderland. In July 2006 the synagogue was used for services for the last time.

Of course, Sunderland wasn't the only town in the North East which the Jews eventually abandoned. Middlesborough, for instance, closed in 1998. As we saw at the beginning, the communities grew up where there was a need for them and they followed the trends in economic fortunes to other locations. North Shields was one of the earliest, but it was no more by 1910, though it was briefly resurrected in the Thirties when a number of German refugees arrived.

In Sunderland the considerable number of Jews who emigrated to Israel went to support a new Jewish nation, in existence for the first time in nearly 2,000 years. They also yearned to be a majority for once. Others succumbed to the attractions of assimilation, as so many of their forebears had done over the centuries. What they never did in the Beth Hamedresh was compromise. There was never a Reform or Liberal synagogue in the town. Either you were in or you were out.

The economic situation in Sunderland towards the end of the 20th century was not attractive. The town needed reinventing badly but the regeneration which eventually improved the situation dramatically - for which Japanese manufacturing should take much of the credit - could not be foreseen. Those members of the community who decided that London, Manchester or Leeds would offer greater opportunities upped sticks and departed.

The inevitable encroachments of old age were also cutting down the former leaders of the community. In 1999 the Hebrew Congregation rabbi in the 1960s died; Bernard Susser had served five years before he went to Johannesburg in 1970. In 2002 Myrella Cohen died at 74. Rabbi Zahn retired in 1999 when the community was down to 80 and died in 2001 when he was 80 years old. His health had deteriorated when his kidneys started to fail and in his last years he was confined to a wheelchair. One of his friends offered to pay for him to have a transplant. Unfortunately his Doctors considered him too old to survive the operation but made sure that the local hospital was prepared to look after him as a patient, rather than give up hope.

Rabbi Zahn had gone back to Gateshead when he left Sunderland but, typically, he came back to the old house for one last weekend towards the end, to "inspire a lone and almost fatherless boy from the Anglo-Jewish community on his Barmitzvah day." He was sincerely mourned by the old members of the Sunderland congregations all over the world. He was buried in Newcastle and it is said that his grave is visited by more people than the rest of the cemetery put together.

In 2006 Rabbi Shlomo Toperoff died. He had given 17 years to the Englisher Shul and only retired in 1951 to go on to Newcastle which he served faithfully until 1973. He retired to Israel and, sadly, went blind. His great heart did not fail him, however, and when he eventually passed away, he was 99 and had four great, great grandchildren.

Today there are fewer than 30 Jews in Sunderland, though they include the inimitable Charles Slater, for so long the head of the Council. As the former leader answered humorously when asked why he still stayed in Sunderland when all about him had gone, he said "If I left, nobody would know me!" In Krottingen in 1989 there were three Jews left. The Joel Intract Home has also been knocked down, the residents having been moved to a new home in Newcastle.

In different parts of the world, however, the same Tehillim are being sung, the same lessons are being taught to the next generation in the Talmud Torahs, the shiurs on the works of Rashi, Maimonides and the Shulkhan Aruch are still attended by Jews eager to learn and intent on carrying on the religion. A lot of the teachers, a lot of the Orthodox families have their roots in what was the fertile Beth Hamedresh soil. For a period of time it happened in Krottingen and Sunderland.

When Mowbray Road was to be closed, one of the members who had gone on aliyah to Israel, Elaine Brewer, wrote of her memories:

> Yes, I wanted to sit in the Ladies Gallery, but I was only four, and it was nice to sit downstairs with Daddy, uncles and the men. My cheder teacher told me that when I was five, I had to join the ladies. There were the usual Shabbos morning rituals: the man who always complained of the draught from the window. The opening and closing of the windows throughout every service. The man who every week picked on yet another member of the community to argue with. The man who always had sweet lollipops in his desk and gave them out to us children. The man who always sang so much louder than anyone else. The Rabbi and the Chazan, who sat in their seats on either side of the 'Aron Ha'Kodesh, like kings upon their thrones. The Rabbi's speeches that didn't sound too much like English to me - he spoke with a 'foreign' accent. Solemnity at Rosh Hashona and Yom Kippur, the smelling salts in the Lady's gallery. On Purim I always thought the ceiling would fall in from the noise of our 'drayers'. They were strict in their religious beliefs and observances, yet the atmosphere was relaxed and at ease.

The memories of the Beth Hamedresh would easily last a lifetime.

Now the study is carried on elsewhere - and particularly up the road in Gateshead from the old synagogue. Gateshead wasn't entirely introspective either though. They certainly wanted to spend their time building up their own institutions, but they realised that persuading other Jews to their point of view was also essential. They formed the Jewish Schools Torah Council after the war to devise curricula for school examinations in Jewish subjects. There are now a number of national qualifications which can be obtained in such areas.

Also, in 1979, they launched Project Seed, a concept that had been in use at the Beth Hamedresh for a few years already. The basic idea was that when Jews wanted to learn more about their religion, they should be able to get personal tuition, without charge, on a one-to-one basis, from someone who knew the subject very well. You could choose whatever topic you wanted and study it at whatever level suited you. There would be someone who could explain it all to you. What you did with the knowledge would be up to you., but you would at least have it. Project Seed attracted a lot of people. Today, it has offices in London and Manchester. The planting of Seed came from Gateshead, Gateshead came from the Sunderland Beth Hamedresh, and the Sunderland Beth Hamedresh came from Krottingen.

It isn't easy to do justice to the enormous amount of excellent work put in by members of that small congregation over 100 years. Fortunately, it has been summed up beautifully in the peroration that Rabbi Israel Levy once gave when he spoke at the time of the Neilah service at the end of Yom Kippur in the 19th century. Rabbi Levy said:

> Just as the shades of night now hover around this synagogue, so must, at some time, the shadow of the valley of death approach each of us; when that time comes for you, for me, may we have lived so that we may conclude our life with the same words as I conclude this discourse. Take thou my spirit I confide , when I sleep and when I wake up, and with my spirit my body also. The Lord is with me, I shall not fear.

The members of the Beth Hamedresh would have asked no more.

Appendix A

Beth Hamedresh Rabbis and Ministers.

Rabbi Shmaryahu Bloch 1894 - 1902
Rabbi Hirsch Hurwitz 1903 - 1910
Rev. Warrantz (acting) 1910 - 1913
Rabbi David Rabbinowitz 1913 - 1923
Rabbi Moishe Rabbinowitz 1923 - 1946
Rabbi Abraham Babad 1947 - 1965

Rabbi Shammai Zahn 1965 - 1999

Bibliography

Bermant, Chaim, *Troubled Eden*, Valentine Mitchell, 1969.

Cohen, Isaac, Unpublished manuscript.

Cohen, Solly, *The man in the bowler hat*, Docostry, 2004.

Dansky, Miriam, *Gateshead*, Targum Press, 1992.

Davis, Harold (Ed), *Sunderland Jews at War*, Arima Publishing, 2009.

Levy, Arnold, *The Behr Tree,* Barnicotts, 1949.

Levy Arnold, *History of the Sunderkand Jewish Community*, Macdonald, 1956.

Levy, Arnold, *The story of Gateshead Yeshivah*, The Wessex Press, 1952.

Olsover, Lewis, *The Jewish Communities of North East England*, Ashley Marks, 1980.

Roth, Cecil, *The rise of provincial Jewry*, The Jewish Monthly, 1950.

Schoenburg, Nancy & Stuart, *Lithuanian Jewish Communities*, Garland Publishing, 1991.

Susser, Bernard, *The Jews of South West England*, University of Exeter Press, 1993.

Thanks to Mordaunt Cohen, Shirley Davis, Dayan Chonoch Ehrentreu, Peter Gillis, Max & Eva Guttentag, Lionel Kopolowitz, Rabbi Abraham Levy, Diane & Jack Lopian, Chaim Pearlman and Meyer Pearlman.

Index

www.ingramcontent.com/pod-product-compliance
Lightning Source LLC
Chambersburg PA
CBHW080552090426
42735CB00016B/3211

* 9 7 8 1 8 4 5 4 9 4 3 5 3 *